STONE TAPESTRY

A VISUAL AND HISTORICAL GUIDE TO THE WEST POINT CEMETERY

Acknowledgments

A book such as this cannot be written in a vacuum, and this one wasn't. I owe a tremendous debt to many people who assisted me in the research, provided encouragement (and occasional prodding) and gave of their valuable time. First and foremost, I want to thank Jenifer McSwain of the Memorial Affairs Office at West Point, whose encyclopedic knowledge of the cemetery and all associated functions was instrumental in completing the book. She shared freely and openly everything she knew and reviewed early drafts of the book. Without her, this book could not have happened.

I also owe a great debt to the staff of the USMA Library, and in particular Elaine McConnell, Corey Flatt and Alicia Mauldin-Ware for their help. No other single source provided as much practical assistance as did the library, and in particular, their deep knowledge of the photographs available, and their willingness to provide them for scanning, made the book possible. It was also a very happy place to do research.

The US Army Heritage and Education Center in Carlisle, PA was also vital in providing materials, especially photographs. Particular thanks go to Tom Buffenbarger who was most helpful and cheerfully gave of his time in multiple research trips to Carlisle.

John Stone and Ian Robertson of Schiffer Publishing have been very helpful in guiding this first-time author through the publishing process. Their vision and practical suggestions have made the book a better product than the initial version.

I must also acknowledge the help and support I received from my wife, Kathy. She was an enthusiastic supporter from the beginning, provided motivation to continue when I grew tired or discouraged, and was indefatigable in finding ways to assist in the process, especially with the photographs. She carefully reviewed early drafts and was always available for discussion of finer points. The book very much reflects her influence throughout.

Any mistakes in the book are, of course, my own.

Est. **SCHIFFER** PUBLISHING 1974

Inspiring through expert knowledge

IF YOU LOVE THIS BOOK,

please take a moment to post a review or tell a friend.

DO YOU HAVE A BOOK IDEA?

We're looking for authors who can inspire with expert knowledge. Submit your proposal:

www.schifferbooks.com/submitabookproposal

Pop Culture | Art & Design | Fine Craft & Technique
Fashion & Fiber Arts | Architecture & Interior Design
Decorative Arts | Regional

Divination | Meditation | Astrology | Psychic Skills
Numerology & Palmistry | Channeled Material
Metaphysics | Spirituality | Health & Lifestyle

Aerospace | Naval | Ground Forces
American Civil War | Militaria | Uniforms & Insignia
Weaponry | Modeling | Transportation

Early Concepts | SEED | STEAM
Laptime & Independent Reading | Interactive Learning
Board Books | Picture Books | Middle Grade

SCHIFFER PUBLISHING, LTD.
4880 Lower Valley Road | Atglen, PA 19310
610-593-1777 | info@schifferbooks.com

www.schifferbooks.com

Printed in China

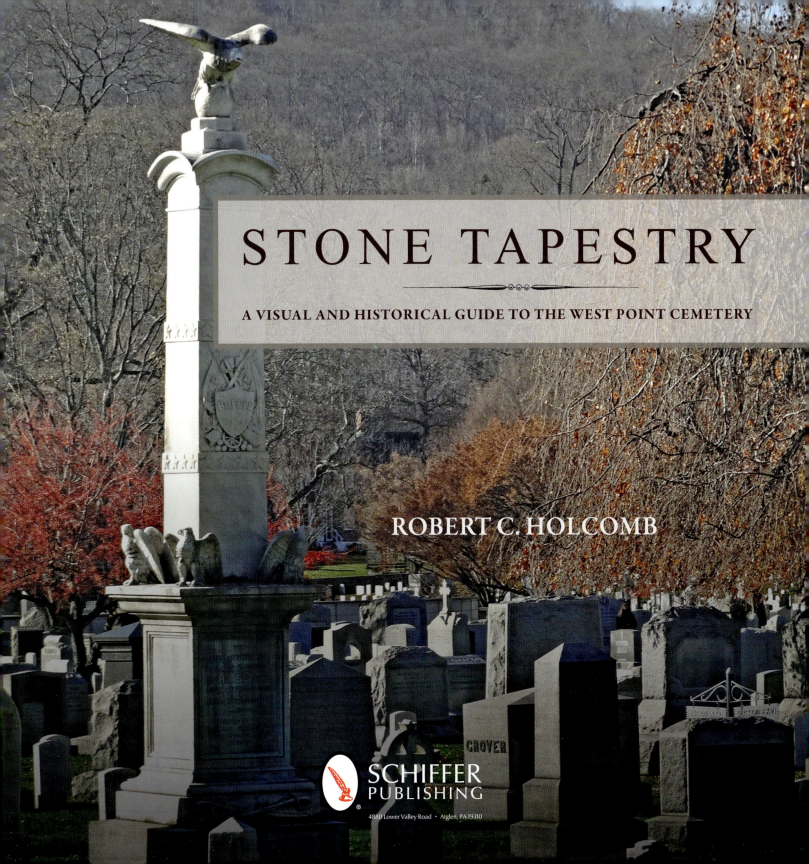

STONE TAPESTRY

A VISUAL AND HISTORICAL GUIDE TO THE WEST POINT CEMETERY

ROBERT C. HOLCOMB

SCHIFFER PUBLISHING
4880 Lower Valley Road • Atglen, PA 19310

Copyright © 2025 by Robert C. Holcomb, Lieutenant Colonel (Ret.), USA

Library of Congress Control Number: 2024941404

All rights reserved. No part of this work may be reproduced or used in any form or by any means—graphic, electronic, or mechanical, including photocopying or information storage and retrieval systems—without written permission from the publisher.

The scanning, uploading, and distribution of this book or any part thereof via the Internet or any other means without the permission of the publisher is illegal and punishable by law. Please purchase only authorized editions and do not participate in or encourage the electronic piracy of copyrighted materials.

"Schiffer," "Schiffer Publishing, Ltd.," and the pen and inkwell logo are registered trademarks of Schiffer Publishing, Ltd.

Edited by Ian Robertson
Designed by Beth Oberholtzer
Cover design by Jack Chappell
Type set in Microsoft Himalaya/Garamond Premier Pro

ISBN: 978-0-7643-6941-4
ePub: 978-1-5073-0515-7
Printed in China

Published by Schiffer Publishing, Ltd.
4880 Lower Valley Road
Atglen, PA 19310
Phone: (610) 593-1777; Fax: (610) 593-2002
Email: info@schifferbooks.com
Web: www.schifferbooks.com
For our complete selection of fine books on this and related subjects, please visit our website at www.schifferbooks.com. You may also write for a free catalog.

Schiffer Publishing's titles are available at special discounts for bulk purchases for sales promotions or premiums. Special editions, including personalized covers, corporate imprints, and excerpts, can be created in large quantities for special needs. For more information, contact the publisher.

Gratefully dedicated to my parents, Lt. Col. James F. Holcomb, USMA '45, and Ann E. Holcomb, who introduced me to the world in the hospital at West Point and who lie together in peace here in the cemetery. Everything I know about love, and about duty, honor, and selfless service to country, I learned from them.

LOVE

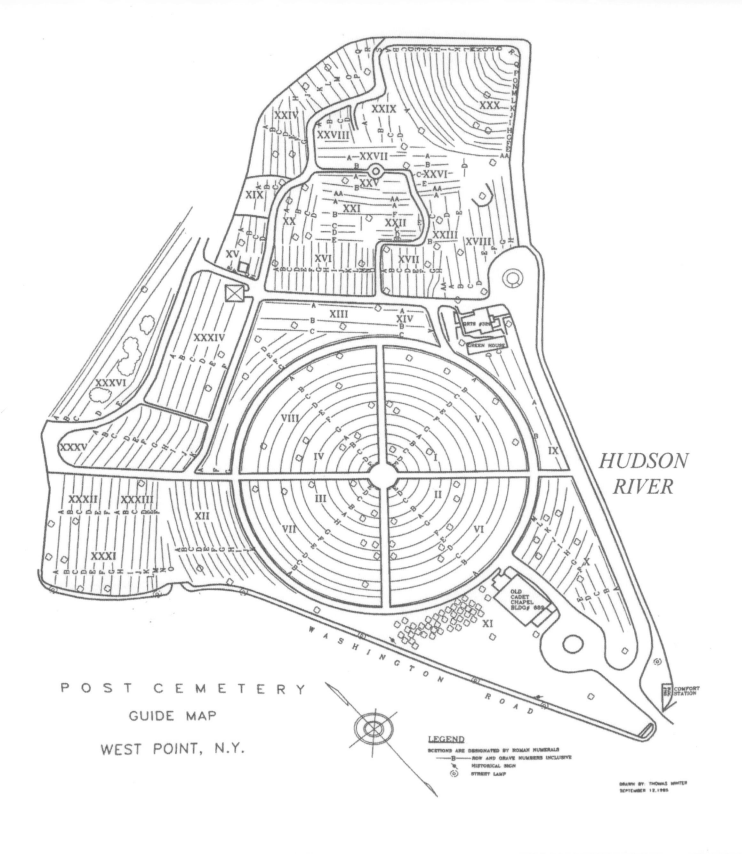

Contents

Foreword	11
Preface	13
Chapter 1: The Entrance and the Old Cadet Chapel	15
Chapter 2: Sections X and IX	29
Colonel Earl H. "Red" Blaik	30
Glenn W. Davis	31
Margaret Mary "Maggie" Dixon	32
Colonel Ronan C. Grady Jr.	33
Major General Lawrence M. Jones Jr.	35
Lieutenant General John Norton	36
Colonel Russell P. "Red" Reeder	37
Major General H. Norman Schwarzkopf Sr.	39
Colonel Lawrence M. "Biff" Jones Sr.	40
General H. Norman Schwarzkopf Jr.	41
Lieutenant General James Gavin	43
Major General Norman "Dutch" Cota	44
Patricia Buyers	46
George R. Pinkerton and Captain Charles C. Pinkerton	47
Lieutenant Colonel Frederick G. Terry and Major Frederick G. Terry Jr.	49
General Paul D. Harkins	50
Chapter 3: The Caretaker's Cottage	51

Chapter 4: Sections XVIII and XXVI	57
Major General Philip R. Feir	58
Lieutenant General Howard D. Graves	59
Brigadier General Richard J. Tallman	60
Lieutenant General Blackshear M. Bryan	62
Lieutenant General Garrison H. "Gar" Davidson	63
Lieutenant General Willard W. Scott Jr.	64
General Wayne A. Downing	65
General Bernard W. Rogers	66
Major General Aubrey S. "Red" Newman	67
Brigadier General Vincent J. Esposito	68
General Sam S. Walker	70
General William C. Westmoreland	71
Major General Edward H. White Sr.	72
General Lucius D. Clay	74
Colonel Edward H. White II	75
Major General George W. Goethals	76
General Donald V. Bennett	78
Major General Samuel W. Koster	79
Major General John Buford	80
Lieutenant Alonzo H. Cushing	82
Major General Judson H. Kilpatrick	83
Major General Frederick D. Grant	84
Chapter 5: Section XXX	87
Brevet Lieutenant Colonel Eleazer D. Wood	88
Edward S. Holden	89
Major John Lillie	90
Ensign Dominick Trant	92

Susan and Anna Warner	93
The Cadet Monument	95
The Unknowns	98
Sergeant Louis Bentz	99

Chapter 6: Sections XXIX, XXVII, XXV, XX, and XXI — 101

Lieutenant General Paul W. Kendall	102
Major General William M. Black	103
Mary Godfrey, Wife of Brigadier General Edward S. Godfrey	104
Captain George Derby (and Family)	105
Lieutenant Colonel George A. Custer	106
Major General Robert Anderson	109
Major General (US Volunteers) Ethan A. Hitchcock	110
Lieutenant General Winfield Scott	112
Brigadier General John S. Eisenhower	113
Major General Clarence S. Ridley	114
Brigadier General Ora E. Hunt	115
Brevet Brigadier General Sylvanus Thayer	117
Brigadier General John C. Tidball	118
Lieutenant Colonel Herman J. Koehler	119
Brevet Major General Alexander S. Webb	121
Brevet Brigadier General Peter Michie	122
First Lieutenant Dennis Michie	123
Major William S. Beebe	125
Brigadier General Thomas Devin	126
Brigadier General Frank Kobes Jr.	127

Chapter 7: Sections XXVIII, XXIV, XIX, XV, and XIII — 129

Brigadier General Charles W. Raymond	130
Brigadier General Cyrus Comstock	131
Brigadier General Bernard J. D. Irwin	132
Professor Albert E. Church	134
Professor William H. C. Bartlett	135
Major Edward B. Hunt	136
Professor Robert W. Weir	138
Colonel James G. Benton	139

Captain Henry Metcalfe	140
Major General Daniel Butterfield	142
Brigadier General (US Volunteers) Egbert L. Viele	143
Professor Dennis Hart Mahan	144
Master Sergeant Marty Maher	146
Coach Joseph M. Palone	147
Brigadier General John T. Thompson	148
Brigadier General George L. Gillespie Jr.	150
Lieutenant Colonel William H. H. Benyaurd	151

Chapter 8: Sections I, II, III, and IV — 153

General Hamilton H. Howze	154
Major General Robert L. Howze	155
General Alexander M. Patch	156
Major General Thomas H. Barry	157
General Joseph W. Stilwell	159
Major General Frank D. Merrill	160
Major General Edward L. King	161
Brigadier General Edward H. DeArmond	163
Major General Fred W. Sladen	164
Professor Louis Vauthier	165
Brigadier General Elliott C. Cutler Jr.	167
Colonel Dean Hudnutt	168
Major General Albert Mills	169
Captain Matthew C. Ferrara	171
Colonel Stuart C. MacDonald	172
Lieutenant General Lemuel Mathewson	173

Chapter 9: Sections V and VI — 177

Brigadier General George S. Anderson	178
General Frank S. Besson Jr.	179
Colonel David H. Barger	180
Brigadier General John R. Jannarone	182
Major General Clarence P. Townsley	183
The James O. Green Family	184
The Heiberg Family	187
Colonel Elbert E. Farman Jr.	190
The Benedict Family	192
The Bunker Family	195

Brigadier General William B. Kunzig	196
Colonel David "Mickey" Marcus	198
The Hayes Family	199
Brigadier General Douglas Kinnard	201
Colonel George "Ike" Pappas	202
Lieutenant Colonel William Rice King	203

Chapter 10: Sections VII and VIII — 205

Brigadier General William H. Wilbur	206
General Michael S. Davison	207
Lieutenant Colonel Andre C. Lucas	208
Lieutenant Colonel Mortimer L. O'Connor	210
First Lieutenant John L. Weaver	211
First Lieutenant Samuel S. Coursen	212
Second Lieutenant Courtenay C. Davis Jr.	213
Second Lieutenant George W. Tow	215
Major General Bryant E. Moore	216
Colonel William H. Schempf	217
Major Chancellor Martin	218
Major General John Biddle	219
The Reverend H. Percy Silver	220
First Lieutenant Todd W. Lambka	221
Brigadier General John W. Heard	222
General Cortlandt V. R. Schuyler	224
Brigadier General Joseph E. McCarthy	225
Lieutenant Colonel George S. Eyster Jr.	226
Captain Robert M. Losey	228
Lieutenant Walter H. Schulze	229
Colonel Charles P. Echols	230

Chapter 11: Sections XII, XXXI, XXXII, and XXXIII — 233

Master Sergeant Pasquale "Pat" Nappi	234
The Infants	235
Major General Norman B. Edwards	237

Technical Sergeant William S. Lewis and Frances W. Lewis	238
Lieutenant Colonel Robert E. Donovan	240
Brigadier General Charles H. Schilling	241
William J. Penny	243
Major General Bruce I. Staser	244
Master Sergeant James B. Mahan	245
Colonel Henry A. Mucci	248
Major Timothy E. Krebs	249
Colonel Roger H. Nye	250

Chapter 12: Sections XXXVI and XXXIV — 253

Colonel Lawrence K. "Red" White	254
General Theodore W. Parker	255
Major General Henry R. McKenzie	256
First Lieutenant Laura M. Walker	257
Second Lieutenant Emily J. T. Perez	258
Command Sergeant Major Mary E. Sutherland	259
Chaplain James D. Ford	261
Lieutenant General John A. Heintges	262
Major General Chih Wang	263
Brigadier General Charles R. "Monk" Meyer	264
Congressman Benjamin A. Gilman	266
Colonel Seth F. Hudgins Jr.	267
Lieutenant Colonel Jaimie E. Leonard	268
Major John A. Hottell III	270
Lieutenant General Ying-Hsing Wen	271
First Lieutenant Thomas E. Selfridge	272
Brigadier General René E. De Russy	273

Epilogue	275
Appendix: Men of the Class of 1973 in the Cemetery	277
Bibliography	285
Photo Credits	295
Index	317

Foreword

A measurement of the greatness of a nation is the manner in which it honors and remembers the service and sacrifice of its soldiers. The historic cemetery at the US Military Academy at West Point is a remarkable example of both virtues. On 14 verdant acres overlooking the Hudson River, this national landmark is the final resting place for soldiers from the Revolutionary War to today; principally West Point graduates who lived their lives committed to the motto of the academy: Duty, Honor, Country.

Here rest leaders of character, compassion, and courage. Anchored by the Old West Point Chapel and laid out in elegant circles and rows of manicured gravesites are generations of cadets, officers, and veterans of our wars. They are generals and sergeants, astronauts, and engineers who served the academy's national and enduring mission. Eighteen recipients of the Medal of Honor share this special space with hundreds of others who served with equal devotion to America in peace and war. They include Sylvanus Thayer, known as the Father of the Military Academy; decorated veterans of every major war of our country; and recent graduates who fought in the campaigns of this century. They are "here in ghostly assemblage" by the unique heritage of the Long Gray Line.

At the beginning of the twenty-first century the leadership at West Point undertook a major effort to improve the physical landscape and the management standards of the cemetery in every possible way to ensure that it will stand in sui generis for many more years. Working in alliance with Arlington National Cemetery, the command has set the best-known protocols to conduct the day-to-day work of this historic site. The Corps of Cadets itself has taken on a part of that responsibility through annual orientations and continuous responsibility for the fundamental upkeep of every section of the cemetery. A new Columbarium is now open, and a major project to expand the cemetery is underway after much detailed planning, US Army and alumni funding, and infrastructure development over the past decade.

A moving symbol of one of the greatest leadership institutions in the world, the West Point Cemetery continues to inspire millions of visitors each year to the academy. Every gravesite tells its own story of fortitude, fidelity, and integrity; collectively they speak to the bedrock values of our military profession. In this exceptional book, my classmate Robert Holcomb, himself a former Army officer, brings to life the story of the cemetery with the scholarship and grace this subject fully merits. In your own visit to this tapestry of stone, you will be inspired by its fascinating history, by its natural beauty, and by the palpable sense of duty, honor, and country that is timeless in this sacred place.

David H. Huntoon Jr.
Lieutenant General (Ret.), US Army
Former Superintendent 2010–13

Preface

The purpose of this volume is to describe in words and photographs the cemetery at West Point, New York, located inside the boundaries of the United States Military Academy. The book takes the form of a walking tour through the cemetery, as one might do to while away a few hours on a sunlit summer day. Along the way I will highlight both the natural beauty of the place and the historic or valorous deeds done by the men and women buried here. By doing so, I hope to illuminate some of the significant contributions to our nation's history through the memories of the participants who rest in this tiny plot of sacred land.

The cemetery is small, only covering 14 acres of ground, with just over eight thousand graves. Nevertheless, it contains more than a dozen Medal of Honor recipients, dozens of general officers, an astronaut, engineers, scholars, athletes and coaches, poets, and authors, as well as their family members. It is doubtful if any other similarly sized plot of ground in the United States represents more historical significance to our country. The cemetery contains more than just famous generals. It is the final resting place of many interesting men and women whose lives collectively represent the values and culture of America in general, and the Long Gray Line of West Point graduates in particular. Many sons and daughters of graduates are buried here, alongside their parents, representing in tangible form the linkage and heritage upon which our nation has depended since the founding of the Military Academy in 1802. And the cemetery is not limited to West Point graduates. There are also many enlisted soldiers here who served at West Point, and their wives, sons, and daughters as well. This is truly sacred ground for our nation, for West Point, and for our military men, women, and families.

The emotions invoked here are palpable. There is a sense of pride and awe at the accomplishments of these men and women. There are strong emotions of sadness at the tiny infant graves, the family tragedies that saw so many young children buried here by their parents. There is a sense of tradition at finding several generations of young men and women who followed their fathers or mothers into military service. There is a sense of duty, seeing so many who served their country in one capacity or another, both great and small, and who now rest. There is a deeply personal sense of loss when finding friends, relatives, and classmates buried here. There is serenity along the pathways in this place, silent, peaceful, and calm.

So take a quiet stroll through American history with me and, along the way, reflect on the deep beauty, the quiet serenity, and the commitment to long, faithful, and honorable service to our nation that resides here.

CHAPTER 1

The Entrance and the Old Cadet Chapel

We will begin at the beginning, at the front entrance gates to the cemetery on Washington Road, across from the West Point Fire Station. Our path will take us first into the Old Cadet Chapel, then into adjoining sections of the cemetery sequentially until we finally return to the starting point. Along the way I will point out interesting sights and graves, along with a little bit of the history that is relevant. Where we can, I'll include descriptions of the trees that dot the cemetery, many of which are unique varietals that were expressly brought here to mark or honor a specific grave or section.

There is a pathway through the cemetery, but one must leave the path to visit many of the graves. A certain etiquette should be maintained here by walking along the back of the headstones. Take care not to inadvertently walk directly over a grave; it is a sign of disrespect and carelessness that the inhabitants would deplore. Speak in hushed tones and admire quietly.

The gates are wrought iron and were originally built early in the 1800s to be the main gates to the Military Academy. In 1897 they were moved to this current position to provide the entrance to the cemetery. Another set of these gates exists farther down Washington Road, near Section XXXI, but there is no longer an active road entrance there.

(*Left*) Cemetery Main Gates. (*Above*) Detail of the main gates, showing the crossed cannons

15

The Old Cadet Chapel is just inside the gates. The building is constructed in the Greek Revival architectural style and was originally built in 1837 near Grant Hall. In 1910 the current Cadet Chapel was built, an iconic building towering high over the Plain, and when that happened this chapel was slated for demolition. Cadets and alumni alike were outraged at the thought and raised money to have the building preserved. It was carefully deconstructed, with every brick, board, and pew numbered in sequence and moved to this location. It reopened in 1911. It served as the Jewish Chapel during the 1970s, until a new Jewish chapel was built, and is currently used for Lutheran services on Sunday. The fountain in the front of the chapel depicts a heron on a flower base and was donated to West Point in memory of Lt. Col. Lester J. Tacy, Class of '24, who died in World War II.

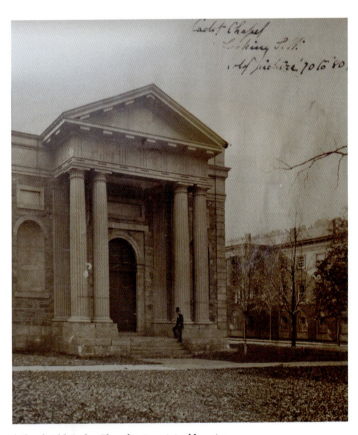

(*Above*) **Old Cadet Chapel in its original location**
(*Right*) **Heron Fountain**
(*Opposite*) **Old Cadet Chapel from the rear**

16 *Stone Tapestry*

The interior of the Old Cadet Chapel is laid out in the classical style, with white-painted pews covered in red velvet cushions. There are eight white Corinthian columns supporting the roof. A large organ fills the balcony. The painting over the altar (the altarpiece) is called a combine, mixing physical objects into the painting. On the right is a furled American flag, and on the left is a classical Greek vase with a gray draping; both are extended into the room by actual cloths painted to match the background, giving a three-dimensional feel to the painting.

(*Prior page*) **Interior of Old Cadet Chapel**
(*Left*) **Detail of Greek vase and drape**
(*Below*) **Detail of flag**

The Entrance and the Old Cadet Chapel   19

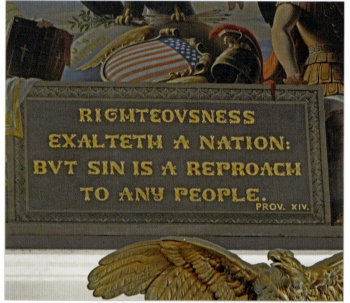

A gilt eagle sits above the center of the altar below the altarpiece, holding a fasces in his talons, an early Roman symbol of power and authority. The fasces consists of a bundle of birch rods bound together for strength, with an ax-head embedded in it. It symbolized magisterial power and was a part of the design on the US Mercury dime in recent memory. Another example of a fasces is on display in the United States House of Representatives chamber in the Capitol.

(*Top left*) **Altarpiece**
(*Above right*) **Detail of lamp on column**
(*Middle right*) **Detail of altarpiece**
(*Bottom right*) **Eagle with fasces**
(*Above*) **Lt. Gen. Winfield Scott's pew nameplate** (see page 112 for a description of General Scott)
(*Overleaf*) **The organ and balcony**

20   *Stone Tapestry*

There are two organs in the chapel: a large one in the balcony and a small one in the front of the chapel. The smaller organ was donated in memory of Lt. Col. John J. Luther, USMA Class of 1977. Luther was an artilleryman who served with distinction in Operation Desert Storm in Kuwait in 1990. He was assigned to the Military Academy staff and while serving here was the president of the Lutheran Church Council. He passed away while stationed here in 2001 and is buried in the cemetery.

Along both walls as you face the altar are dark bronze plaques of varying sizes, mounted in between several large cannons that are embedded in the walls. These are actual cannons, spoils of war captured from the enemy and brought back to be displayed as trophies. Along the right wall the plaques and cannons memorialize the Revolutionary War; along the left wall they honor the Mexican War, the Indian Wars, and the Spanish-American War. The cannons and plaques on the right wall were part of the original Cadet Chapel when it was built in 1837. Those on the left were added to it shortly thereafter, after the Mexican War.

(*Above*) **Right wall of chapel, showing plaques and cannon**
(*Right*) **Detail of a captured cannon, showing the "GR" script symbol identifying the cannon as belonging to "George, Rex," or King George III of England during the Revolution.**

22   *Stone Tapestry*

We'll spend a moment on the right wall first. This wall is dedicated to the generals, officers, and men of the Continental army who fought in the Revolutionary War. There are, of course, no West Point graduates named on this wall, since the Military Academy was not established until 1802, well after the Revolutionary War was finished. The place of honor on this wall is the upper left plaque, which is dedicated to General George Washington, the commander of the Continental army. Similar plaques dot the walls for the major generals who served under Washington. Some of the more noteworthy include Major General Nathaniel Greene; the German Baron von Steuben, who came to help the American cause; and Major General Artemus Ward.

General Greene was second only to Washington in the Continental army, both as a strategist and as an able commander. He effectively led all colonist forces from Delaware to Georgia during the last years of the war. General Greene commanded the highly successful march through the Carolinas in 1780 and 1781 and fought perhaps the decisive battle at Guilford Courthouse (near Greensboro, North Carolina, named after him), defeating General Cornwallis. He put an end to the British "Southern Strategy" and contributed directly to their surrender at Yorktown.

Baron Friedrich Wilhelm von Steuben was a drillmaster and professional soldier in the Prussian army. He came to the colonies to aid Washington in organizing and training the Continental army during the dreadful winter at Valley Forge. A strict disciplinarian, his drive, organizational skills, and attention to detail turned the colonial militias into a competent professional soldiery. He authored the *Regulations for the Order and Discipline of the Troops of the United States*, which was the original field manual for the American army and remained in effect, unchanged, until the War of 1812.

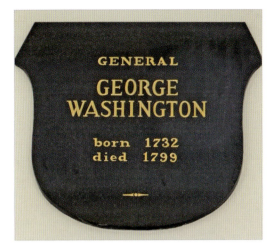

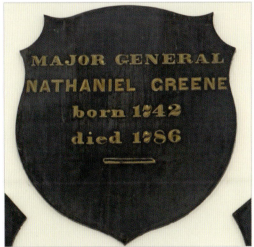

(*Top*) **Plaque for General Washington**
(*Middle*) **Plaque for General Nathaniel Greene**
(*Bottom*) **Plaque for Baron von Steuben**

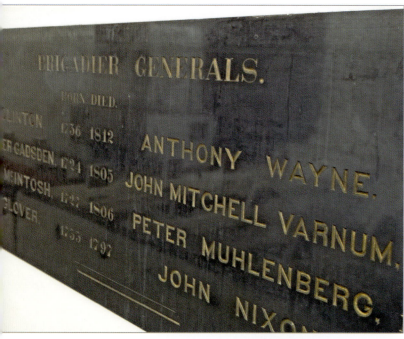

In addition to the individual plaques for major generals, there is a single plaque for the brigadier generals in the service during the Revolution. Prominent among the names is "Mad" Anthony Wayne, the commander at the Battle of Stony Point, just south of West Point. Wayne staged a daring raid on a British fort, with both the approach march and the battle taking place entirely at night. He instructed his men not to fire their weapons, but to assault the fort entirely with the bayonet for silence and surprise. The attack was a remarkable success, taking only thirty minutes to kill seventy British soldiers and capture the rest, securing the fort. Wayne went on to a successful career after the war as a legislator, until he was pressed back into service by then president Washington to participate in the Indian Wars. He led a successful campaign against the Western Indian Confederacy, culminating in a victory at the Battle of Fallen Timbers in Ohio.

Perhaps the most interesting of the plaques on this wall is on the far right, up near the balcony. It identifies a major general with a date of birth, but the name and the date of death have been effaced. It is intended for Benedict Arnold, who was one of the rising stars in the Revolution stable of generals until his betrayal and traitorous attempt to hand over the fort at West Point to the British. West Point occupied a strategic position on the Hudson leading to New York by virtue of its commanding position on the heights above the two 90-degree turns in the Hudson River. Because of the importance of the Hudson River to transport men and supplies quickly between their base in Canada and New York City, the fort at West Point was the most valuable terrain in the whole of the Northeast. Arnold later died in British service.

(*Above*) **Plaque honoring the brigadier generals of the Revolutionary War**
(*Below*) **Plaque for Benedict Arnold**

24   *Stone Tapestry*

In addition to the individual plaques honoring the generals of the Revolution, there is a single plaque on the right front wall of the chapel honoring the officers and men both of the Continental army and the Continental navy. The Daughters of the American Revolution (DAR) of the State of New York commissioned this plaque. The New York state chapter of the DAR was established in 1896 to promote historical preservation, education, and patriotism.

The altar is simple, made of plain wood, befitting a Lutheran chapel. It is accompanied by a beautifully carved mahogany altar rail and lectern. Two louvered doors that go to the sacristy flank the altar.

Moving to the other side of the Old Cadet Chapel, we find a matching plaque on the left front wall, honoring the officers and men of the US Army during the Spanish-American war of 1898–99. This plaque was also commissioned by the DAR of the State of New York.

(*Left*) Plaque on the right front wall honoring the officers and men of the Revolution
(*Right*) Matching plaque on the left front wall honoring the officers and men of the US Army in the Spanish-American War
(*Overleaf*) Altar and altar rail

26 *Stone Tapestry*

The opposite wall is dedicated to the Mexican War, with additional plaques in place for the Florida (Seminole) War and one euphemistically titled "Minor Actions."

The cannons in the wall were trophies taken from the Mexican War; the four are engraved with the names of the battles in which they were captured, along with the dates. They include Mexico City, Vera Cruz, Resaca de la Palma, and Monterey.

The black plaques represent individual battles of the war and list the names of the officers who lost their lives in them and the date of the battle.

"Minor Actions" refers to small-scale engagements that did not rise to the level of full-scale battles between the armies. Nonetheless they could be deadly, as evidenced by the high number of captains and lieutenants who lost their lives in such actions.

Captain Seth B. Thornton, first on the list in minor actions, was originally captured in the opening battle of the Mexican War, called the "Thornton affair." He was paroled back to the United States. He was subsequently killed in a skirmish near Mexico City.

(*Above*) **Plaque and cannon from the Mexican War**
(*Below*) **Plaque memorializing the deaths of officers in minor actions.**

The Entrance and the Old Cadet Chapel 27

The Mexican War was the first in which graduates from the Military Academy played significant roles in the fledgling American army. The American army was commanded by Winfield Scott, who had already served a long and distinguished career before the Mexican War (Scott is buried in Section XXVII A of the cemetery and will be covered in more detail later in this tour).

He conceived and executed a brilliant flanking maneuver against the Mexicans through an amphibious assault at the port of Vera Cruz, on the Gulf coast. After seizing Veracruz, Scott marched the American army overland, following the route taken by Cortez in his earlier conquest of Mexico. Scott concluded the war by an assault upon Chapultepec, the fortress in Mexico City. After the Mexicans surrendered, Scott was named the military governor of Mexico, and he was considered a just and fair governor both by the Americans and the Mexicans.

The plaques on the wall cover all the major battles of the Mexican War, including Veracruz, Resaca de la Palma, Chapultepec, Mexico City, Molino del Rey, Churubusco, Buena Vista, and others. They list the names of the officers killed in the engagements.

Many West Point graduates distinguished themselves in the Mexican War in their roles as relatively junior officers. The story of our Civil War history is filled with names of men who achieved fame and glory in the Mexican War as junior officers, including Robert E. Lee, Ulysses S. Grant, James Longstreet, Thomas "Stonewall" Jackson, Philip Sheridan, and William T. Sherman.

Additional plaques on this wall refer to the Florida Seminole Wars and the Spanish-American War. The Florida War is also memorialized by the Dade Monument outside the chapel.

(*Above and below*) **Detail from the cannons captured in the Mexican War**

28 *Stone Tapestry*

CHAPTER 2
Sections X and IX

Next we will step outside and begin our tour among the sections. Section X is on the immediate left as one exits the rear doors of the chapel, and consists of thirteen rows labeled A through M. This is one of the most diverse sections in the cemetery and contains several prominent sports figures that have connections to West Point, as well as distinguished and innovative generals, authors, heads of academic departments at the academy, and two former superintendents.

Probably the third-most-recognizable monument in the cemetery (after the Viele pyramid and the Butterfield "cake topper," which we will see soon) is the black football-shaped stone memorializing Earl "Red" Blaik, the famous Army football coach. We will begin our tour there.

After we pass out of Section X, we'll move to the next section of the cemetery, Section IX. From General Cota's gravesite we will walk counterclockwise along the circle formed by the columbarium until we reach the small sliver of grass that runs north to the Caretaker's Cottage. In this section we will find several examples of the Long Gray Line, with two brothers buried together and a father-son team, both killed in action in their respective wars.

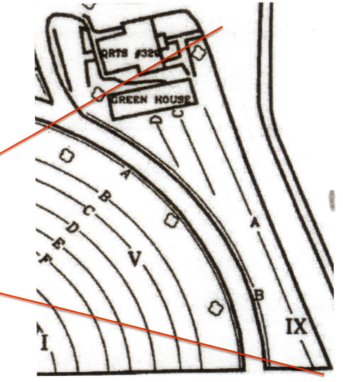

29

Colonel Earl H. "Red" Blaik
Section X, Row G, Grave 131

Red Blaik graduated from USMA in 1920 and achieved lasting fame for his successful coaching of the Army football team. Already a graduate of Miami University in Oxford, Ohio, when he entered West Point, Blaik's class graduated in 1920 instead of 1922 because of World War I. Blaik served two years on active duty, then resigned his commission and began work as an assistant football coach at the University of Wisconsin.

In 1927, Biff Jones, the football coach at Army at the time (whom we shall also see in these pages), brought Blaik back to West Point to serve as an assistant coach. There he excelled until 1934, when he was hired away by Dartmouth to be the head coach. He was considered for the Army head coaching position, but at the time Army required their football coach to be an active-duty officer, which Blaik no longer was. He coached successfully at Dartmouth for seven years, building a record of 45-15-4, winning the Ivy League championship in 1936 and 1937, and raising Dartmouth up to seventh in the nation.

He returned to West Point in 1941 (accepting a commission as a colonel in the bargain) and began his stellar career there. The year before he arrived, Army finished 1-7-1. He turned that around to a 5-3-1 record the next season, then went on to win the national championship in 1944 and again in 1945. He also won the Eastern championship four times, won the Lambert Trophy seven times, and had six unbeaten seasons. His overall record at Army was 121-32-10. In twenty-five years of coaching college football, Red Blaik had only one losing season.

In 1964, Blaik was installed in the National Football Hall of Fame, and in 1986 President Reagan awarded him the Presidential Medal of Freedom.

Stone Tapestry

Glenn W. Davis
Section X, Row H, Grave 150

Glenn Davis was one of the most gifted athletes ever to attend West Point, and he achieved lasting fame under football coach Red Blaik as a part of the backfield duo Mr. Inside and Mr. Outside. Davis was Mr. Outside and was joined by Doc Blanchard as Mr. Inside. Davis graduated from West Point in 1947.

In addition to his superb skills on the football field, he also excelled in baseball, basketball, and track. He held the Military Academy record for the sports aptitude test, which was given to all cadets, scoring 962.5 points out of a possible 1,000. His aptitude for mathematics was not quite as high, and he was sent home after his first semester for tutoring. He rejoined the Corps the following year and teamed up with Doc Blanchard for the remainder of his football career at West Point.

Davis scored twenty touchdowns in 1944 and was the runner-up for the Heisman Trophy that year. In 1945 he scored eighteen touchdowns and again finished as the runner-up in the Heisman voting, second to Doc Blanchard. In 1946, Davis won the Heisman Trophy and scored thirteen touchdowns when Army went 9-0-1 (the tie was to Notre Dame, a 0-0 slugfest in Yankee Stadium). As part of his legacy the Class of 1947 never saw their football team defeated during their entire tenure at West Point.

Davis went on to a pro career after his military commitment expired, joining the LA Rams, but it was cut short by a knee injury in 1951. Davis was inducted into the College Football Hall of Fame in 1961. After his football career ended, he joined the *Los Angeles Times* as a director of special events and served there for more than thirty years. He is buried here within a few yards of his coach, Red Blaik.

Margaret Mary "Maggie" Dixon
Section X, Row I, Grave 174A

Maggie Dixon is a rarity in the cemetery, being neither a West Point graduate nor the spouse of one. She was a women's basketball star at the University of San Diego from 1995 to 1999, then went on to be an assistant coach at DePaul University from 2001 to 2005.

Dixon was hired (at age twenty-eight) as the head coach of the Army women's basketball team a mere eleven days prior to the start of the 2005–06 season. She didn't let that slow her down, as she led the cadets to a 20-11 season in her first year, then won the Patriot League conference tournament. She took the team to the 2006 NCAA Women's Division I Basketball Tournament, Army's first-ever appearance in an NCAA tournament in basketball. They lost in the first round, being beaten by the University of Tennessee. Dixon returned to West Point, where she collapsed and died from cardiac failure the day after the women's championship game.

In November 2006, West Point held the 1st Annual Maggie Dixon Classic, a mini tournament now held in her honor. In addition to the tournament, there is a Maggie Dixon Award presented by the Women's Basketball Coaches Association for the best coach in their first year as a Division I head coach.

It is worth noting that Maggie's brother, Jamie Dixon, is the head basketball coach at Texas Christian University. They became the first-ever brother-sister coaching team to take their teams to the NCAA Division I Men's and Women's tournaments in 2006, with Jamie leading the Pitt Panthers at the time.

This is but one example of women and men of excellence and character who lie here in the cemetery. This is not solely a place of repose for warriors on the battlefield or generals.

Colonel Ronan C. Grady Jr.
Section X, Row A, Grave 33

Ronan Grady graduated in the Class of June 1943 and had a distinguished career as an infantry officer. In World War II he was assigned to the 17th Airborne Division, where he was awarded a Silver Star for valor in combat, as well as a Purple Heart. He later served as defense attaché in Paraguay and was on the Military Assistance Command Vietnam (MAC-V) staff in 1968–69. Grady retired in 1972 as a colonel after twenty-nine years in service.

His major contribution to the merriment of cadets, however, was as the author of the classic West Point book *The Diary of Ducrot Pepys*. It was written in the style of the famous *The Diary of Samuel Pepys*, and Grady recorded for four years the amusements, foibles, tragedies, and joys of being a cadet at West Point in the 1940s. The book is still a classic among graduates, and there is much truth in those pages for modern cadets as well. The term "ducrot" is French; it roughly translates as "mister" and was a common slang term for plebes at that time. Grady wrote hilariously of parades, football, weekends away from West Point, and living with roommates (referred to as "wives" in the cadet vernacular; Grady classified his two roommates as "his sane wife" and "his other wife"). The book was illustrated by a classmate.

Grady is also an example of the Long Gray Line by his association with family members who were also West Point graduates. Grady's brother-in-law was Maj. Gen. Lawrence M. Jones Jr., whom we will meet later in this section. In turn, Jones was the son of Biff Jones, the former Army football coach introduced a few pages ago, and of whom we will hear more shortly. There is a thread of continuity in this cemetery among fathers and sons, wives and daughters, uncles, and nephews (and nieces in more-recent years).

Sections X and IX   33

34   *Stone Tapestry*

Major General Lawrence M. Jones Jr.
Section X, Row A, Grave 24

Larry Jones graduated from West Point in 1945 and was commissioned in the field artillery. He returned to the academy as a professor of physics and later went on to command the Americal Division Artillery in Vietnam as a colonel. During the war he was awarded a Legion of Merit and twelve Air Medals. He was promoted to brigadier general and served in Europe as the assistant division commander of the 1st Armored Division, and upon his promotion to two-star rank he went on to command the 21st Support Command in Kaiserlautern. His final assignment in the Army was as the deputy commanding general of the First Army.

While a cadet, Larry was known to his classmates as a congenial colleague, and he lettered in football and lacrosse. It is not surprising that he was a football player; his father was Biff Jones, the Army football coach in the 1920s. We will hear more of Biff Jones later in this chapter. He was also the brother-in law of Colonel Ronan Grady, of the previous page.

During his tour as West Point as a professor, his toddler son, Lawrence M. Jones III (known to the family as "Chipper"), fell ill and died. Chipper was buried here in the cemetery, in Grave 25 of this section. He was joined by his father and mother years afterward.

This is just the first example (we shall see many others later) of fathers, sons, and grandsons buried here in the cemetery. This is a physical manifestation of the Long Gray Line of West Point, where service to the nation extends down through family ties for many generations.

Sections X and IX 35

Lieutenant General John Norton
Section X, Row A, Grave 1

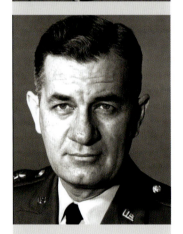

John Norton was the first captain of the USMA Class of 1941. Known by his nickname, "Jack," he was commissioned in the infantry and was immediately sent off to World War II. Assigned to the 82nd Airborne Division, Norton earned three Bronze Stars and a Legion of Merit in combat in Europe. He participated in all four of the division's combat parachute assaults, jumping into Sicily, Salerno, Normandy, and Arnhem.

After the war, Norton became the commander of the 505th Parachute Infantry Regiment. He served on the Howze Board on Tactical Airmobility, a commission that was established to investigate ways in which helicopters could be useful in land combat operations. He was instrumental in devising ways to implement the concepts of air mobility, including aerial gunships, air assault tactics, and logistical resupply. After promotion to major general, Norton went on to command the 1st Cavalry Division in Vietnam in 1966, implementing those tactics with great success. Norton was continually examining new ways in which developing technology could be used to solve Army problems.

When his tour in Vietnam ended, Gen. Norton commanded Project MASSTER at Fort Hood. MASSTER stood for Mobile Army Sensor System Test, Evaluation and Review, which explored potential uses for night observation and intelligence sensors for use in the war. General Norton was promoted to three-star rank and went on to command the Army's Combat Developments Command, where he oversaw all aspects of new equipment development, testing, and fieldings.

Gen. Norton's son, John Jr., is also a graduate of the Military Academy, from the Class of 1970. He was also an airborne infantry officer, another example of the Long Gray Line.

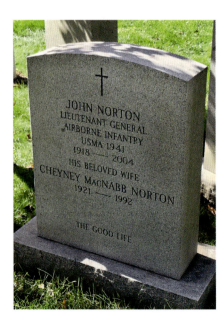

Colonel Russell P. "Red" Reeder
Section X, Row K, Grave 213

"Red" Reeder was an icon among West Point lore from the 1940s through the 1970s. Born at Fort Leavenworth in 1902 into an Army family, Reeder graduated with the Class of 1926 after being turned back twice (for failing mathematics and mechanics). He was commissioned in the infantry. Reeder was an athlete while a cadet in both baseball and football, and he even took leave from the Army in 1928 to try out for the New York Giants baseball team. He made the Giants second team but decided to return to his Army career instead.

He became a highly decorated Army officer in World War II, winning the Silver Star for gallantry in action in New Guinea, and subsequently was transferred to the War Department General Staff in Washington under General George C. Marshall. While in the War Department, Reeder was sent to Guadalcanal to draft a short treatise on lessons learned from the soldiers and marines in combat there, which was published throughout the Army and Marine Corps. He submitted a suggestion to General Marshall that the Army should have an award similar to the Air Medal authorized for the Air Corps, and shortly afterward the Bronze Star medal was created for ground combat soldiers to recognize valor in combat.

As a colonel, Reeder commanded the 12th Infantry Regiment of the 4th Infantry Division and came ashore on Utah Beach on D-day. A few days later he was hit in the ankle by fragments from a German 88 mm shell, ultimately losing his left leg. He was awarded the Distinguished Service Cross for his actions at Normandy.

Red retired from the Army as a colonel in 1946 and joined the West Point staff as the assistant athletic director and assistant baseball coach. He became an author, writing a series of books about a fictitious cadet named Clint Lane as he navigated West Point life in the 1940s. He also wrote his autobiography, titled *Born at Reveille*.

In 1997 the West Point Association of Graduates awarded Red Reeder the Distinguished Graduate Award.

Major General H. Norman Schwarzkopf Sr.
Section X, Row I, Grave 160

H. Norman Schwarzkopf Sr. lies here near his more famous son, whom we shall meet in a few pages. "Schwarzie" was a graduate of the Class of April 1917 along with several other famous officers, such as Mark Clark, Matthew Ridgway, Ernie Harmon, and "Dutch" Cota (of whom more later in this chapter). Upon graduation he was immediately sent to France for service in World War I with the American Expeditionary Force. He was assigned to the 3rd Infantry Division, where he earned a Purple Heart for wounds suffered in action.

Upon his return from the war, Schwarzkopf resigned his commission in the Army and was appointed as the first superintendent of the New Jersey State Police by Governor Edward I. Edwards. He personally trained the first twenty-five candidates for the police force and went on to head the force until 1936. Schwarzkopf took lessons from the Royal Canadian Mounted Police, the Texas Rangers, and the Pennsylvania Highway Patrol and used them to formulate the training for the New Jersey force.

In March 1932, Schwarzkopf was called upon to investigate the kidnapping of Charlie Lindbergh, the twenty-month-old son of Charles and Anne Lindbergh. The case attracted nationwide attention, and he led the search until poor Charlie's body was found on May 12. Schwarzkopf's investigation led to the arrest of Bruno Hauptmann for the kidnapping and subsequent murder of Charlie, resulting in Hauptmann's execution in 1936.

Schwarzkopf returned to active duty in the Army in 1939 with the advent of World War II. He spent the war in Iran, where he had responsibility for the organization of the Iranian national military police force. He was promoted to brigadier general after the war and became the provost marshal for the US forces in occupied Germany. After promotion to major general, he served as the commanding general of the 78th Infantry Division in the New Jersey Army Reserve. The elder General Schwarzkopf passed away in 1958, two years after the graduation of his son, General H. Norman Schwarzkopf Jr.

Colonel Lawrence M. "Biff" Jones Sr.
Section X, Row J, Grave 189

Lawrence M. "Biff" Jones was a West Point graduate, Army colonel, and football coach extraordinaire. We have already met his son in these pages, Major General Lawrence M. Jones Jr., and his grandson Chipper, who passed away so tragically and so young. Biff Jones was a member of the Class of August 1917, accelerated because of US involvement in World War I. His class entered as the Class of 1918 but graduated ten months early; interestingly, they retained the 1918 image upon their class crest rather than revising it.

Biff Jones played tackle on the Army football team and was the team captain in his final season. Upon graduation he saw service as an artilleryman with the American Expeditionary Force in France, serving as an aerial-artillery spotter. After the war he returned to West Point, where he served as a member of the Tactical Department with the additional duty of assistant football coach. In 1926, Biff was named as the head coach of the Army football team, and he remained in that capacity until 1929.

From West Point, Biff moved to Louisiana State University, where he served as the head football coach from 1932 to 1934. Jones ran afoul of Senator Huey Long at LSU; Long had originally helped Biff get the coaching job. He came down to the locker room during a game against Oregon State in 1934. LSU was losing the game, and Senator Long wished to address the players at halftime; Biff refused. Long told him if LSU lost the game, Biff would then be fired. Jones told him, "Win, lose, or draw, I will resign at the end of this game," and closed the locker room door. He was as good as his word.

He then went on to be the head coach at Oklahoma University in the 1935 and 1936 seasons. During this time he remained on active duty in the Army, serving in the ROTC departments at both LSU and OU. In 1937, Biff retired from the Army and took the head coaching job at Nebraska University, which he led to the Rose Bowl in 1941. When WWII arrived, Biff returned to active duty as a colonel and became the graduate manager of athletics at West Point, helping create the vaunted Army football dynasty of the 1940s. Biff is a member of the National College Football Hall of Fame and the hall of fames at both Louisiana State and Nebraska.

40 *Stone Tapestry*

General H. Norman Schwarzkopf Jr.
Section X, Row L, Grave 244

The son of Major General Schwarzkopf, whom we met a few pages ago, achieved his own measure of fame in his career and will be well known to visitors to the cemetery. A member of the West Point Class of 1956, Norman Schwarzkopf Jr. was commissioned in the infantry. He earned a master's degree at USC in 1964 and taught in the Mechanics Department at West Point before heading to Vietnam. There he served as an advisor to the Vietnamese Airborne Brigade, earning two Silver Stars, a Bronze Star, and a Purple Heart before returning to West Point and the Mechanics Department.

Schwarzkopf then began a rapid advancement, commanding an infantry battalion back in Vietnam, where he earned a third Silver Star, a second Purple Heart, and a Distinguished Flying Cross. He went on to command successively larger units, including the 24th Infantry Division and I Corps, before he was appointed as the commander of US Central Command in 1988.

When Saddam Hussein invaded Kuwait in 1990, General Schwarzkopf became the commander of the multination coalition assembled to defeat him. Moving his headquarters to the Middle East, Schwarzkopf led an impressive array of US and allied military might into Saudi Arabia. He brought the VII US Corps down from Europe, XVIII Airborne Corps from Fort Bragg, and elements of Army, Air Force, and Navy commands together with British and French in Operation Desert Shield. At its height, Schwarzkopf commanded 750,000 soldiers, sailors, airmen, and Marines, of which two-thirds were American.

On January 17, 1990, Schwarzkopf began the air campaign of Operation Desert Storm, designed to eject Hussein from Kuwait. On February 24 the ground assault began, concluding successfully in only one hundred hours.

General Schwarzkopf retired in 1991 and was awarded the Association of Graduates Distinguished Graduate Award in 1994.

Lieutenant General James Gavin
Section X, Row L, Grave 235

"Jumpin' Jim" Gavin enlisted in the Army in 1924 and was stationed in Panama. He passed the entrance exams for West Point despite not having completed high school and was a member of the Class of 1929. Gavin was commissioned in the infantry and spent his early career in various infantry regiments at Fort Benning, Fort Sill, and the Philippines.

He came back to West Point to serve in the Tactics Department, where he studied German tactics from early World War II extensively, including their use of airborne troops in the capture of Fort Eben-Emael in Belgium.

Gavin attended the Parachute School at Fort Benning in August 1941 and became involved in the design and creation of the first US airborne divisions. In 1942 he commanded the 505th Parachute Infantry Regiment at age thirty-five. During WWII he led parachute troops throughout and made four combat jumps with the 82nd Airborne Division at Sicily, Salerno, Normandy, and Arnhem. The parachute wings on his headstone have four small stars on them to indicate his combat jumps.

In 1944, Gavin assumed command of the 82nd, becoming the youngest division commander in the Army at age thirty-seven. After the war he continued to command the division on occupation duty in Berlin.

After he returned to the United States, Gavin went on to higher postwar command. He participated in the Howze Board, which resulted in the creation of airmobile divisions in Vietnam, and headed up the Army's Research and Development command. The M113 Armored Personnel Carrier was developed during his tenure there, and he retired in 1958 as a lieutenant general.

He became an author, writing *War and Peace in the Space Age*, and served as president of the Arthur D. Little company. In 1961 he came back to service to be the US ambassador to France. Gen. Gavin died in 1990.

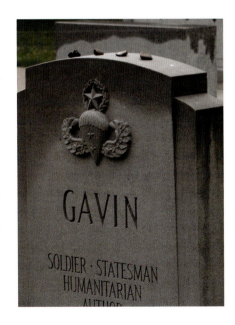

Major General Norman "Dutch" Cota
Section X, Row M, Grave 287

Norman Cota, nicknamed "Dutch" as a boy, graduated from West Point in the Class of April 1917, along with H. Norman Schwarzkopf Sr., seen earlier in these pages. He served in a variety of infantry, finance, and chemical assignments prior to World War II.

In WWII he was assigned as a brigadier general to the 29th Infantry Division as assistant division commander and, as such, was the first general officer to come ashore on D-day. He landed with the second wave, about an hour after H-hour. Cota found the troops on the beachhead disorganized and frozen in place with fear. He first rallied the 5th Rangers with the cry "Rangers lead the way!," which became the motto of the Ranger Regiment and remains so up to the present day. He is also credited with the cry "Gentlemen, we are being killed on the beaches. Let's go inland and be killed!" Under his personal leadership while under fire on the beachhead, the 29th Division managed to breach the seawall and open vehicular exit paths out of the beachhead for the subsequent forces. General Cota won both the Distinguished Service Cross and the Silver Star for his valorous actions at Normandy.

After D-day, Cota was promoted to major general, took command of the 28th Infantry Division, and led them through the campaign across France and into the Hürtgen Forest. He won a second Silver Star and a Purple Heart during the breakout at St. Lo.

The only American soldier executed for desertion in World War II, Private Eddie Slovik, was in the 28th Infantry Division, and General Cota personally reviewed and approved his death sentence. He later said Slovik's execution was the "toughest fifteen minutes of my life."

44   *Stone Tapestry*

Patricia Buyers
Section IX, Row A, Grave 16

The first gravesite we will linger at in Section IX is that of Patricia Buyers, one of the Cadet Hostesses.

Pat Buyers (*at center in photo*) was married to Major John Buyers of the West Point Class of June 1943. Major Buyers was an engineer officer who passed away following surgery in 1966. After his death, Pat moved to West Point to join the Hostess Office, which was in the gingerbread house just below the Plain level, off Thayer Road.

Pat was one of three Cadet Hostesses between the years 1968 and 1974. The Cadet Hostess office, which still exists, has the mission to "support the social development of the Corps of Cadets," which could also be described as "making a silk purse of a sow's ear." These women are responsible for teaching the finer things in life to cadets, such as ballroom dancing, how to go through a receiving line, dress codes for different social events, and social etiquette. Many a cadet learned how to handle dreaded social occasions through the patient and kind tutelage of Pat. She was also a valuable resource for cadet dates during a time when the academy was an all-male institution. Most dates had little comprehension of the social activities required of an Army officer, and Pat was a wealth of practical knowledge.

The house where the Hostess Office was located was itself noteworthy at West Point, having been the home of Master Sergeant Marty Maher and his wife, Mary, whom we shall meet later in another section of the cemetery. Maher had spent fifty-five years at West Point as an enlisted man and a civilian. His book *Bringing Up the Brass* describes his life here. The house was featured prominently in the movie *The Long Gray Line*, based on his book. After Maher's passing, the house was used as the office for the Cadet Hostesses.

46 *Stone Tapestry*

George R. Pinkerton and Captain Charles C. Pinkerton
Section IX, Row A, Graves 10 and 11

The Pinkerton brothers are another example of the Long Gray Line in action. Charles Pinkerton was commissioned in the Class of January 1943 and became a flier in the Army Air Corps. Pinkerton served in the European theater of operations, flying sixty-five missions in B-26 bombers. After the war he was assigned to the Wright Field Engineering School in Ohio, which later became the Air Force Institute of Technology.

Charles's brother, George Pinkerton, wanted to emulate his older brother and applied for admission to West Point. George won an appointment in 1947 from his local congressman but, tragically, died six days later in his sleep while visiting the home of his sister.

Charles had previously decided he wanted to be buried at West Point and had reserved two plots in the cemetery for himself and his future wife. Upon hearing of George's death, Charles felt he should be interred at West Point to complete the journey he had just begun, and he petitioned Protestant chaplain John B. Walthour for permission. Walthour raised the matter with Superintendent General Maxwell D. Taylor, who approved it even though George had not yet been sworn in as a cadet.

Charles himself lived only a short time past his brother, dying in an airplane accident in Ohio in 1949 when his P-51 Mustang crashed in bad weather.

Sections X and IX   47

Lieutenant Colonel Frederick G. Terry and Major Frederick G. Terry Jr.

Section IX, Row A, Graves 3 and 4

This father and son exemplify the Long Gray Line, similar to the Pinkerton family we just met. Fred Terry Sr. was a member of the Class of 1930 and was commissioned in the field artillery. In 1936 he was newly married and assigned to West Point to teach history. While he was there, his son, Fred Jr., was born in the post hospital. Fred Jr. represented the fourth generation of West Point graduates in their family.

During World War II, Fred Sr. was killed in an air accident on Saipan in June 1944. He had volunteered to go up as an aerial observer and call for artillery fire from the aircraft. While aloft, his aircraft was struck by a B-25 bomber who did not see them, killing all aboard. Fred Jr. was a lad of seven at the time. He went on to be admitted to the Class of 1960 and graduated as an armor officer.

Fred Jr. then volunteered for the 1st Special Forces Group, and during 1962–64 he spent time in Laos and Vietnam, where he was awarded the Silver Star for gallantry in action. Returning to the United States, he went to flight school and became an Army aviator, just like his father. He returned to Vietnam in 1965 as a pilot and won four Distinguished Flying Crosses and twenty-nine Air Medals during this tour.

Returning home in 1966, Fred Jr. became an instructor pilot at Fort Rucker and attended the Infantry Advanced Course. In 1968 he returned to Vietnam for his third tour, as commander of an air cavalry troop. During a mission to rescue wounded soldiers from a mine strike, Fred Jr.'s aircraft was struck midair by a second helicopter also coming to assist. There were no survivors. Fred Jr. was awarded the Bronze Star and sixteen additional Air Medals from his final Vietnam tour.

The Terry family represents an honored tradition of service to the nation, volunteering for difficult and dangerous assignments and heroic deeds in combat. It is a tragic coincidence that both died in flight after being struck by another US aircraft.

General Paul D. Harkins
Section IX, Row A, Grave 53

General Paul D. Harkins had a distinguished career spanning three wars that culminated in his serving as the commander of the Military Assistance Command, Vietnam (MAC-V), during the early phases of the Vietnam War. General Harkins enlisted in the Massachusetts National Guard in 1922, rising to the rank of sergeant in a cavalry regiment.

At age twenty-one he entered West Point, graduating with the Class of 1929. Commissioned in the cavalry, he began his career at Fort Bliss, Texas. By 1939, General Harkins joined the 3rd Cavalry Regiment and while here began a close association with General George Patton that lasted until Patton's death in 1945. He began his participation in World War II with the invasion of North Africa and continued with the planning of and then the invasion of Sicily. He continued to accompany Patton in the Third Army and landed in France in 1944 six days after D-day. General Harkins played a pivotal role in the decisive left-turn movement of the Third Army during the Battle of the Bulge. After General Patton died in a traffic accident in 1945, he escorted Mrs. Patton back to the United States.

General Harkins became the commandant of cadets at West Point in 1948 and served in that capacity until 1951. He then was assigned to Korea as the chief of staff of the Eighth Army under General Maxwell Taylor. Ultimately he was promoted to major general and commanded the 45th and then the 24th Infantry Divisions. General Harkins returned to the Army staff in Washington until he was promoted to lieutenant general and assigned to Turkey as the commander of the Allied Land Forces, Southeastern Europe.

In 1962, General Harkins was promoted to four stars and left the United States to command MAC-V in Vietnam. For two and a half years he held that assignment, until his retirement in 1964. After retirement, General Harkins worked as a military advisor to the movie *Patton* and authored a book, *When the Third Cracked Europe*.

50 *Stone Tapestry*

CHAPTER 3
The Caretaker's Cottage

Taking our leave of General Harkins, we continue northward out of Section IX and toward the Caretaker's Cottage. The cottage was originally built in 1872 as a one-story dwelling and was renovated in 1905, when a second story was added. It is the only other building in the cemetery other than the Old Cadet Chapel. Originally built to house the caretaker's family, it has had many functions over the years, and it currently houses the West Point Cemetery Memorial Affairs offices.

The two photographs below show how little changed the cottage has been since the second story was added in 1905. To the left of the house (*in the top picture*) can be seen an old greenhouse that was a part of the groundskeeper's domain. That is now gone, eliminated as the cemetery began to expand. The half-timbered frame on the second story is striking. The gable roof is slate, and the natural grains form a zigzag pattern. The house features two side walkways, with granite pillars supporting the roof. The whole building looks to be in Elizabethan style, matching much of the architecture at West Point.

To the left of the cottage as you face it is a very large tree, a London planetree (*Platanus × acerifolia*). The tree is a cross between an American sycamore and an oriental planetree. It is estimated to be 70 to 100 feet tall.

In front of the cottage, in the traffic circle, is the Anderson Fountain, named in honor of General Robert Anderson, USMA Class of 1825. Anderson, whom we shall see in more detail later in our walk, was the officer commanding the garrison at Fort Sumter, South Carolina, at the beginning of the Civil War. Anderson resisted the bombardment of Fort Sumter as long as he could, finally surrendering the fort on April 14, 1861. He continued to serve throughout the Civil War, and on April 14, 1865, precisely four years to the day after surrendering, Anderson was on hand to raise the very same flag he had lowered four years earlier.

The Caretaker's Cottage   53

CHAPTER 4

Sections XVIII and XXVI

Continuing northward from the Caretaker's Cottage, we enter a section known for having a high density of West Point leadership throughout most of the twentieth century. No fewer than ten superintendents and commandants are buried in Section XVIII, with their tenure covering many of the years between 1954 and 1996. The commandant position at West Point is usually a brigadier general who is responsible for the training and discipline of the Corps of Cadets, including all their military instruction and their summer training. The dean, also a brigadier general, is responsible for all academic instruction, and the superintendent, formerly a major general but now a lieutenant general position, is responsible for everything that happens at West Point, including the operation of the garrison. Two renowned military authors also lie here: Aubrey Newman and Vincent Esposito. An entire generation of cadets learned their military history from the textbook authored by Esposito, the *West Point Atlas of American Wars*.

In an interesting juxtaposition, astronaut Ed White (killed in the Apollo 1 fire at Cape Canaveral) lies next to George Goethals (builder of the Panama Canal). The canal and the Apollo moon-landing program represent two of the most impressive technological and engineering achievements in the century, and they lie side by side.

In Section XXVI we begin our journey into the Civil War era. We will meet two veterans of the Gettysburg campaign: John Buford, who began the initial delaying engagement as the senior cavalry commander on-site (played superbly by actor Sam Elliot in the movie *Gettysburg*), and Alonzo Cushing, only two years out of West Point when he was killed repulsing Pickett's Charge, dying as he fired the last shot of his last cannon on Cemetery Ridge. Cushing is the first Congressional Medal of Honor winner we shall meet on our tour, but by no means the last. Men who have won the Medal of Honor are indicated in these pages by a small replica of the medal in the upper right corner of the page. There are two designs of the Medal of Honor: one early design and one more modern design. The one relevant at the time of award will be shown.

Major General Philip R. Feir
Section XVIII, Row B, Grave 12

Major General Philip Feir, Class of 1949, was the fifty-fifth commandant of cadets at West Point, from 1972 to 1975. General Feir was a tackle on the national championship Army football team, along with "Doc" Blanchard, Glenn Davis, and Earl Blaik (whom we met in chapter 2). Feir was an all-around athlete, making all-state in basketball prior to coming to West Point and lettering in football and lacrosse while a cadet.

After graduation, Feir was commissioned in the infantry and began a series of infantry command and staff assignments. He was both Airborne and Ranger qualified and served in Italy and Korea, as well as in stateside assignments. He attended graduate school at Georgia Tech, graduating in 1960 with a master's degree in electrical engineering. He then came back to West Point to serve as an instructor in the Department of Electrical Engineering. As noted on his headstone, there was a saying among the cadets in the sections he taught that the "only thing to fear is Feir himself."

General Feir commanded the 2nd Battalion, 35th Infantry, in combat in Vietnam as a lieutenant colonel, then returned overseas to command the 1st Brigade, 4th Infantry Division, as a colonel. He also commanded another brigade (1st Brigade, 25th Infantry Division) and subsequently became the assistant division commander of the 25th Infantry Division.

General Feir returned to West Point in 1972 to assume his duty as the commandant of cadets. This time the entire Corps became familiar with the motto now engraved upon his headstone. Well noted as a disciplinarian, General Feir was nonetheless respected by the cadets as being "tough but fair."

His subsequent assignments included command of the 7th Infantry Division at Fort Ord, and finally as the deputy commanding general of Vth Corps in Frankfurt, Germany.

58 *Stone Tapestry*

Lieutenant General Howard D. Graves
Section XVIII, Row C, Grave 19

Lieutenant General Howard Graves is the first superintendent we shall meet on our path, serving from 1991 to 1996. A member of the Class of 1961, General Graves graduated as the second man in his class in academic standing and was a Rhodes scholar. General Graves had a distinguished military and academic career and was named a Distinguished Graduate of West Point in 2001.

Commissioned in the Corps of Engineers, General Graves began his career studying at Oxford as a Rhodes scholar from 1961 to 1965. He then returned to the United States, where he had early assignments in engineer units, including in the Dominican Republic, where he earned a Bronze Star medal. Graves returned to Oxford for a master of letters degree in medieval and modern languages.

General Graves was then assigned as a battalion operations officer and assistant engineer of the 1st Cavalry Division in Vietnam in 1968–69, where he earned two more Bronze Stars and five Air Medals. He then returned to West Point, where he taught in the Social Sciences Department. After his tour on the faculty, General Graves returned to the field, holding engineer and staff assignments of ever-increasing responsibilities, including commanding the 54th Engineer Battalion in Germany and the 20th Engineer Brigade, and finally as the assistant division commander of the 1st Infantry Division.

Graves served as the vice director of the Joint Staff in Washington before being named the commandant of the Army War College in Carlisle, Pennsylvania. After three years of leading the Army's senior service college, General Graves returned to the Joint Staff as the assistant to the chairman. It was from this position that he was tapped to return to West Point to be the fifty-fourth superintendent.

After General Graves's service as superintendent, he retired from the Army and became a visiting professor at the University of Texas. In 1999, General Graves was named the chancellor of Texas A&M University in College Station, where he served until he passed away from cancer in 2003.

Brigadier General Richard J. Tallman
Section XVIII, Row C, Grave 21

Brigadier General Richard Tallman was a soldier's soldier. As an enlisted machine gunner in World War II, he earned both a Combat Infantryman's badge and a battlefield promotion to second lieutenant while serving in the 42nd Infantry Division. After the war he resigned his commission to attend West Point, graduating in the Class of 1949. He served in the Korean War as a company commander, where he earned two Bronze Stars for valor. In 1960, Tallman returned to West Point, where he served in the Tactical Department.

General Tallman served four tours in Vietnam, including one in the headquarters of the Military Assistance Command, Vietnam, and one as an advisor with the Vietnamese army. He returned as a battalion commander in the 101st Airborne Division.

After his return from his third Vietnam tour, General Tallman was assigned again to West Point as the commander of the 2nd Regiment in the Corps of Cadets, and later as the deputy commandant.

General Tallman was on his fourth tour in Vietnam as the deputy commanding general of the 3rd Regional Assistance Command in 1972 when he was killed in action during the battle of An Loc. He was the last US general officer to give his life in Vietnam.

General Tallman's legacy in the Long Gray Line includes two sons (one of whom was the first captain of the Class of 1973), two granddaughters, two grandsons, and three sons-in-law. General Tallman had a bridge named after him in his hometown of Honesdale, Pennsylvania.

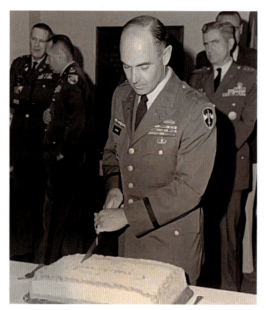

Lieutenant General Blackshear M. Bryan
Section XVIII, Row C, Grave 24

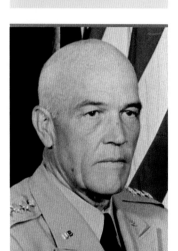

General Bryan served as the forty-third superintendent of the Military Academy, serving from 1954 to 1956. He had a long and distinguished career prior to returning to West Point. Bryan graduated in the Class of 1922, although he was originally in the Class of 1923. During WWI, several classes were accelerated, and the cadets in the Class of '23 were given the option of graduating early with the Class of 1922. Bryan was one of thirty members who opted to graduate early.

General Bryan was attending the Virginia Military Institute in Lexington when he received his appointment to West Point. He was an excellent athlete while a cadet, and after his commissioning as an artillery second lieutenant he returned to West Point to serve as the assistant football coach during the 1925 and 1926 seasons. Bryan coached alongside "Biff" Jones, whom we met earlier. Bryan returned twice more to West Point to teach, from 1928 to 1929 and again from 1933 to 1934.

During World War II, General Bryan headed up the Prisoner of War Division within the Provost General's Office and was responsible for the internment of Japanese citizens and all prisoner-of-war camps within the United States. During the Korean War, General Bryan commanded the 24th Infantry Division, his first combat command. He subsequently took command of the XVI Corps in Japan and had a leading role in the armistice talks that ended the Korean War in 1953. He returned to Korea to command I Corps until he was appointed as the superintendent.

General Bryan, as superintendent, appeared on a popular television show at the time called *What's My Line*, where contestants tried to guess the occupation of the mystery guest on the basis of a few clues given to them. That was certainly the first, and most likely the last, time a superintendent had so appeared!

General Bryan returned to the regular Army after his tour as superintendent, commanding first the US Army, Pacific, in Hawaii and then the First United States Army in New York City. He retired in 1960 and went on to serve as the first president of Nassau Community College on Long Island. Two of his sons also served in the Army, and both perished in aircraft accidents.

Stone Tapestry

Lieutenant General Garrison H. "Gar" Davidson
Section XVIII, Section D, Grave 27

It is fitting that General Davidson and General Bryan lie so close together in the cemetery, since "Gar" Davidson was the superintendent who immediately followed Blackshear Bryan, serving from 1956 to 1960. Davidson had the unique distinction of being the Army football head coach for five seasons, in addition to his stellar military achievements. Commissioned from the Class of 1927, he went into the engineer branch. In 1930 he returned to West Point as an instructor in philosophy and became the assistant football coach. In 1933 he was appointed the youngest head coach in Army football history (while still serving as a commissioned officer) and ran the Black Knights for five seasons, amassing a 35-11-1 record. He never had a losing season as head coach.

In World War II, General Davidson returned to his engineer duties and served in Patton's army as an engineer during the invasions of North Africa, Sicily, and Italy. In September 1943 he was promoted to brigadier general, and General Patton pinned one of his own stars on Davidson's shirt. At the conclusion of the war, General Davidson served as the first president of the Nuremberg War Crimes Tribunal in Germany.

General Davidson served in the Eighth Army in the Korean War, directing construction of a defensive perimeter line near Pusan. After the war he began an extensive career as an Army educator, first by commanding the Army Command and General Staff College at Fort Leavenworth, then by becoming superintendent at West Point.

After his tour as superintendent, General Davidson returned to troop duty, commanding the Seventh Army in West Germany. He was in that command during the Berlin Wall crisis in 1961. He then returned to the United States, where he again followed General Bryan by commanding the First United States Army in New York before his retirement. General Davidson continued as an educator after his retirement, serving as the vice president of the University of California at Berkeley.

Lieutenant General Willard W. Scott Jr.
Section XVIII, Section D, Grave 30

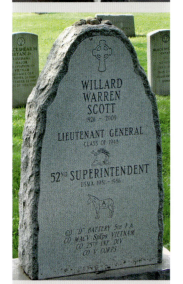

"Scotty" was one of the best-known, best-liked, and longest-serving superintendents in the academy's history. During his tenure as the fifty-second superintendent, General Scott oversaw the recovery from an unfortunate cheating scandal prior to his arrival, the turnaround of the football program back to success, and the introduction of women into the Corps of Cadets. Scotty served for five years in the assignment, from 1981 to his retirement in 1986.

General Scott graduated in the Class of 1948 and was commissioned in the field artillery. During the Vietnam War, General Scott commanded the 23rd Artillery Group and the Headquarters, Military Assistance Command, Vietnam Special Troops in Saigon. After the war he was selected to command the 25th Infantry Division in Hawaii, and finally to command V Corps in Germany.

Interestingly, there were two W. W. Scotts at West Point when he was a cadet. In the Class of 1950 there was a Winfield W. Scott, who rose to prominence in the US Air Force. When Scotty was the superintendent at West Point, the other General Scott was the superintendent at the Air Force Academy. Scotty also shared the name of a noted TV personality and weatherman, Willard Scott. General Scott took this in stride and used to introduce himself as "the other Willard Scott."

General Scott had three themes while he was the superintendent: to improve the athletic program, especially football; to reground the Honor Code among the Corps; and to introduce women into the Corps in a manner befitting the traditions of West Point. He accomplished all three in his tenure. He was noted for attending, along with his wife, Dusty, six or seven athletic events each weekend, and he took great pride in his ability to ride the mule during football games.

After his retirement, General Scott served on the staff at the Institute for Defense Analyses in Alexandria, Virginia. There he participated in operational testing of many Army systems, assisting in providing objective results to the secretary of defense.

64 *Stone Tapestry*

General Wayne A. Downing
Section XVIII, Row D, Grave 32

Two graves away from Scotty we find General Wayne Downing's simple headstone. General Downing was a special-operations expert who served in several positions of increasing importance in the shadowy world of special operations.

General Downing graduated with the Class of 1962 and was commissioned in the Infantry branch. After Ranger school he joined the 173rd Airborne Brigade in Vietnam, where he served as a platoon leader and as the aide to the commanding general. After an additional assignment at the Infantry School, General Downing returned to Vietnam as a company commander in the 25th Infantry Division, followed by tours as an operations officer for both a battalion and a brigade.

General Downing then joined the Ranger Regiment for several tours as an operations officer, battalion commander, and, finally, as the regimental commander. He went into the special-operations community, initially as the commander of the Joint Special Operations Command at Fort Bragg. During this tour he commanded all the special-operations forces that participated in the invasion of Panama in Operation Just Cause. Subsequently, General Downing commanded a task force of special-operations forces who operated behind enemy lines during the first Gulf War, tracking and attacking SCUD missile sites.

In 1991, General Downing was appointed to command the US Army Special Operations Command, and two years later he was elevated to the four-star position of commander in chief, US Special Operations Command. In this position General Downing was responsible for training, equipping, and deploying more than 47,000 personnel from all services to accomplish special-operations missions.

After his retirement in 1996, General Downing served on the National Commission on Terrorism and was the deputy national security advisor for combating terrorism. In 2006 the West Point Association of Graduates presented General Downing with the Distinguished Graduate Award.

General Bernard W. Rogers
Section XVIII, Row D, Grave 38

General Bernie Rogers served as the fifty-third commandant of cadets at West Point from 1967 to 1969. Rogers graduated in the Class of June 1943, one of the accelerated wartime classes during World War II. He was a distinguished cadet, rising to the rank of first captain of the Corps of Cadets. He also graduated twelfth in his class and was selected for a Rhodes scholarship.

During the Korean War, General Rogers commanded the 3rd Battalion, 9th Infantry, in combat. He later commanded the 1st Battalion, 23rd Infantry, and then a brigade within the 24th Infantry Division.

General Rogers served during Vietnam as the assistant division commander in the 1st Infantry Division and was awarded the Distinguished Service Cross—second only to the Medal of Honor—for personal valor in leading a counterattack against Vietcong raiders on a South Vietnamese special-forces camp. It was after this assignment that Rogers came back to West Point to be the commandant.

Following his assignment at West Point, Rogers was selected to promotion to major general and commanded the 5th Infantry Division at Fort Carson. From there he became the US Army's deputy chief of staff for personnel. After promotion to the rank of general, Rogers became the commander of the Army's Forces Command. In 1976, General Rogers was named to be the Army's chief of staff, a post he held until 1979. During this time he began a period of renaissance within the Army, rebuilding morale and capability after the decline following Vietnam.

Following his tenure as chief, General Rogers continued on active service, moving to Europe to become the supreme Allied commander, Europe (SACEUR), leading all the armies of the NATO Alliance. Rogers served as SACEUR for eight years, longer than any other in the post. Simultaneously he was the commander in chief of the United States European Command. He is another selectee for the Distinguished Graduate award, like General Downing, whom we met previously. Rogers was granted the distinction in 1995.

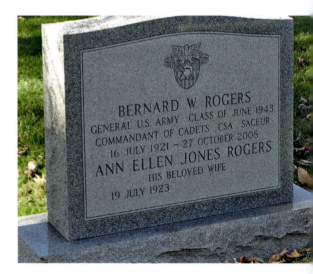

66 *Stone Tapestry*

Major General Aubrey S. "Red" Newman
Section XVIII, Row E, Grave 42

Aubrey Newman, known as "Red," graduated in the Class of 1925. A gifted athlete, like so many of the men and women buried here, he competed in the pentathlon in the 1928 Olympics. Newman served in a variety of assignments in the Pacific army prior to World War II, including company commands in the 26th Infantry and the 19th Infantry. He was the chief of staff of the 24th Infantry Division shortly after the outbreak of the war. Following a short assignment to the Command and General Staff College, he returned to the 24th Division to take command of the 34th Infantry Regiment for the invasion of Leyte in the Philippines in 1944.

During the invasion the regiment was pinned down on the beaches. Then colonel Newman arrived on the scene and quickly realized that the only way to escape was to drive directly ahead into the jungle and get away from the killing fields on the beach. Standing up and crying, "Follow me!," Newman led his men in a charge up off the beaches. The cry "Follow me!" has become the battle cry of the American infantryman ever since and is still the motto of the Infantry School at Fort Benning. Newman was awarded the Distinguished Service Cross, the Silver Star, and the Purple Heart for his leadership on Leyte.

Newman rose in the service to become a major general, including assignments as the assistant division commander of the 82nd Airborne Division and as the deputy commandant of the Infantry School. He was an accomplished writer, penning a treatise on leadership titled *Follow Me: The Human Element in Leadership*, in three volumes. He also wrote a second book on character development in the Army, titled *What Generals Are Made Of*. General Newman was a contributor to *ARMY* magazine for more than twenty years, writing a monthly column called "The Forward Edge."

Sections XVIII and XXVI   **67**

Brigadier General Vincent J. Esposito
Section XVIII, Row F, Grave 62

General Esposito, known as "Mike" to family and friends for some unknown reason, was a classmate of Aubrey Newman's in the Class of 1925. Esposito enlisted in the Army in 1919, prior to his attending West Point, and rose in the ranks from private to battalion sergeant major in the period of seven months while serving in the Army Occupation Forces in Germany.

After graduation, General Esposito was commissioned in the Army Air Corps but shortly afterward decided to transfer to the Corps of Engineers. During his early years in the Army, he served in a variety of assignments, one of which included the opportunity to get a second bachelor's degree in mechanical engineering from the Massachusetts Institute of Technology. During World War II, Mike served on the War Department General Staff in Washington as a colonel.

Esposito represented the War Department General Staff at several important wartime conferences, including those held in Quebec, Malta, Yalta, and Potsdam. At the conclusion of the war, he served as one of the first instructors at the National War College and was there until 1947, when he was assigned back to West Point. He reported as professor and deputy head of the Department of Military Art and Engineering (the deputy heads of departments at the academy have long been known as the "knot heads" to distinguish them from the department heads). Esposito served in this capacity until 1956, when he was promoted to be the head of the department.

He served as the head of department until his retirement in 1963. During his sixteen-year span in the Department, General Esposito became known as one of the foremost educators in the theory and practice of the military art and was the principal editor of the *West Point Atlas of American Wars*. This volume has been a mainstay of instruction at West Point ever since its introduction and is still in use today. He followed shortly afterward with a companion volume on the Napoleonic campaigns.

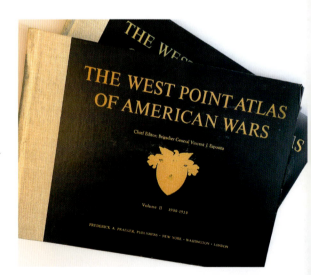

68   *Stone Tapestry*

General Sam S. Walker
Section XVIII, Row F, Grave 65

Sam Sims Walker was another member of the Long Gray Line similar to those we have seen before. His father was Walton Walker, also a general officer, who was killed in a jeep accident in Korea while serving as the commander of the Eighth Army. Sam was born at West Point in 1925, while his father served as a tactical officer. Walker enrolled at the Virginia Military Institute in 1941 but transferred to West Point the following year. After graduation with the Class of 1946, General Walker was commissioned in the infantry and was serving as a company commander in the 24th Infantry Division in Korea when his father was killed. He escorted his father's body back to the United States for burial. Walker himself earned a Silver Star for battlefield valor while in Korea.

General Walker then went on to distinguished assignments as he rose in ranks, serving as a tactical officer at West Point and as aide to the chief of staff of the Army, and was a distinguished graduate of his War College class in 1963.

General Walker then volunteered to go to Vietnam, where he earned a second Silver Star for gallantry and a Distinguished Flying Cross. He was promoted to brigadier general in 1968 and came back to West Point to serve as commandant from 1969 to 1972. After his tour as commandant, Walker was promoted to major general and took command of the 3rd Infantry Division in Germany.

In 1977, General Walker was selected to be promoted to four-star rank, the youngest full general in the Army at the time. He was appointed to a NATO command with the unwieldy name of commanding general, Allied Land Forces Southeast Europe (COMLANDSOUTHEAST), in Turkey. During that time, our relations with our Turkish ally were acrimonious, and we ultimately initiated an arms embargo against Turkey for political reasons (they had deployed troops to Cyprus earlier in 1974). In 1978 the commanding general position was rotated back to a Turkish general, and General Walker retired.

After his retirement, Sam Walker returned to VMI and became the superintendent, where he served from 1981 to 1988. In 2005, General Walker was awarded the Distinguished Graduate Award by the West Point Association of Graduates.

70   *Stone Tapestry*

General William C. Westmoreland
Section XVIII, Row F, Grave 66

General William Westmoreland needs no introduction in these pages. "Westy" was the commander of the US forces in Vietnam from 1964 to 1968 and became the face of the unpopular war to millions of citizens. It is worth noting that General Westmoreland had a brilliant career in the Army besides his Vietnam tour, including as superintendent at West Point and as chief of staff of the Army. He was named a Distinguished Graduate in 1996.

Westmoreland began his career at the Citadel, where he attended his first year (similar to General Walker at VMI). The following year he was appointed to West Point, where he became the first captain of the Class of 1936. After graduation he was commissioned in the field artillery. He served as the commander of B Battery, 1st Battalion, 18th Field Artillery, at Fort Sill (a distinction that the author of this book can also claim) prior to WWII. During the war, Westmoreland served in North Africa, Sicily, France, and Germany. After the war he attended Airborne School and served in a series of assignments with airborne units, including the 504th Parachute Infantry Regiment as a colonel. He became one of the youngest brigadier generals in the Army in 1952, when he was promoted at age thirty-eight. He commanded an airborne regimental combat team in the Korean War and went on to command the 101st Airborne Division in 1958, and then the XVIII Airborne Corps in 1963.

It was after his corps command that Westy went to Vietnam to command the US forces there. He served in Saigon from 1964 until 1968, when he turned over command to one of his classmates, General Creighton Abrams. Westy returned to the United States, where he became the Army chief of staff. His biggest responsibility as CSA was to transition the Army from the Vietnam era to an all-volunteer force, which he did successfully. The Army remains an all-volunteer force today. He retired in 1972. Westmoreland ran for the governor of South Carolina in the 1974 election but lost.

Westmoreland became embroiled in a legal battle after an interview with CBS's Mike Wallace, during which he was accused of ordering his staff officers to lie about enemy infiltration figures. He sued for libel, and the case was ultimately settled to his satisfaction out of court.

Major General Edward H. White Sr.
Section XVIII, Row G, Grave 78

General White is another example of the Long Gray Line in action and, like the senior Schwarzkopf we met earlier, had his son eclipse his own exemplary career. "Eddie" White graduated in the Class of 1924 and was commissioned in the fledgling Army Air Corps. After attending both Primary and Advanced Flying Schools, he went on to attend the Balloon and Airship School as well. He made the first successful landing of a dirigible on water, landing to rescue a stranded balloonist. From 1931 to 1933, General White commanded the 6th Pursuit Squadron at Wheeler Field in Hawaii.

General White then went on to graduate from the Army Industrial College in Washington and began a successful move into the procurement side of the Army Air Corps. He was selected to attend Harvard Business School, where he earned a master's degree in business administration.

General White soon found many uses for this newfound knowledge, spending most of World War II in budgeting, fiscal, and materiel matters in the Air Materiel Command and later in the Air Force when it was established in 1947. He also managed a brief tour in Burma during the war in a special mission assignment related to flying supplies over "the Hump" into China.

After the war ended, General White took command of the 1503 Air Transport Wing, based in Japan, where his area of responsibility extended from Honolulu to Karachi, Pakistan. During the Korean War, White's wing was responsible for transporting wounded soldiers back to the United States, and he was the first to utilize pressurized aircraft for the severely wounded. His next assignment was to command the Army–Air Force Exchange Service, the famous PX service that spanned the globe with retail stores for the military.

General White's sons also joined the military. We shall meet Ed White Jr. in a few pages. James Blair White was in the Air Force and lost in action in 1969 in a combat mission over Laos. He was added to this memorial, but his body was never recovered.

72 *Stone Tapestry*

General Lucius D. Clay
Section XVIII, Row G, Grave 79

Lucius Clay graduated from West Point in the Class of November 1918, a war-shortened course. In his early career he was a civil engineer and worked on several substantial projects, such as dams and airports within the United States. During the period 1940 to 1941, he was responsible for selecting and supervising the construction of over 450 airports in this country.

During World War II, Clay was promoted to major general and was placed in charge of supervising the rebuilding and operation of the port of Cherbourg in France, crucial to the race across France. At the end of the war, General Clay was the deputy to General Eisenhower, and he became the deputy governor of Germany in the early occupation.

By 1947, General Clay had been promoted to four stars and was the military governor of Germany. Clay's headquarters prepared and published a detailed set of recommendations designed to reconstruct Germany and keep her as a valuable NATO partner and first line of defense against the Soviet Union in the Cold War. His report, titled *A Report on Germany*, served as a basis for the later Marshall Plan, which addressed multiple countries.

The following year he initiated the Berlin Airlift in response to the Soviet government's blockade of Berlin. For 324 days, aircraft flew into Berlin's Templehof Airport around the clock to bring needed supplies and food both for the military and the civilians in the city. At one point an airplane landed every four minutes for twenty-four straight hours. General Clay was featured on the cover of *Time* magazine during the airlift, one of two times he was awarded that distinction. His grave is marked by an additional marker, placed there in 1978 by the people of Berlin, which reads "We thank the guardian of our freedom" and is signed by the city leaders of Berlin.

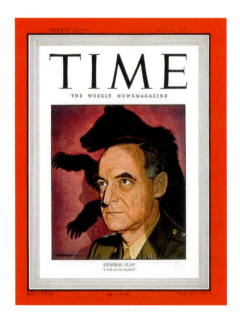

74 *Stone Tapestry*

Colonel Edward H. White II
Section XVIII, Row G, Grave 80

Ed White tragically died very young at age thirty-six in the Apollo 1 fire at Cape Kennedy. His father, whom we met previously, had to bury both of his sons before he himself passed. Ed White II graduated from West Point in the Class of 1952 and joined the Air Force as a fighter pilot. He served in Germany both in F-86 and F-100 aircraft before getting a master's degree in aeronautical engineering in 1959. He was then assigned to the Air Force Flight Test Center at Edwards Air Force Base in California.

White was selected in the second group of astronauts behind the "Mercury Seven." This second group was to fly the Gemini missions in earth orbit as part of the effort to reach the moon in 1969. White flew as the pilot on Gemini 4, along with command pilot James McDivitt, and has the distinction of being the first American to walk in space. He opened the hatch and left the spacecraft, tethered with a gold-wrapped umbilical cord, to demonstrate that extravehicular activity (EVA) was possible and practical. NASA understood that EVA procedures would be necessary in the race to the moon, and Ed White was the first to try it. After Gemini 4, White was selected to be the backup command pilot for Gemini 7, behind Frank Borman. He was slated to become the command pilot himself on Gemini 10 but instead began training for the fledgling Apollo program.

Because of his skilled performance in Gemini, White was selected to be senior pilot of the Apollo 1 mission, along with "Gus" Grissom and Roger Chaffee. Grissom had been one of the original Mercury Seven astronauts, and Chaffee was in the second group, along with White. Grissom had flown both on Mercury and Gemini spacecraft, while Chaffee was a rookie and had not yet flown in space.

Apollo 1 was slated to fly in February 1967. About five weeks before launch, the entire crew perished in a fire inside the command module while on the pad at Cape Kennedy during a systems test. White was subsequently awarded the Congressional Space Medal of Honor.

Major General George W. Goethals
Section XVIII, Row G, Grave 81

Geothals (*right*)

Right next to Apollo astronaut Ed White we find General George Goethals. General Goethals is well known for having built the Panama Canal, but like so many of the residents of this cemetery, he also had other distinguished achievements in his life. General Goethals first attended the College of the City of New York and completed three years of study before he went on to West Point. Academics presented no difficulty to him there, and he graduated second in the Class of 1880. He was commissioned in the Corps of Engineers and remained at West Point for two additional years as an instructor in astronomy.

Goethals had several assignments as an engineer officer in the United States, first at Vancouver and later along the Tennessee River. He designed and supervised the building of the Riverton Lock at Colbert Shoals in Alabama, which set a world record for lock height at the time. During the Spanish-American War, Goethals was a lieutenant colonel and served as the chief of engineers for the United States Volunteers, where he came to the attention of future president Teddy Roosevelt.

In 1902 the French began building a canal across Panama but soon went bankrupt. In 1904 the United States took control of the French property involved in building a canal across the isthmus at Panama, but initially let a contract to a civilian corporation. Eventually, after a visit by President Teddy Roosevelt (the first visit outside the country by a sitting president), the job was awarded to army engineers. In February 1907, Roosevelt appointed Colonel George Goethals to complete the canal. Seven years later, in 1914 (two years ahead of the target date of June 10, 1916), the canal was completed and opened to traffic. Goethals was promoted to major general and appointed as the first governor general of the Canal Zone. Shortly afterward he resigned from the post and retired.

In 1917, General Goethals was recalled to active duty and made the quartermaster general of the Army, with the duty to coordinate and improve the logistical support of the two million Army troops in France for World War I. Goethals immediately took charge of the immense and complicated supply chain, streamlining, consolidating, and standardizing it until it was running smoothly. General Goethals retired from this post in 1919, after being called a "great engineer, a great soldier, and the greatest Chief of Supply produced by any nation in the World War."

76 *Stone Tapestry*

General Donald V. Bennett
Section XVIII, Row G, Grave 84

General Bennett was the forty-seventh superintendent of the Military Academy. A graduate of the Class of 1940, he saw extensive combat service in Europe during World War II as an artilleryman, including landing in the second wave on Omaha Beach on D-day. He was the battalion commander of the 62nd Armored Field Artillery Battalion during the landing and personally rallied his men and other disorganized units to make an assault against a German-held ridgeline that was holding up the expansion from the beachhead. General Bennett went on to win the Distinguished Service Cross, a Bronze Star, and two Purple Hearts as the 62nd assisted in the drive across France and into Germany. Bennett later coauthored a book of his experiences in WWII called *Honor Untarnished*, published in 2003.

After the war, General Bennett continued with command of two additional artillery battalions and attended a sequence of Army schools, including the Command and General Staff College and the Army War College. He continued to alternate between artillery command assignments of increasing importance and service on the Army staff in Washington. By 1966, General Bennett was promoted to two stars and named as the superintendent.

Like Generals Bryan and Davidson, whom we met earlier, Bennett turned over the superintendent's office to the man who lies next to him in the cemetery, General Sam Koster. General Bennet was promoted to lieutenant general and given command of VII Corps in Germany. In 1969 he returned to the United States and took command of the Defense Intelligence Agency in Washington. After promotion to four-star rank, General Bennett assumed command of the United Nations Command in Korea. His final assignment was as the commander, US Army Pacific, responsible for all Army forces in the Pacific region.

Major General Samuel W. Koster
Section XVIII, Row G, Grave 84C

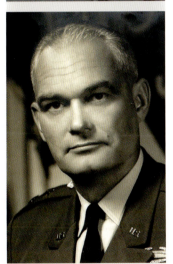

"Sam" Koster graduated from the Military Academy in 1942 and was commissioned in the Infantry branch. He served with the 413th Infantry Regiment throughout World War II, in campaigns through northern France, the Rhineland, and central Germany. During his combat service, General Koster served at every level, from platoon leader through battalion commander and regimental executive officer, and was awarded a Silver Star for heroism, two Bronze Stars, and a Purple Heart.

In 1949, Koster returned to West Point to serve as a tactical officer, and when the Korean War broke out he deployed to Asia, serving in the Far East Command and then Headquarters, Eighth US Army, where he directed their guerrilla warfare campaign. General Koster continued to be assigned operations and command jobs, including a tour as the chief of staff of the Infantry School.

In Vietnam, Major General Koster assumed command of the 23rd Infantry (Americal) Division in 1967. In 1968, an infantry company of the Americal, commanded by Captain Ernest Medina and with 2nd Lieutenant Calley as one of the platoon leaders, killed hundreds of South Vietnamese civilians in the My Lai massacre. Koster was not present at the massacre, although he did fly over the village later in a helicopter. He ordered an investigation done, but the reports were not forwarded any higher than his headquarters. He went on to West Point to assume the position as superintendent after General Bennett.

During a subsequent Army investigation into My Lai, the Army secretary decided that General Koster's investigation of the massacre was insufficient, and relieved him of his duties at West Point. He was also reduced in grade by one rank and reassigned within the Army. General Koster fought his grade reduction in court but ultimately lost his case and retired in 1973. His monument here reflects his highest grade achieved, rather than his retired rank.

Major General John Buford
Section XXVI, Row A, Grave 6

And now we take leave of Section XVIII, and all of its Military Academy leadership, and stroll over to Section XXVI, where many of the Civil War veterans from the Union army lie (there are no soldiers from the Confederate army buried in this cemetery). The first of many distinguished and gallant soldiers we will see is John Buford, cavalry leader and scout, and the one whose determined stand at Gettysburg set the stage for that climactic struggle. Buford's monument is one of the most distinctive in the cemetery and graces the title page of this book.

General Buford was in the Class of 1848 from West Point and served in the US Dragoons after graduation. He served in Texas and Utah in the Indian campaigns prior to the Civil War. Despite being from Kentucky, Buford elected to remain with the Union after the war began. He saw active service in early campaigns, including a cavalry brigade command at the Second Battle of Bull Run, where he was wounded in the knee. When he returned to the war, he became the chief of cavalry under Generals McClellan and Burnside during their tenure as commanders of the Army of the Potomac. Buford then took command of the Cavalry Division and led it in the battles at Brandy Station and Upperville.

It was at Gettysburg that Buford played his pivotal role. As the commander of the cavalry division on the scene at Gettysburg, Buford was the first to realize that he was facing a large Confederate force of infantry and artillery, so he quickly deployed his men to defend the critical high ground south of the town. His skillful and tenacious defense allowed the I Corps of the Army of the Potomac to reach the battlefield and to take possession of Cemetery Ridge near the town.

Buford continued to play a major role in the cavalry force until his untimely death from typhoid fever in December 1863. In the movie *Gettysburg*, Buford was played by Sam Elliott.

80 *Stone Tapestry*

Lieutenant Alonzo H. Cushing
Congressional Medal of Honor
Section XXVI, Row A, Grave 7

Alonzo Cushing had a short but glorious career. He is the first Medal of Honor winner we shall meet on our walk, earning the nation's highest award for valor at Gettysburg in 1863. Buford's delaying action on the first day at Gettysburg meant the Union retained the high ground on Cemetery Ridge, where Cushing was to die two days later. Now they lie side by side in the cemetery.

Cushing was a member of the Class of June 1861 and received both his commission as a second lieutenant and a promotion to first lieutenant on the same day. He immediately set off to the war in the artillery service and saw action in Chancellorsville, where he won a brevet (temporary) promotion to major. Lieutenant Cushing then was sent to command A Battery, 4th US Artillery.

At the battle for Gettysburg, Cushing's battery was situated on the top of Cemetery Ridge, near the center of the Union line. General Lee had tried on the first day to take the Union position from its right flank, and on the second day he tried the left flank. On the third day he resolved to break the Union line in the center, and as luck would have it, Pickett's Charge was to crest the ridge directly in front of Cushing's guns. Lieutenant Cushing was wounded three times in the battle: the first a bullet through one shoulder, and then a second shot sliced open his abdomen. Unable to shout, he whispered commands to his first sergeant, who was holding him, sitting upright. Refusing commands to go to the rear, he remained at his guns, firing into the teeth of Pickett's Charge until a final bullet struck him in the head and killed him as he fired his last round.

Cushing was given a brevet promotion to lieutenant colonel and cited for gallantry after the battle. In the late 1980s, a campaign was begun to have Cushing awarded the Congressional Medal of Honor, culminating in the award being presented on November 6, 2014.

82   *Stone Tapestry*

Major General Judson H. Kilpatrick
Section XXVI, Row B, Grave 17

"Judd" Kilpatrick was an aggressive cavalry commander in the Union army in the Civil War. He graduated from West Point one month before Alonzo Cushing, whom we just met, in the Class of May 1861. Kilpatrick had the dubious distinction of being the first Regular Army officer to be wounded in the Civil War, being struck in the leg by cannister shot during the Battle of Big Bethel in June 1861. He was a mere thirty-four days into his military career.

Kilpatrick soon rose in the ranks to become a lieutenant colonel, and then a full colonel as he led the 2nd New York Cavalry. His tactics were direct, fearless, and wasteful. He frequently took excessive losses and drove his men (as well as himself) mercilessly. His troopers soon gave him the derisive nickname "Kill Cavalry" for his seeming indifference to their losses.

By 1863, Kilpatrick had taken command of the 1st Brigade, 2nd Cavalry Division, within General Stoneman's Cavalry Corps. During the Chancellorsville Campaign, Kilpatrick's brigade was ordered to swing behind General Lee's army and do as much damage and destruction to railroads and supplies as they could. Kilpatrick took to the task and ended up riding completely around Lee's army (duplicating Jeb Stuart's ride around McClellan the year prior).

Kilpatrick played a minor role at Gettysburg, launching an attack on Longstreet's corps after the Pickett's Charge failure. When one of his subordinate commanders questioned the attack order, Kilpatrick responded by saying if he was afraid to go, then Kilpatrick himself would lead the charge. Thus shamed, his subordinate led the charge and was killed in the attempt.

Kilpatrick became the American ambassador to Chile after the war and died at Valparaiso in 1881.

Sections XVIII and XXVI 83

Major General Frederick D. Grant
Section XXVI, Row D, Grave 39/40

Fred Grant was the eldest son of General (later President) Ulysses S. Grant. Even as a young boy, he accompanied his father on field duty during the Civil War and was even wounded once during the siege at Vicksburg. He recovered from that wound, and also the subsequent typhoid fever. Fred Grant graduated from West Point in the Class of 1871 and was commissioned in the cavalry. He served on frontier duty against the Indians in his early career and became aide-de-camp to General Sherman. He also served with General Sheridan and was with George Custer during the Black Hills expedition (although not at Little Big Horn).

Grant resigned from the Army and went into business while assisting his father with his *Memoirs*. In 1894 he became the commissioner of police in New York City, and he held that post until 1898. In 1889 he was appointed by President Benjamin Harrison to be the US minister to Austria-Hungary and remained there until 1893.

During the Spanish-American War, Grant returned to service and became a brigadier general of volunteers. He participated in the occupation of Puerto Rico and later in the Philippines, where he commanded a brigade. In 1901 he was given a commission as a brigadier general in the Regular Army and was promoted to major general in 1906. He was given command of the Eastern Division, which included the Department of the East and the Department of the Gulf portions of the US defenses.

At the time of his death in 1912, General Grant was the second-most-senior officer in the Army after Major General Leonard Wood.

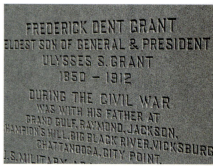

84   *Stone Tapestry*

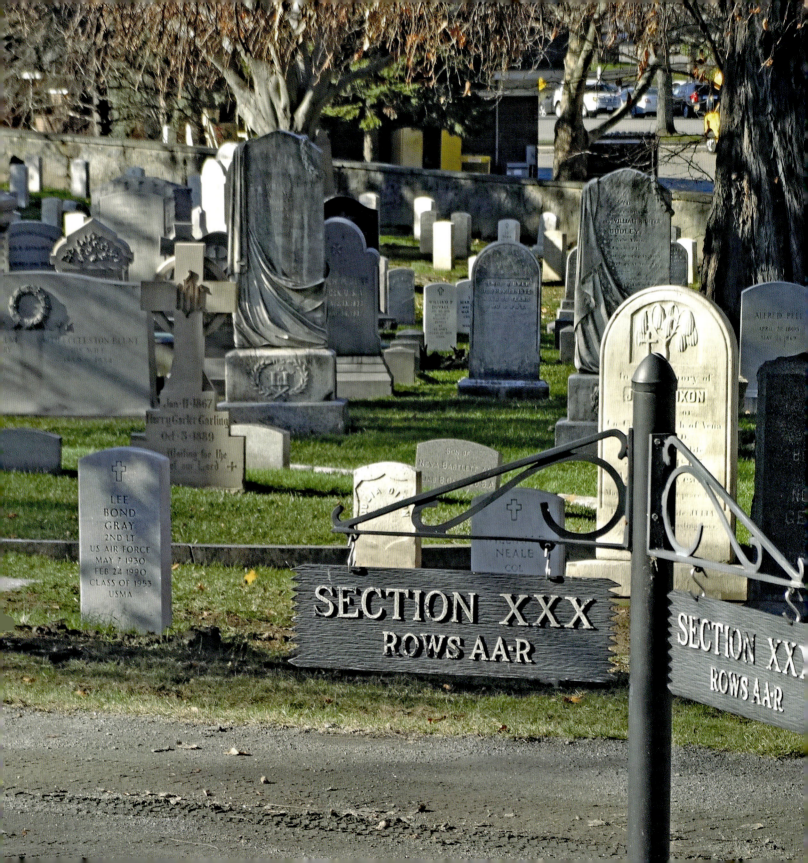

CHAPTER 5

Section XXX

Section XXX is the oldest and, in many ways, the most interesting of the sections within the cemetery. Many of those interred here lived and died before the Military Academy was founded. The oldest grave in the whole cemetery is here, that of Ensign Dominick Trant, buried in 1782 during the Revolutionary War, when Washington had his headquarters near here. The monuments are many and conspicuous in their variety. The Cadet Monument is here, dedicated to the many young men who perished before they could graduate. There are many families in this section and, heartbreakingly, many unknowns.

When this cemetery was founded in 1817, Sylvanus Thayer had just been chosen as the new superintendent. This ground was previously known as German Flats because Pennsylvania Dutch militia units were encamped here during the Revolutionary War. The grounds of West Point had been expanded by purchase from private owners, and a building program was begun to expand and solidify the academy. As ground was taken over and construction was begun, many family gravesites were uncovered, and those people were moved here to this cemetery. Some came with markers and family histories; others came simply as "unknown." Ensign Trant was one of those who was moved here, but in his case his remains came with a headstone.

So those we shall meet here are the very beginnings of the Long Gray Line, those who passed on before they could wield their sword in their country's defense (in the words of one early officer), those who never knew that there was a West Point, or what it would contribute to the nation. Many family members are here, officers and enlisted with wives and small children, who resided in this spot before it was famous and who now lie in peace surrounded by thousands of graduates, most lacking fame themselves, but sharing in the fame around them.

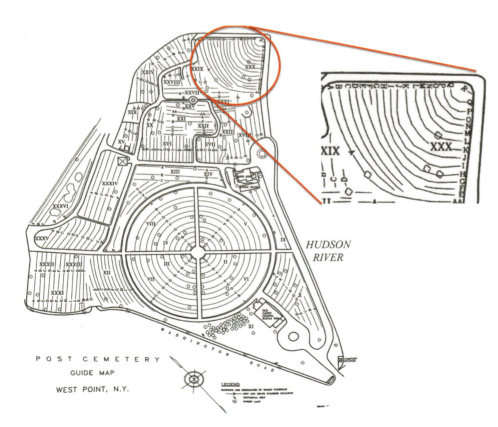

87

Brevet Lieutenant Colonel Eleazer D. Wood
Section XXX, Row E, Grave 171

The monument to Eleazer Wood is the oldest marker for a graduate in the cemetery. Wood was the seventeenth graduate of West Point, graduating in the Class of 1806. It is unclear if his body is, in fact, buried here. This marker was first built up on the Plain level of West Point and was used as a navigation marker by passing ships on the Hudson. The monument was built in 1816 and was moved to the current location around 1911, when the Old Cadet Chapel was erected here.

Wood was admitted to West Point in 1805 and graduated a year later as an engineer officer at age twenty-three. He served as an engineer in the construction of the defenses at Governor's Island, in the harbor of New York. He was promoted to first lieutenant in 1806 and was assigned to various engineering duties in Virginia. By the start of the War of 1812, Wood had been promoted to captain and was responsible for the construction of two forts used in the defense of Lake Erie.

By May 1813, Wood had been recognized for his superior work in construction of the defenses and was awarded a brevet promotion to major. Wood participated in several battles in the War of 1812, including the Battle of the Thames, the Battle of Chippewa, and the Battle of Lundy's Lane. In the latter two battles, Wood commanded an artillery section despite his commission as an engineer. After Lundy's Lane, his valor was again recognized and he was promoted to brevet lieutenant colonel, a mere seven years after his graduation.

The American army withdrew to Fort Erie after the Battle of Lundy's Lane, and Wood was given command of one of the defensive sectors of the fort. During the enemy's attack on August 15, 1814, Wood's battalion successfully repulsed a British brigade assault. He was mortally wounded the following month during a sortie against the British camped outside Fort Erie.

A fort on Bedloe Island in New York Harbor was named Fort Wood in his honor. Bedloe Island was afterward re-named Liberty Island, and Fort Wood now serves as the base for the Statue of Liberty, which stands there.

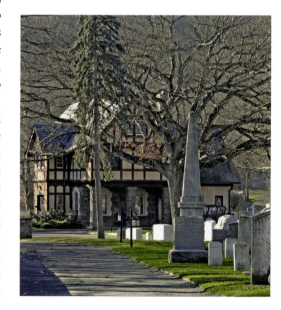

Edward S. Holden
Section XXX, Row E, Grave 173

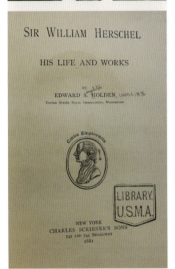

Next to Wood's monument we find the small but distinctive marker for Edward Singleton Holden. Holden graduated from West Point as the third man in the Class of 1870 and immediately became an assistant professor of mathematics, where he served until 1873. Apparently not impressed with military life, he resigned his commission and went to serve as a professor of mathematics at the US Naval Observatory. There he was an assistant to the primary astronomer and participated in the discovery of the two moons of Mars. He later moved to the Washburn Observatory at the University of Wisconsin–Madison.

In 1885, Holden moved to California, where he became the fifth president of the University of California. His interest in astronomy never disappeared, and by 1888 he was the first director of the Lick Observatory in California, where he served until 1897. While there he also served as the founder of the Astronomical Society of the Pacific.

Holden was a prolific author, writing many books on a variety of subjects, including a biography of Sir William Herschel, a history of the Mogul emperors of Hindustan, and a children's reader on science. He has an asteroid, a crater on the moon, and a crater on Mars all named after him in recognition of his service in astronomy.

But Holden had another role to play, and in 1901 he returned to West Point to become the librarian. He served in that capacity until his death in 1914. In the *Annual Report of the Superintendent* of 1914, Col. Clarence P. Townsley (we will meet him again later) wrote of Holden: "He was for thirteen years librarian and during his incumbency he changed the library from a more or less chaotic state as to cataloguing, arrangement, reference, &c., to one of the best equipped and most convenient of all college libraries.... The Academy was most fortunate to secure this distinguished graduate as its librarian and to him the thanks of the cadets and alumni of West Point are due for his wise, untiring and successful efforts to improve the library and awaken an interest in the valuable and comprehensive works in its collection."

Major John Lillie
Section XXX, Row F, Grave 244

Major John Lillie was the commander of the West Point garrison in June 1801, prior to it becoming the Military Academy. Major Lillie had distinguished himself in the Revolutionary War and, as garrison commander, was supervising young cadets in their military instruction here before the law that established the Military Academy. Major Lillie died of an "apoplectic fit" in September 1801 and was superseded after his death by Jonathan Williams, the first true superintendent, who arrived in December 1801. On March 16, 1802, the order establishing the Military Academy was signed by President Thomas Jefferson.

John Lillie came from Boston. At the outbreak of the Revolutionary War in 1775, he joined the militia and was commissioned as a second lieutenant in artillery. He was in several units, notably commanded by capable officers such as Henry Knox and Richard Gridley. By 1782, Lillie had become an aide-de-camp to Knox, who was the chief of the Continental artillery. He was stationed at Newburgh, north of West Point, with General Washington's headquarters. In 1783 he received a commendation from Washington himself for his meritorious service, and he received a ceremonial dress sword from General Lafayette of France as well.

After the Revolutionary War, Lillie married and raised a family while searching for steady employment outside the Army. For a time he was a merchant in Boston, making several sea voyages to Europe. On February 16, 1801, he was appointed as commander of the artillery unit stationed at West Point and was instructed to begin training young cadets there. Discussions about a military academy were already underway, and Lillie (and others) thought he might take command of the new school. Unfortunately he died before that could happen.

Lillie had a son, also named John, who was enrolled at West Point after his father's death. The younger John remained a cadet in the Class of 1805 for more than four years but did not graduate.

90 *Stone Tapestry*

Ensign Dominick Trant
Section XXX, Row H, Grave 317

Ensign Trant has the distinction of being the oldest grave in the cemetery. He was a young Irish immigrant who enlisted in the 9th Massachusetts Regiment and died at the tender age of eighteen of an illness on November 7, 1782.

Not very much is known about the young man, although a family history text of the Trant family has some details. He was born in Cork, Ireland, and came to the United States when he was in his teen years. He immediately enlisted in the 9th Massachusetts and was subsequently raised to the grade of ensign and given command of the second platoon of his company. Colonel Henry Jackson, the commander of the regiment, recommended Trant for his promotion to ensign in a letter to John Hancock dated June 23, 1781.

The newspaper titled *New York Packet and American Advertiser* of November 14, 1782, describes the funeral procession for young Ensign Trant: "On Friday succeeding the remains of this worthy youth were conveyed to the garrison at West Point, from whence they were conducted to the grave in the following manner. Preceding the bier, a platoon of regular troops from the regiment to which he belonged marched in open order with arms reversed, followed by a band of music playing a solemn dirge, the bier borne by six sergeants, and attended by six officers as pall bearers, and followed by His Excellency, General Washington, Major-General Knox, a respectable number of military and civil gentlemen, to the place of interment."

Within a month of poor Trant's death, King George III had announced to his Parliament that he had decided to recognize the independence of the United States. While that effectively concluded the war, it took the rest of the winter before the word officially made it back to the US. In the meantime the garrison had to endure another difficult winter, and finally the officers and men could take no more. Rumors of a mutiny began to spread in February 1783 and finally had to be put to rest by General Washington himself. On March 15, 1783, Washington met with his officers in Newburgh to read them a letter from Congress. His quiet confidence, undisguised emotion, and physical frailties earned in the line of duty won over the men, and the assemblage dispersed.

Stone Tapestry

Susan and Anna Warner
Section XXX, Row Q, Graves 586 and 587

The sisters Susan (*bottom*) and Anna Warner (*top*) lived across the river from West Point, on Constitution Island, and were renowned authors. Their uncle, Thomas Warner, served as the chaplain at West Point from 1828 to 1838. The Warner sisters' father, Henry, had originally built the house on the island as a summer home, but after suffering financial reverses in New York City he and the family moved there full time.

The sisters were well-recognized authors, each in their own way. Anna wrote the lyrics to the hymn "Jesus Loves Me" as well as thirty-one novels, including *Dollars and Cents*, *In West Point Colors*, and *Gold of Chickaree*. She also wrote a biography of her sister, Susan, and a gardening book for women called *Gardening by Myself*.

Susan Warner wrote *The Wide, Wide World*, which was the country's first bestseller, and the first book by an American author to sell over a million copies. She also wrote *Queechy*, *The Old Helmet*, *A Story of Small Beginnings*, and *The Hills of Shatemuc* (which sold 10,000 copies on the day of publication).

The women taught Sunday school in their little home on Constitution Island to cadets, who would row across the Hudson to attend. Susan began the classes in 1875, and after she passed away ten years later, Anna took over the classes. A biography of the two sisters, written in 1925, states that "after each of the boys had read a Bible verse, Miss [Susan] Warner, choosing her subject from some New Testament text, talked to them for perhaps half an hour until her enthusiasm and interest and obviously exhausted her small strength . . . she always gave to the boys the brightest and most optimistic side of the faith she loved so well."

After her passing in 1915, Anna bequeathed a portrait of George Washington, painted by Gilbert Stuart, to the West Point library.

The Cadet Monument
Section XXX, Row R, Grave 600

The Cadet Monument is on the far northeastern corner of the cemetery and is dedicated to those cadets who passed away while still cadets. It was designed and purchased by the officers and cadets of West Point themselves and placed here in 1818. The first cadet to be honored by this monument was Vincent M. Lowe of New York, who was killed in an accidental cannon discharge during the twenty-four-gun salute on New Year's Day 1817.

Since that time, numerous cadets have died in accidents, drownings, or mishaps across the years. The first ones were honored by having their names added to the monument in limestone blocks, but eventually they ran out of space. In addition to this monument, there are approximately two dozen other graves in Section XXX that were for young men who perished as cadets.

This photograph is a page from the 1876 *Surgeon's Report* on the health and sanitation at West Point, apparently submitted annually. The entry below reads, "The Cadet's monument is as a unique but sad memento of those 'youths to fame unknown' who quietly resigned their young lives ere they were permitted to enjoy the privilege of wielding the sword in their country's service."

96 *Stone Tapestry*

The Unknowns
Section XXX

In Section XXX there are dozens of graves marked simply "unknown." This has to be the saddest portion of the cemetery. These people lie among some of the most famous of our country's history yet are completely unknown to us. When West Point expanded its boundaries, several times over the years before the Revolutionary War and on into the early 1800s, many gravesites were uncovered during construction. They could be local families who lived here, Revolution-era soldiers and militia, or infants of families who lived here. As graves were uncovered during construction, they all were moved to the "new" cemetery here on German Flats and were reburied. Those that had no stone were placed in plots marked "unknown," so they rest here today, mute, without history, without visitors.

Passersby should stop and reflect on these graves as they stroll by the more famous. They are part and parcel of this place too, and of our country's history as well, even if they lack the recognition others have. We cannot speak about their achievements, for we do not know of them. We cannot speak of their heritage, or even their very names. They do not have the honors that we show to the Tomb of the Unknowns in Arlington. Yet, like those in Arlington, they certainly lie in good company.

98 *Stone Tapestry*

Sergeant Louis Bentz
Section XXX, Row C, Grave 116

Another oddity about Section XXX is the large number of bandsmen who are buried here. West Point has had a band here since the beginning, and much of Army communications in the nineteenth and twentieth centuries was done by bugle calls. Sergeant Louis Bentz served here at West Point for forty years, from 1834 to 1874. He was an immigrant from Germany and became a master at the keyed bugle. Bentz was so highly thought of that the Corps of Cadets purchased his headstone when he passed away. The original headstone had a silver bugle on it, but over time that disappeared and was replaced with a stone replica.

One of Sergeant Bentz's duties was to blow "Reveille" at five o'clock in the morning to wake up the cadets, so it is hard to see why they would have such fond memories of him, but he was very widely liked while he was in the band at West Point. He is reported to have always had a plug of beeswax in his mouth to chew and had a faithful dog named Hans who accompanied him everywhere. Bentz's wife, Rachel, is also buried here in the cemetery.

Section XXX 99

CHAPTER 6

Sections XXIX, XXVII, XXV, XX, and XXI

Next we will stroll through several of the oldest sections within the cemetery and visit with some of the most famous people to be buried here. Here we find Sylvanus Thayer, called the Father of the Military Academy, along with General Winfield Scott, affectionately known as "Old Fuss and Feathers." President Eisenhower's son lies here, himself a brigadier general and author of some fame. We will see Custer, Devin, Tidball, and Webb, all veterans of the Civil War, along with General Robert Anderson, who defended Fort Sumter and lived to see Old Glory raised again over her. The Michie family is here, including young Dennis Michie, for whom the football stadium is named.

This is a most eclectic group of residents of the cemetery. They span from its earliest days (Thayer himself graduated in 1808) to the modern era. Winfield Scott embodied the Army itself, from the War of 1812, through the Mexican War, and up to the Civil War. General Eisenhower wrote a bestselling book about his father's biggest battle in World War II and is also the author of a biography of Winfield Scott, who lies next to him.

We see some educators here as well. Herman Koehler led the Physical Education Department, a position titled the Master of the Sword, up to and through World War I. Frank Kobes lies here as well, who led that same department from the Korean War through the Vietnam War. The engineer who supervised the building of the Lincoln Memorial in Washington, DC, is here, along with the grandson of Ethan Allen. There are several Medal of Honor awardees here, and the wife of yet another. The man who founded the Association of Graduates lies here as well, and several of the residents we will visit were the oldest living graduates of their respective classes.

While eclectic, this grouping of sections carries much of the history of the Army, and of West Point, beneath its shade trees. Much of the heart and soul of the cemetery lies here.

101

Lieutenant General Paul W. Kendall
Section XXIX, Row A, Grave 3

General Paul Kendall is but one example of the unsung heroes who lie in this cemetery. A casual visitor would walk by his grave without a second glance. A standard, government-issued headstone, it has nothing to indicate anything special about General Kendall. He graduated with the Class of November 1918, just at the end of the First World War.

While he thought he would not get to see any combat, in fact 2nd Lieutenant Kendall participated in the last battle involving American troops in the First World War—in Siberia, no less. An Allied contingent of American, Czech, British, Italian, and French troops commanded by a Japanese general were sent to Vladivostok, Russia, to assist the Russian Tsarist White Army in their fight against the Bolsheviks, who were trying to take over Russia. Kendall commanded a platoon of infantrymen in the 27th Regiment, known as the Wolfhounds. He was assigned to guard a portion of the Trans-Siberian Railroad and was attacked by a Bolshevik armored train. Kendall's platoon successfully defeated the Bolshevik troops in a vicious night battle in subzero temperatures. The Distinguished Service Cross is our nation's second-highest award for valor in combat, and Lieutenant Kendall's platoon earned three of them that night, including his own.

After the war, General Kendall went on to teach at West Point in the Department of English and History, and during the summer training he was responsible for teaching cadets the art and science of fighting with the bayonet. In 1937 he was assigned to the 15th Infantry Regiment in Tientsin, China, and was evacuated with that regiment in 1938.

General Kendall went on to an even more lustrous career in World War II, rising to command the 88th Infantry Division throughout the Italian campaign and earning three Silver Stars and a Purple Heart in so doing. When the Korean War broke out, General Kendall was sent to command I Corps, which was a composite unit composed of Army, Marine, Korean, and Commonwealth units. For his service in Korea, General Kendall earned the Distinguished Service Medal. After the war he was sent to Turkey, where he commanded the Allied Forces Southeast in a NATO command.

Not a word of this is evident on his simple soldier's headstone.

Major General William M. Black
Section XXIX, Row B, Grave 20

Major General Black was a distinguished engineer who rose to be the chief of engineers in the Army throughout the First World War, from 1916 to 1919. He graduated as the first man in his class in the Class of 1877 and set a stellar example of both scholarship and command ever after. He developed into a respected specialist in the arts of river and harbor engineering, and in port development. He was known as "the man who cleaned up Havana" for his work there after the Spanish-American War. There he was responsible for the removal of the wreck of the battleship USS *Maine*.

General Black began his career by returning directly to West Point after graduation to serve as an assistant instructor in Practical Military Engineering. He returned a second time as a full instructor, in addition to duty with the engineer battalion stationed there. General Black also graduated from the Engineer School of Application, then located at Willets Point, New York, and returned there as an instructor as well.

Black was then appointed as the engineer commissioner of the District of Columbia. While there, he developed the plans for the construction of the tunnel under Capitol Hill, as well as the design of Union Station. He supervised the construction of the iconic Lincoln Memorial.

During the Spanish-American War, Black was a captain in the Regular Army but was promoted to be a lieutenant colonel of US Volunteers, and he commanded the first landing of the Army in Puerto Rico. From Puerto Rico he moved to Havana for the first of two tours there, organizing a department of public works in a mere three days. He conducted a military survey of the island of Cuba, which became the basis for all subsequent maps of the island. In 1916, General Black became the chief of engineers and established the Engineers Officers' Reserve Corps. He retired from the Army in 1919. In 1946 the Navy commissioned a transport ship in his name, USS *General W. M. Black*.

Mary Godfrey, Wife of Brigadier General Edward S. Godfrey
Congressional Medal of Honor
Section XXIX, Row C, Grave 29

Mary Godfrey's grave offers us a glimpse into a storied career, that of her husband, Brigadier General Edward Settle Godfrey. Mary was Godfrey's first wife, who passed away while they were stationed at West Point in 1883. Godfrey was a famed cavalryman of the Indian Wars and was awarded the Medal of Honor in 1894 for his service against Indians at Bear Paw Mountain, Montana, in 1877. Godfrey himself is buried in Arlington National Cemetery.

General Godfrey began the Civil War as an enlisted man in the 21st Ohio Infantry and was admitted to West Point in 1863. He graduated in the Class of 1867 and was commissioned in the cavalry. Godfrey was assigned to the 7th Cavalry, and he served in that regiment through the grades of first lieutenant, captain, and major.

Godfrey served in more than forty engagements against the Indians in the West and was severely wounded once. He became one of the most experienced and successful Indian fighters, seeing action against the Sioux, Cheyenne, and Nez Perce, among others. He was a participant in the Battle of Little Big Horn, in which a portion of Custer's command was massacred, serving as a troop commander under Major Reno. It was his troop, which dismounted and provided a strong fire in a delaying tactic, that permitted the safe retirement of the remainder of Major Reno's squadron. In September 1877, Godfrey's troop of the 7th Cavalry made an attack on the Nez Perce at Bear Paw Mountain. Godfrey had his horse shot out from underneath him, remounted another horse, and then was seriously wounded and had to be evacuated from the battle. Godfrey's unit had lost 53 men out of 115 officers and men engaged, a horrific casualty rate. For this action he was awarded the Medal of Honor.

He served as an instructor in the Mounted Service School, and as an instructor in mounted tactics at West Point from 1879 to 1883. It was during this tour that his first wife, Mary, passed away and was buried here. In later life he commanded Fort Riley, Kansas. Godfrey later served as the leader of an honor guard made up of Medal of Honor recipients at the burial of the Unknown Soldier from World War I.

Stone Tapestry

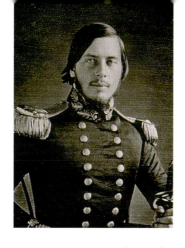

Captain George Derby (and Family)
Section XXIX, Row C, Grave 33

George Horatio Derby graduated in the Class of 1846 and had a short but intense career as a humorist. In his military career, he served briefly in the Mexican War in combat both at Vera Cruz and Cerro Gordo. He wrote humorous articles under the pen names Squibob, John P. Squibob, and John Phoenix.

Derby was assigned to San Diego after the Mexican War, and he married Mary Coons there. He began to write humorous articles for the *San Francisco Herald* and the fledgling *San Diego Herald*. His articles were generally poking fun at the high society that inhabited California in the day. In 1855, Derby bought the *San Diego Herald*, but the newspaper went out of business in 1860. He moved to New York but died the following year.

He consistently poked fun at the weather and temperature in his writings. In one article he wrote, "One of our Fort Yuma men died, and unfortunately went to hell. He wasn't there one day before he telegraphed for his blankets." In another article, referring to the Oregon and Washington Territory, he wrote, "It rains incessantly twenty-six hours a day for seventeen months of the year."

Despite his short-lived career, Derby's family is an example of the Long Gray Line. His son George McClellan Derby graduated from West Point in the Class of 1878, his grandson George T. Derby in the Class of 1927, and three other grandsons (not buried at West Point) in the Classes of 1904, 1917, and 1932. In addition he had a great-grandson, George K. Derby, graduate from the Naval Academy in 1951.

Buried with Derby is his daughter Mary Townsend Derby, who never married. His first daughter, Daisy Derby, is buried nearby as the wife of General William M. Black, whom we met a couple of pages ago in our stroll.

Sections XXIX, XXVII, XXV, XX, and XXI

Lieutenant Colonel George A. Custer
Section XXVII, Section A, Grave 1

George Custer needs no introduction; all of America knows of his brilliant career and death at Little Big Horn. He is probably the most famous of all those who are buried in the cemetery. His monument is an obelisk with four bronze plates around the base. Custer graduated from West Point at the very beginning of the Civil War, as the last man in the Class of 1861. His record at the academy was shoddy; he amassed a total of 726 demerits while a cadet, which was a Military Academy record at the time. Despite his troublesome disciplinary record, and his low academic standing as a cadet, Custer was quickly recognized as an able cavalryman and was made a brevet brigadier general of volunteers. He fought in numerous engagements in the Civil War, including one at Gettysburg, where he commanded a Michigan cavalry brigade.

Custer also served in the Shenandoah River valley under Sheridan and was promoted to brevet major general and given command of a cavalry division. His division blocked the final retreat of the Army of Northern Virginia, and Custer was on hand at the McLean House at Appomattox when General Robert E. Lee surrendered to General Ulysses S. Grant.

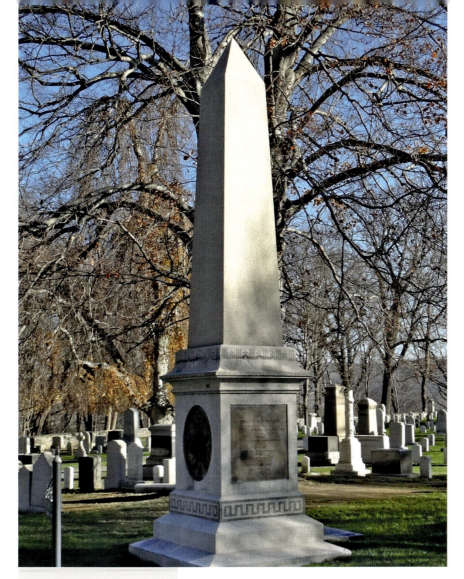

After the Civil War ended, Custer was promoted to lieutenant colonel in the Regular Army and began his campaigns against the Indians, where he commanded the 7th Cavalry. On June 25, 1876, Custer led the 7th Cavalry into the Battle of Little Big Horn in Montana. Fatefully, he divided his command into three groups: one commanded by himself, one commanded by Major Reno (where Lieutenant Edward S. Godfrey, recently met, commanded a troop), and one commanded by Captain Benteen. With Custer was his brother Thomas Custer.

During the subsequent Indian attack, Custer and his small portion of the command (about two hundred men) fought desperately, slowly giving ground until they came to a small knoll. About forty men were left alive at this point in the battle, but all were ultimately killed. Both Custer and his brother were buried on the battlefield. Soldiers returned a year later to discover that the graves had been broken into by animals and the bones scattered. Some of the bones were gathered, and Custer was reinterred here at West Point in 1877, alongside his wife, Libby.

Sections XXIX, XXVII, XXV, XX, and XXI **107**

Major General Robert Anderson
Section XXVII, Row A, Grave 4

General Anderson had the distinction of commanding the Union Fort Sumter in Charleston Harbor when it was shelled by Confederate forces to begin the Civil War. Anderson came from a military family; his father, Richard Anderson Sr., served as aide-de-camp to the Marquis de Lafayette during the American Revolution. Anderson graduated tenth out of thirty-seven in the West Point Class of 1825. He was commissioned as a second lieutenant in the 3rd Artillery. He was assigned as an artillery instructor at West Point from 1835 to 1837. Interestingly, one of his students then, cadet Pierre G. T. Beauregard, later was the Confederate commander who shelled Anderson at Fort Sumter.

During the Black Hawk War, Anderson served as a brevet colonel of Illinois volunteers. He reportedly was the officer who mustered Abraham Lincoln into service during the Blackhawk War, when Lincoln was elected captain of his company of volunteers. Anderson later served as assistant adjutant general on the staff of Winfield Scott, whom we will meet. He served in the Mexican War in the siege of Vera Cruz, and in the Battle of Molino del Rey, where he was wounded.

Anderson then served in garrison duties while he recovered from his wounds and was on the Board of Officers that wrote *A Complete System of Instruction for Siege, Garrison, Seacoast, and Mountain Artillery*. He also authored *Instruction for Field Artillery, Horse, and Foot* in 1839. In large part because of his expertise in coastal forts and artillery, in November 1860 Anderson was assigned command of the forces around Charleston Harbor, including Fort Sumter. By February 1861 the Confederate States of America were established, and their president, Jefferson Davis (himself a West Point graduate in the class of 1828), ordered Beauregard to capture Fort Sumter.

Beauregard attacked on April 12, 1861, and Anderson, outgunned, outnumbered, and cut off from supplies, surrendered two days later. Anderson lowered the flag of the United States and kept it in safekeeping until the end of the Civil War, when he took it back to Fort Sumter and saw it raised once more in 1865.

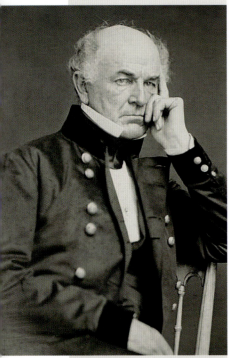

Major General (US Volunteers) Ethan A. Hitchcock

Section XXVII, Row A, Grave 7

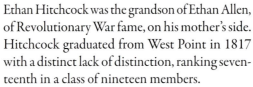

Ethan Hitchcock was the grandson of Ethan Allen, of Revolutionary War fame, on his mother's side. Hitchcock graduated from West Point in 1817 with a distinct lack of distinction, ranking seventeenth in a class of nineteen members.

He was commissioned in the field artillery and returned to West Point in 1829 as the commandant of cadets. He served with somewhat more distinction in the Seminole War in Florida, and again in the Mexican War, where he was the inspector general on Winfield Scott's staff (where he must have been acquainted with Robert Anderson). By 1851, Hitchcock had been promoted to be the colonel of the 2nd Infantry Regiment, followed by command of the Pacific Division, and later the entire Department of the Pacific.

Ethan Hitchcock resigned from the army in 1855, following a dispute with then secretary of war Jefferson Davis (the same Jefferson Davis who was ten years behind him at West Point, and who later became the president of the Confederacy). Hitchcock had requested a four-month leave of absence to recover his health, and Davis refused to grant it, so Hitchcock resigned instead.

At the beginning of the Civil War, Hitchcock requested to return to active duty but was rejected (presumably for his age). He appealed to Winfield Scott, himself past mandatory retirement age at the time, and with Scott's intercession Hitchcock was commissioned a major general and became a special assistant to the secretary of war. For a period in 1862, Hitchcock served as the chairman of the War Board, advising President Lincoln during the absence of a commander in chief for all the Union armies. Ultimately this position was revoked by the appointment of Henry Halleck as the general in chief.

Hitchcock served as the president of the court-martial of Major General Fitz John Porter, which convicted Porter of disobedience and cowardice. General Hitchcock then went on to serve as the commissioner for prisoner-of-war exchange, and the commissary-general for prisoners. He had a lifelong interest in alchemy and wrote a masterly treatise on the subject called *Remarks upon Alchemy and the Alchemists*, in which he argued that alchemists were, in reality, religious philosophers.

Stone Tapestry

Lieutenant General Winfield Scott
Section XXVII, Row A, Grave 16

General Winfield Scott, though not a West Point graduate, was the most distinguished soldier in American history prior to the Civil War. In addition to his numerous other honors, he served as the commanding general of the US Army for twenty years, from 1841 to 1861.

Scott was commissioned in 1808 in the Regular Army as a captain of light artillery. He served in Canada in the War of 1812 against the British, being badly wounded at the Battle of Lundy's Lane, and was promoted to brigadier general in 1814. One of his distinctions is that he served on active duty as a general officer longer than any other soldier, a total of forty-seven years at flag rank. In 1835, Scott authored *Infantry Tactics, or Rules for the Exercise and Maneuvre of the United States Infantry*, which served as the standard manual for the Army until 1855.

In 1841, Scott became the commanding general of the US Army and remained in that post until he retired in 1861. In the Mexican War, Scott took to the field with the Army and led the entire campaign, from the landings at Veracruz to the march to Mexico City. Scott's biographer, John Eisenhower (whom we shall meet on the following page), wrote that the amphibious landing in Mexico was "up to that time the most ambitious amphibious operation in human history." Scott then defeated Santa Ana's forces in Veracruz, Cerro Gordo, and Churubusco. Mexico began peace negotiations, but the two sides were so far apart in terms that Scott continued his march to Mexico City, ultimately capturing the key fort at Chapultepec to bring the war to a close.

Scott was also active in political circles, even as a serving general, and was a candidate for the Whig Party presidential nomination in 1840, 1844, and 1848, finally becoming the nominee in 1852. He was defeated in that election by Franklin Pierce.

In 1855, Scott was promoted to the grade of lieutenant general, the first American to hold that rank since George Washington. He remained loyal to the Union, and in the early days of the Civil War he offered command of the Union army to Robert E. Lee, who declined and joined the Confederacy. Scott retired in 1861 and lived at West Point until he passed away. He was a frequent visitor to the chapel and had a silver nameplate put on a pew to reserve his spot.

112 *Stone Tapestry*

Brigadier General John S. Eisenhower
Section XXVII, Row A, Grave 18

John Eisenhower graduated from West Point on June 6, 1944, while his father was commanding the D-day invasion of France. He initially served in Europe before the close of the war, but his assignments were hampered by being the son of the supreme Allied commander. This shadow of his famous father also hampered his assignment to combat in the Korean War, when his father was president. Eventually, Eisenhower served a fourteen-month combat tour in Korea in the 3rd Infantry Division.

Eisenhower was a graduate of the Armor Advanced Course and the Command and General Staff College and returned to West Point to be an instructor in English after taking a master's degree from Columbia University. He also served in the White House during his father's presidency as an assistant to Andrew Goodpaster, the staff secretary.

Eisenhower's passion was writing, and he became a very successful historian after he left the Army. In 1961 he took a two-year leave of absence from active duty, without pay, to help his father edit his presidential memoirs. After the two years was up, the book was not yet finished, and Eisenhower was faced with returning to the active Army for his next assignment or giving up his help on the book. Deciding instead to continue the book, he resigned his commission a mere year before he would have been eligible for retirement at half pay. Instead he joined the Army Reserve and he continued to advance there, ultimately retiring as a brigadier general. He finished the presidential memoirs in 1964.

Eisenhower authored thirteen historical books, including *The Bitter Woods* about the Battle of the Bulge. His first four books all dealt with World War II, while his next three dealt with the Mexican War, including *Agent of Destiny*, the biography of Winfield Scott. It is appropriate that the author of Scott's definitive biography should lie next to him here in the cemetery.

In 1969, Eisenhower was appointed ambassador to Belgium, where he "kept the peace with Belgium" (in his words) for two and a half years.

Major General Clarence S. Ridley
Section XXVII, Row B, Grave 23

General Clarence Ridley was a 1905 graduate of West Point, commissioned in the Corps of Engineers. He began his career, as many engineers did, doing land defense surveys or harbor work in Hawaii and the Philippines. By 1916 he was assigned to the Chief of Engineers office in Washington, and in 1917 he was assigned as the military aide to President Wilson. After this prestigious assignment, he remained in Washington as superintendent of the State, War and Navy Building, the forerunner to the Pentagon.

General Ridley was next sent to the Canal Zone, where he became the assistant engineer of maintenance. He returned to the United States for schooling, first at the Command and General Staff College (where he was the Honor Graduate) and then to the Army Industrial College, where he taught. He returned to the Canal Zone as the engineer of maintenance, and in 1936 he became governor of the Panama Canal.

In 1941, at the outbreak of the Second World War, Ridley returned to the United States as a major general and became a division commander, serving at Fort Lewis, Washington, and Fort Leonard Wood, Kansas, in command of divisions in training. In 1942, General Ridley was sent to Tehran, where he served as the chief of the military mission with the Iranian army. He remained there until his retirement in 1947.

His headstone reflects his award of the US Distinguished Service Medal, but in addition he was awarded the Officer Order of the Leopold by King Albert of Belgium, the Iranian Medal of Merit, and the Iranian Order of Harmayon, Second Class.

Brigadier General Ora E. Hunt
Section XXVII, Row B, Grave 25

Ora Hunt graduated in the West Point Class of 1894 and was commissioned in the infantry. He began his field service in the Philippine Insurrection. He then was assigned to the Infantry and Cavalry School at Fort Leavenworth as a student, where he was the distinguished graduate of the course in 1906. One of his classmates at Fort Leavenworth was future Army chief of staff General George C. Marshall.

General Hunt then returned to his alma mater to be an instructor in the Department of English and History. It was during his time at West Point that Hunt served as a contributor and an editor of volume V of *The Photographic History of the Civil War*.

When World War I broke out, then colonel Hunt was made commander of the 320th Infantry Regiment for training. Prior to departure for France, Hunt was promoted to brigadier general and given command of the 6th Brigade, 3rd Infantry Division.

Hunt served with distinction in combat in France. His brigade participated in the premier American contribution to the war, the St. Mihiel and Meuse-Argonne Offensives. Hunt's classmate at Leavenworth, George Marshall, was the author of the operations plan for both offensives, and Hunt's brigade played a pivotal role in their successful execution.

For his service in World War I, General Hunt was awarded the Distinguished Service Medal and a Silver Star for gallantry in action. Upon the 3rd Division's return to the United States, General Hunt was given command of the division.

Hunt retired from active service in 1923. Five years later, in 1928, President Calvin Coolidge asked General Hunt to serve on the Joint American Electoral Mission to supervise the elections in Nicaragua. He again returned to the service of his country, and the mission resulted in the first scandal-free elections in the South American country. For this service, General Hunt was awarded the US Marine Corps Medal.

Brevet Brigadier General Sylvanus Thayer
Section XXV, Row A, Grave 22

Sylvanus Thayer is known as the "Father of the Military Academy" for his inspiring leadership and his design of the academic system, which remains in place to this day. Thayer graduated from Dartmouth College in 1807 as the valedictorian of his class and received an appointment to West Point from President Jefferson. He graduated from West Point in 1808 after only one year and was commissioned in the engineers.

Thayer's early military service was spent in port fortifications in Norfolk, Virginia, and Boston Harbor. He was granted a two-year leave of absence to study at the French military academy, the École Polytechnique. While there, he established a large collection of scientific and engineering texts that would later form the basis for the USMA Library.

He had early service in the War of 1812, during which he was promoted to brevet major, and by 1817 he had returned to the Military Academy as the fifth superintendent, with the rank of captain. He remained the superintendent for sixteen years and transformed the institution into one of the foremost technical schools in the country. The demerit system, the emphasis on honor and responsibility, the summer encampment, high academic standards, and small class size all were part of Thayer's improvements, as well as his insistence on military bearing. "Every cadet shall recite in every class every day" was one of his maxims. The cadets who served under Thayer's guidance went on to lead the country through both the Mexican War and the American Civil War.

Thayer retired as a brevet brigadier general, US Army, in 1863 by Abraham Lincoln. In 1869, Thayer met with Brigadier General Robert Anderson, whom we met, and they established the USMA Association of Graduates, with Thayer as the first chairman. Part of their motivation for the AOG was to help heal the wounds of the Civil War, and the first reunion of Civil War veterans who were graduates took place under the auspices of the AOG at West Point in 1870.

Brigadier General John C. Tidball
Section XXV, Row B, Grave 35

General Tidball graduated in the Class of 1848 from West Point. He was commissioned in the Artillery branch and saw service in the Seminole War in Florida. He was a part of the US Army expedition sent to Harpers Ferry during the John Brown raid, along with Robert E. Lee and Stonewall Jackson.

But it was during the Civil War that Tidball achieved his most-lasting fame. He was a member of the horse artillery throughout the conflict and received five brevet promotions throughout the war. He was personally complimented by President Lincoln after the Battle of Gettysburg, where he commanded the 2nd Brigade Horse Artillery. After the battle, the chief of the Union artillery said of both Tidball and his colleague James Robertson that both men "are now performing the duties of general officers with only the rank of captain, and I most urgently that they be promoted to the rank of Brigadier General."

While General Dan Butterfield (whom we shall meet in the next chapter) is credited with writing the haunting air "Taps," it was Tidball who first had it played at the end of military funerals. Interestingly, after the Wilderness Campaign of 1864, Tidball was reassigned to West Point, where he was the commandant of cadets. Three months later he returned to active field service, commanding the IX Corps artillery.

After the war, Tidball became recognized as the Army's best artilleryman, and he wrote several books and articles, including *The Artillery Service in the War of the Rebellion* and *The Manual of Heavy Artillery Service*. He was promoted to brigadier general in the Regular Army and served as the third commander of the Department of Alaska—a post akin to today's governor. He also served as an aide-de-camp to General William T. Sherman when he was the general in chief of the US Army. Tidball was the last surviving member of the Class of 1848.

118 *Stone Tapestry*

Lieutenant Colonel Herman J. Koehler
Section XXV, Row B, Grave 37

Herman Koehler was not a graduate of West Point but was the head of the physical education department for thirty-eight years. Koehler graduated from the Milwaukee Normal School of Physical Training in 1882 and was immediately hired as the director of school gymnastics. He competed in gymnastics both in national and international competitions. In 1885 the West Point superintendent, General Wesley Merritt, appointed him to the position of Master of the Sword, the title of the head of the physical education department. Koehler served in that position until 1923.

He revitalized the department quickly and established a physical-training program for the cadets that included swimming, gymnastics, fencing, dancing, horsemanship, and strength testing. He began a rigorous calisthenics routine with cadets in mass formation and stressing precision and posture. He authored a textbook, *A System of Calisthenic Exercises for Use in the School of the Soldier*, which became the Army standard manual in 1892.

Koehler was given a direct commission as a first lieutenant of infantry in 1900 and subsequently was promoted to the grade of lieutenant colonel prior to his retirement. He was always a strong proponent of college athletics, including intramural sports, and was named the head Army football coach in 1897 for four years. During his tenure as head coach, Army amassed a record of nineteen wins, eleven losses, and three ties. His team played Navy twice (1899 and 1900) and won both games.

Koehler's physical-training program soon expanded to include boxing and wrestling and was made mandatory for all four years at the Military Academy. The cadets he trained became the junior officers of World War I and the general officers of World War II. In addition to his Army duties, Koehler also established a recruit school for the New York Police Department, among other assignments. In World War I, Koehler developed a physical-training program for 200,000 new soldiers in several training camps. He wrote a second book, *Koehler's West Point Manual of Disciplinary Physical Training*, in 1919, which included rifle exercises, bayonet training, and obstacle courses.

Sections XXIX, XXVII, XXV, XX, and XXI **119**

Brevet Major General Alexander S. Webb
Congressional Medal of Honor
Section XXI, Row C, Grave 32

General Alexander Webb earned a Medal of Honor during the Civil War at Gettysburg and in later life went on to be the president of the City College of New York, a post he held with distinction for thirty-three years.

Webb graduated from West Point in 1855, was commissioned in the artillery, and immediately went off to the Seminole Wars in Florida. He then returned to West Point, where he became an assistant professor of mathematics. When the Civil War broke out, Webb was assigned to Battery A, US Artillery. He participated in the Battle of Bull Run, and by August 1862 he had been promoted to lieutenant colonel. Before another year had passed, Webb was promoted to brigadier general in the US Volunteers and took command of the 2nd Brigade, 2nd Division, in the II Corps of the Army of the Potomac.

At Gettysburg, Webb's brigade was centrally located in front of the famous "Copse of Trees," which marked the center of the Union line on Cemetery Ridge during Pickett's Charge and was also the high-water mark of the Confederacy. As Armistead's brigade closed with the Union lines, Webb rallied the Pennsylvanian troops under his command and pushed back, personally leading a counterattack that ended with Armistead's death and the repulse of Pickett's Charge. Interestingly, Webb's heroics took place mere yards away from Alonzo Cushing (whom we met earlier), when Cushing was fatally struck firing the last rounds from his last cannon. It is probably fair to say that Webb and Cushing earned their respective Medals of Honor about as far apart on the battlefield at Gettysburg as they now lie buried from one another in the cemetery. Webb went on to be promoted to major general of volunteers and stayed in the Army until 1870. His final year of active service found him again at West Point as an instructor, having reverted to his permanent rank of lieutenant colonel. After his discharge, Webb became only the second president of the City College of New York, where he remained until 1902. He succeeded another West Point graduate, Horace Webster.

Webb authored a history of the Civil War's Peninsula Campaign in 1881, titled *The Peninsula: McClellan's Campaign of 1862*. A life-size bronze statue of Webb stands at the center of the Union lines on the Gettysburg battlefield.

Brevet Brigadier General Peter Michie
Section XXI, Row D, Grave 54

General Michie (pronounced *MIKE-ee*) graduated from West Point in the middle of the war years, in the Class of 1863 (a few weeks before General Webb and Lieutenant Cushing earned their Medals of Honor at Gettysburg). Michie showed his academic aptitude early, graduating second in his class of twenty-five. While still a cadet he was detailed as an acting assistant professor of mathematics and was praised for his teaching performance by Professor Albert Church (whom we shall meet in more detail farther along in our walk).

Michie was commissioned in the Corps of Engineers upon graduation and immediately joined the Union Army of the James. Within a year he was named chief engineer of the Army of the James and participated in the campaign against Richmond, and finally Appomattox. In 1865, a mere two years after his graduation, Michie was a brevet brigadier general.

In 1867, after the war was over, General Michie rejoined the faculty and staff at West Point as an assistant professor of engineering. His supervisor, Professor Dennis Hart Mahan (whom we shall also meet), had Michie teaching practical military and civil engineering, as well as chemistry, mineralogy, and geology. Michie demonstrated an active and curious mind and quickly rose to prominence within the faculty.

In 1871, Professor Michie was promoted to be the chair of the Natural and Experimental Philosophy Department, replacing Professor Bartlett (the third professor we shall meet in the next chapter), and he retained that post for thirty years. At this point in his life, Professor Michie was only thirty-two years old. In addition to his teaching duties, Professor Michie was named to be on the board that oversaw the creation of the Thayer School of Civil Engineering at Dartmouth College. That institution was established in accordance with the Thayer system of teaching engineering and was named for its most famous graduate, Sylvanus Thayer, whom we met a few pages ago.

Michie was granted a doctor of physics degree from Princeton University. He published several books, both about the Civil War and about physics, including *Analytical Mechanics*, *Hydrodynamics*, and *General McClellan*. Next on our walk we shall meet his son Dennis.

122 *Stone Tapestry*

First Lieutenant Dennis Michie
Section XXI, Row D, Grave 59

Dennis Mahan Michie is the son of Professor Michie. The younger Michie was born at West Point while his father was assistant professor of engineering, and he was named after his father's mentor and professor, Dennis Hart Mahan. Dennis Michie did not inherit his father's aptitude for scholarship; he was fifty-third out of sixty-two in the Class of 1892. However, he did have an aptitude for sports and heroism.

Michie was chosen to be the first head football coach of Army in 1890, while still a cadet, and he served as captain of the team in 1891 during his second-class year. He returned as head coach as a first classman in 1892. His overall coaching record at Army was 3-2-1.

Michie graduated in 1892 and was commissioned in the infantry. He spent his early commissioned years in the 17th US Infantry Regiment, on duty in Wyoming and Ohio. In 1897, Lieutenant Michie was on duty at the Cavalry and Infantry School at Fort Leavenworth when the Spanish-American War broke out. Michie rejoined the 17th Infantry in Tampa and embarked for Cuba. While en route he was assigned for duty to be the aide-de-camp for Brigadier General Hamilton Hawkins, who commanded the 1st Brigade, 5th Division, V Corps.

During the early days of the campaign, Michie was killed by enemy fire while in the battle for Santiago, near the San Juan Hills. His body was returned to West Point, where his father, by now professor of natural and experimental philosophy, buried him in the cemetery.

Michie Stadium, the Army football team's home at West Point, was named for Dennis Michie.

Sections XXIX, XXVII, XXV, XX, and XXI 123

Major William S. Beebe
Congressional Medal of Honor
Section XX, Row A, Grave 10

Major Beebe graduated in the Class of 1863, along with Peter Michie. Beebe was commissioned in the ordnance branch and immediately went off to war. His first assignment was to the arsenal at Saint Louis, and then, at his request, he was sent to be the chief ordnance officer of the Red River expedition. Not commonly known, the Red River campaign took place in 1864, in Louisiana. The basic plan was for Union forces to move north from New Orleans along the Red River and capture Shreveport. The campaign itself was a failure for the Union, but several successful battles were fought, and Lieutenant Beebe participated in all of them. He was wounded in action, had his horse shot out from underneath him, and was promoted to brevet captain.

In April 1864, at the Battle of Cane River Crossing, Captain Beebe was on board a small steamer with a load of powder and shells attempting to resupply some Union mortar batteries. He led an assault against the Confederate cavalry in front of him and was recognized as being the first Union officer inside Confederate lines. For his gallantry, Beebe was promoted to major and awarded the Medal of Honor.

Major Beebe went on to serve in the remainder of the war and afterward commanded the Mount Vernon Arsenal in Alabama, then the Frankford Arsenal in Pennsylvania. He continued to serve honorably at all the major Army arsenals until his retirement in 1874.

When war was declared against Spain in 1898, Major Beebe petitioned the government to be commissioned again to serve in Cuba, despite having been retired for twenty-four years. He was appointed a major of volunteers and was assigned to the staff of Major General Wade. He traveled with Wade to Havana for the war but contracted yellow fever and died before he could participate in the campaign.

Brigadier General Thomas Devin
Section XX, Row B, Grave 21

General Thomas Devin is a bit of a rarity here in the cemetery, in that he is not a West Point graduate. A very distinguished cavalryman, he served under General John Buford and General Judson Kilpatrick, both of whom we have already met.

Devin was not a college graduate, and prior to the Civil War he was not even in the military. When the war began, he formed a small militia cavalry company that he led as their captain. By 1862, Devin had been promoted to colonel and given command of the 6th New York Volunteer Cavalry. He led this regiment up to and through the battle at Antietam Creek, and by the time of the Battle of Fredericksburg, Devin had been moved up to command a brigade of cavalry.

During the Chancellorsville Campaign, Devin's cavalry brigade led three Union corps in a flanking movement around Confederate lines. During the large cavalry action at Brandy Station, Devin temporarily moved up to command John Buford's cavalry division when Buford was moved up to command the right wing of the Army.

At Gettysburg, Devin again led his brigade under Buford's command, and as we have seen, his unit under Buford was decisive in choosing the high ground on which to fight and in forcing the Confederates to deploy and fight before General Lee was ready. By 1864, Devin's brigade was placed under General Kilpatrick's command for a raid against Richmond.

Devin was wounded once during the war, in 1864. By late 1864, President Lincoln had appointed Devin to brigadier general of volunteers. After the war he reverted to his regular rank of lieutenant colonel and commanded the 8th US Cavalry. Devin died in 1867 and was buried in New York. His wife moved to Highland Falls, outside West Point, and upon her death both were buried here in the cemetery, at her wish.

CAVALRY RALLY.

126 *Stone Tapestry*

Brigadier General Frank Kobes Jr.
Section XXI, Row D, Grave 60

General Kobes graduated from West Point in 1939 and was commissioned in the infantry. He was a noted athlete, both in high school and at West Point, and lettered in football, basketball, and track while a cadet. After graduation he remained at West Point as the assistant coach of the football team.

In 1941, Kobes joined the 15th Infantry at Fort Lewis, Washington, and he went on to command the 2nd Battalion, 15th Infantry, in combat in North Africa and Italy. He was medically evacuated from his command after a knee injury. He returned to the United States, where he served as an instructor at the Infantry School, then back to West Point as a tactical officer. In 1946 he retired from the Army with a medical disability.

After his retirement, Kobes became the commandant of cadets at Valley Forge Military Academy and began graduate studies at Villanova. In 1951 he was recalled to active duty in the Army, with duty at West Point as an instructor in physical education and as the executive officer of the 1st Regiment, United States Corps of Cadets.

In 1953, then colonel Kobes was named the director of the Physical Education Department at West Point, and he remained there until 1974. In 1957, Colonel Kobes was named a permanent professor and head of the Physical Education Department. Like Herman Koehler, Kobes's influence on generations of cadets was impressive. He devised a complete physical-fitness program for the cadets, and, like Koehler's, it was soon adopted Army-wide. He devised a physical-fitness program for the New York City Boy Scouts, which later grew to be a program for Explorer Scouts. He served on the Physical Education Committee for the National YMCA and was active in the American College for Sports Medicine. He also worked on the Athletic Board for West Point and on the Admissions Committee. Kobe retired in 1974 as a brigadier general.

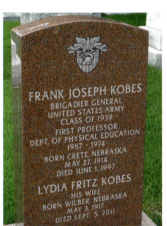

CHAPTER 7

Sections XXVIII, XXIV, XIX, XV, and XIII

In this chapter we again will visit one of the oldest sections in the cemetery, and one of the most interesting. We will meet here first-rate educators; instructors in physics, mathematics, and ordnance; inventors; coaches; swimming teachers; and more. The man for whom the Comstock Prize in Physics is named lies here, along with the inventor of the tommy gun. We will meet the Civil War general who wrote "Taps" and the engineer who laid out Manhattan. We will meet two distinguished Medal of Honor winners who lie side by side, as they served in life. Two of the most ornate and distinctive monuments in the entire cemetery will be on our walk today. Two of the academic buildings at West Point (Mahan Hall and Bartlett Hall) are named for two of the instructors we shall meet. We will spend a little time with Marty Maher, an Irish immigrant who rose from a waiter in the Mess Hall to be a master sergeant in the Physical Education Department. Maher spent more than fifty years at West Point and authored a book called *Bringing Up the Brass*, which was later made into a movie called *The Long Gray Line*. We will begin by meeting the progenitor of his own Long Gray Line, Brigadier General Charles Raymond, who had no fewer than seventeen of his descendants follow him to West Point.

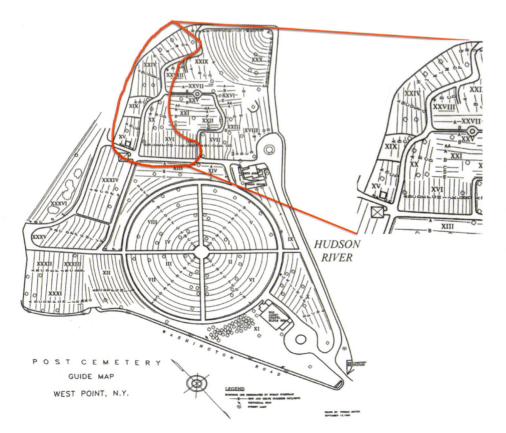

129

Brigadier General Charles W. Raymond
Section XXVIII, Row B, Grave 11

General Raymond graduated from West Point as the first man in his class in 1865. He was appointed as a first lieutenant immediately upon graduation as a reflection of his capabilities, skipping entirely the grade of second lieutenant. He had several assignments after graduation working with or supervising field fortification and harbor defenses in Boston, Alcatraz Island in San Francisco, and Fort Stevens, Oregon.

In 1869 he was selected to command an expedition up the Yukon River in Alaska, surveying the region with an eye toward its defense. He then returned to West Point in 1871 and spent three years there as assistant professor of natural and experimental philosophy during Peter Michie's tenure as department chair. He earned a PhD from Lafayette College, Pennsylvania, during this time as well.

In 1874, Raymond was selected to command an expedition to Tasmania that was part of a worldwide effort to survey the transit of the planet Venus across the face of the sun. The various expeditions were sent around the globe to make their observations in an effort to calculate more precisely the distance between the earth and the sun, using triangulation of the Venus observations at the same moment in time.

In later years, General Raymond supervised a board that recommended a route for a deep waterway from the Great Lakes to the Atlantic Ocean.

General Raymond had a total of seventeen of his relatives attend West Point, and many of them are buried here in this "family plot." He had two sons, four grandsons, six great-grandsons, and five great-great-grandsons graduate from West Point, spanning a total of a hundred years from the Class of 1893 to the Class of 1993. According to the Association of Graduates Annual Register, this is the highest number of descendants to come from a single graduate.

130 *Stone Tapestry*

Brigadier General Cyrus Comstock
Section XXVIII, Row C, Grave 25

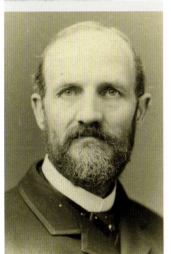

General Comstock was also the first man in his class, but he graduated ten years prior to General Raymond, in the Class of 1855. Comstock distinguished himself as a field engineer early in the Civil War, participating in battles in the Peninsular Campaign, as well as at Antietam, Fredericksburg, and Chancellorsville. He ultimately rose to be the chief engineer officer in the Army of the Potomac and later served as the chief engineer in the Army of the Tennessee.

In 1864, General Comstock became the senior aide-de-camp to General U. S. Grant when Grant assumed command of all the Union armies (*to the far right in photograph*). He served in that role until the end of the war and participated in the taking of Fort Fisher in North Carolina, and in the surrender of Mobile, Alabama. Comstock was promoted to brevet brigadier general in the Regular Army by the end of the war.

After the war, Comstock served on the Military Commission to oversee the trial of John Wilkes Booth. As the commission's work dragged on, Comstock felt that they were conducting the trial with excessive secrecy, which he believed violated the rights of the accused. He argued that the commission ought to remove the trial to a civilian court, and was removed from his position by President Andrew Johnston.

Comstock served after the war on several boards and commissions, including the Mississippi River Commission, and was a member of the National Academy of Sciences and the American Academy of Arts and Sciences. He bequeathed a fund of $20,000 to be awarded to a scientist who conducted innovative work in electricity, magnetism, or radiant energy. Known as the Comstock Prize in Physics, it is awarded every five years. Previous awardees include Robert Millikan, William Shockley, and Ernest O. Lawrence. The most recent award was made in 2019 to Michal Lipson.

Brigadier General Bernard J. D. Irwin
Congressional Medal of Honor
Section XXVIII, Row D, Grave 35

General Bernard Irwin was not a West Point graduate but was an Irish immigrant. He attended New York University and served in the New York State Militia. He graduated from medical college in 1852.

General Irwin was the first person to be awarded the Congressional Medal of Honor, chronologically by date of action, for his valorous service during the Indian Wars. The Medal of Honor was first authorized in 1862, but Irwin's heroics, which took place in 1861, were remembered and he was submitted for the award. Irwin was a surgeon but led a relief mission against Cochise of the Apaches to rescue a besieged Army unit.

Irwin later served in the Civil War as a medical officer responsible for establishing field hospitals. He was captured in 1862 but was paroled within a month. From 1863 to the end of the war, he was the superintendent of the military hospital in Memphis, Tennessee. After the war, Irwin was the senior medical officer at West Point, serving there from 1873 to 1878.

General Irwin also had an interest in science and wrote a monograph titled *The History of the Great Tucson Meteorite*, which he presented to the Smithsonian Institution.

General Irwin had one son and one grandson graduate from West Point. The son, George LeRoy Irwin (*left*), was a member of the Class of 1889. He retired as a major general and was a distinguished field artilleryman, at one point commanding the Field Artillery School. He lies here next to his father. The US Army National Training Center in the Mojave Desert is named after George Irwin.

The grandson, Stafford L. Irwin, graduated in 1915 and retired as a lieutenant general; he commanded XII Corps in Italy during World War II. Lieutenant General Irwin is buried in Arlington National Cemetery.

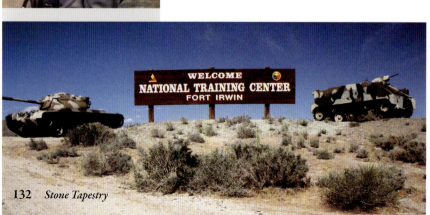

132   *Stone Tapestry*

Professor Albert E. Church
Section XXIV, Row L, Grave 240

In this small section of the cemetery we shall meet four intellectual giants who together led their respective departments, side by side, for more than forty years. Professor Church was one of these giants, along with Professors Bartlett, Weir, and Mahan. Church led the Mathematics Department, Bartlett the Department of Natural and Experimental Philosophy, Weir the Department of Drawing, and Mahan the Department of Military and Civil Engineering. Between them they oversaw the education of over two thousand graduates who attended West Point between 1830 and 1878. These graduates then came to prominence in our country's history from the Mexican War to the Civil War and up to the turn of the century.

Like two others of the four, Church attended West Point under the tutelage of Sylvanus Thayer himself, with Church graduating first in the class in 1828. He was commissioned in the artillery, there being no vacancies in the Corps of Engineers. But Church's destiny was at West Point, not in the artillery, and he stayed on as an instructor of mathematics after graduation. In fact, except for a short two-year tour in an artillery unit, he spent his entire career at West Point in the Mathematics Department.

Church wrote four textbooks on differential and integral calculus, analytical geometry, descriptive geometry, and plane and spherical trigonometry. All four were used as texts for many years at West Point, as well as at other colleges and universities, such as Union College and the University of Michigan.

Church's father was a chief justice of the Supreme Court of Connecticut; Church himself also studied law in his spare time. He was the judge advocate at West Point in addition to his duties in the Mathematics Department. A man of gentle habits and with a calm demeanor, he was a friend to all and was widely liked by the cadets, as well as his colleagues, throughout his life. In 1878 he read a paper describing his fifty years at West Point to an audience of the US Military Service Institute, and he passed away a mere two days later.

134   *Stone Tapestry*

Professor William H. C. Bartlett
Section XXIV, Row P, Grave 286

Like Church, Professor Bartlett (for whom Bartlett Hall is named) was the first man in his class, the Class of 1826. Bartlett excelled in academics while still a cadet and served as an acting assistant professor of mathematics during his last two years. He was commissioned a brevet second lieutenant upon graduation and assigned to the Corps of Engineers. He did not leave the Military Academy; his initial orders were to serve as an assistant professor of engineering. In 1829, Bartlett was sent to duty with the Engineer Corps, and he served on the project that constructed Fort Monroe in Virginia (where Jefferson Davis was subsequently held prisoner) and Fort Adams, Rhode Island.

He then was assigned to the staff of the chief of engineers in Washington, DC, where he remained until posted back to West Point in 1834. He began his tenure as the acting professor of natural and experimental philosophy, but within six months he became the head of the department, where he remained until 1871. During this time, Bartlett wrote several textbooks (like Professor Church), including *Analytical Mechanics*, which went through nine editions. He also wrote *Treatise on Optics*, *Acoustics and Optics*, and *Bartlett's Spherical Astronomy*. Like Church's textbooks, many were used widely in other colleges and universities.

According to his obituary, his course at the academy was always regarded as the "most difficult," but he had a kindly and considerate manner and was well liked by his pupils.

In 1871, Professor Bartlett left West Point to become the chief actuary at the Mutual Company of New York; he served there until he was eighty-five years old. While there, he published *Mortuary Experience of the Mutual Life Insurance Company of New York, from 1843 to 1874*. Professor Bartlett died in 1893.

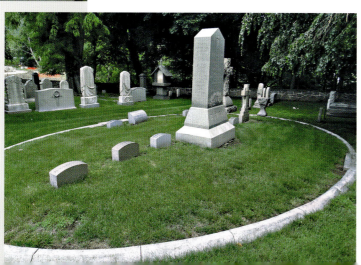

Sections XXVIII, XXIV, XIX, XV, and XIII

Major Edward B. Hunt
Section XXIV, Row O, Grave 278

Hunt and his wife, Helen Hunt Jackson, are a husband-and-wife pair who both achieved some measure of fame. Edward Hunt graduated second in the Class of 1841 and, as was common at that time, came back to West Point to teach early in his career. A superb engineer, he taught in the Engineering Department from 1846 to 1849, then went on to assist in construction of Fort Warren in Boston Harbor. Hunt then went on to work in the Chief of Engineers office in Washington, then on coastal duty in a variety of forts and harbors around the East Coast of the United States.

During the Civil War, Hunt was the engineer of the Department of the Shenandoah until 1862, when he was sent on special duty assigned to the Navy Department. Hunt was instrumental in devising and testing a weapon that could fire underwater, in essence the first torpedo. Named "Sea Miner," the prototype failed during its first underwater test, and the resulting explosion and toxic gases snuffed out Hunt's life.

Hunt was married to his wife, Helen, in 1852, and the couple had two sons. One, Murray, died of a brain disease in 1854 and is buried here in the cemetery with his father. The other son died in 1865. Helen Hunt remarried in 1875 and became famous as Helen Hunt Jackson, an author and poet. Her early writings reflected her loss and suffering through the premature deaths of her husband and children. She published her poetry in *The Atlantic* and in *The Century*. She then began writing novels and published three between 1876 and 1879. No less than Ralph Waldo Emerson used several of her poems in his public readings.

In 1879 she became interested in the American treatment of the various Indian nations, and she wrote her most famous work, a book titled *A Century of Dishonor*. She sent a copy to every member of Congress. She followed that with a novel called *Ramona*, intended to do for the Indians what *Uncle Tom's Cabin* did for Black people, and her book was called "unquestionably the best novel yet produced by an American woman" by the *New York Times*. Helen Hunt Jackson is buried in Colorado.

Professor Robert W. Weir
Section XIX, Row A, Grave 3

Professor Weir is the third of our quartet of long-tenured and famous instructors. He is a relative rarity in this cemetery—a man who never graduated from any college. He left school at a very early age and instead began pursuing an interest in art and painting. He studied art in New York until 1824, then departed overseas to continue his studies in Italy. Weir alternated between Florence and Rome, where he studied the works of the great Italian artists.

In 1834, Weir came to West Point to teach drawing to the cadets. He was promoted to professor in 1846 and remained until 1876. Drawing was an essential engineering skill for Army officers prior to the invention of photography, and all officers were expected to be able to survey, draw detailed maps by hand, and contribute sketches of fortifications, bridges, and other items of military interest.

Some of the students whom Weir taught included James A. M. Whistler, the famous American artist, and Seth Eastman, who achieved fame as an artist of Indian culture. In 1837, Weir was commissioned to paint one of the four paintings that today hang in the rotunda of the US Capitol. His entry is titled *The Embarkation of the Pilgrims* (*below left*). He also did several portraits, including one of Winfield Scott (*below right*, and whom we have already met) and one of the few pre–Civil War paintings of Robert E. Lee.

Weir was married twice and fathered sixteen children; two of his children went on to be famous artists: John Ferguson Weir and Julian Alden Weir.

After he left the Military Academy in 1876, Weir established a studio in New York City and continued to paint extensively.

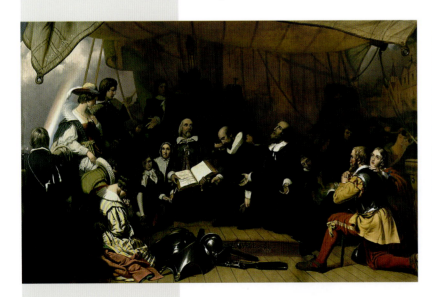

Stone Tapestry

Colonel James G. Benton
Section XIX, Row B, Grave 18

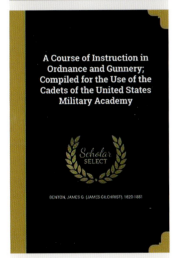

Colonel Benton was an Ordnance officer extraordinaire who commanded ordnance installations around the country and, like so many others we have seen, taught and developed textbooks for the Military Academy.

Benton graduated in the Class of 1842 and was classmates with many of the famous generals who served in the Civil War, including Generals Pope, Longstreet, Rosecrans, Doubleday, and Sykes. He was commissioned in the Ordnance Corps and served there continuously for forty years until his death. From 1853 to 1857 he served on the Ordnance Board in Washington, DC, and was instrumental in the experiments that resulted in the new rifled musket that saw service in the Civil War.

He then moved up to West Point, where he was an instructor of ordnance and gunnery from 1857 to 1861. During his time at West Point, he authored the text on the course of instruction (*left*). Upon the outbreak of the Civil War, Benton was again moved to Washington, where he served as the assistant chief of ordnance, and as a member of the Ordnance Board. In 1863 he took command of the Washington Arsenal, where he remained until 1866.

He assumed command of the National Armory in Springfield, Massachusetts, where he remained until his death fifteen years later. While in command at Springfield, he served on several boards and commissions, including those that examined the use of 15-inch guns, the selection of the proper caliber for small arms in the Army, the use of metallic cartridges in revolvers, and the use of a new design of artillery shell, the Perrine shell. His final contribution to the Ordnance Corps was an investigation into the selection of a magazine-fed gun for the Army, a forerunner to the semiautomatic rifles to come.

Captain Henry Metcalfe
Section XIX, Row C, Grave 21

Captain Henry Metcalfe is another Ordnance officer who worked under Colonel Benton. Metcalfe was first appointed to West Point by President Lincoln in 1863, in a slot that had been reserved for Southern states then in rebellion against the United States. Metcalfe was among the most junior in age of all his classmates and was nicknamed "Babe." He unfortunately fell ill and had to sit out for a year to recover, so instead of being in the Class of 1867, he became a member of the Class of 1868. It is noteworthy of the man that he was so popular that both classes claimed him as their own, and he was active in class functions for both.

Metcalfe was assigned as an Ordnance officer upon graduation and sent to the National Armory at Springfield. Recall from previously that Colonel Benton was then commanding the Armory. Metcalfe assisted Benton in the development of a magazine-fed rifle for the US and obtained a series of patents on a design.

In 1877, Captain Metcalfe was assigned as the assistant ordnance officer at Frankford Arsenal, and there he began development of a new system of shop ordering and management, including time-and-motion studies. Metcalfe's work here was groundbreaking, and he authored a book on the subject called *The Cost of Manufactures and the Administrations of Workshops, Public and Private*. His book was influential, and when Frederick Taylor published his seminal work *Shop Management* in 1903, he acknowledged Metcalfe's contribution to his work. The field of management science grew largely from Taylor, and hence, Metcalfe's work.

Metcalfe went on to be an instructor in Spanish at West Point, and later as aide-de-camp to Major General Halleck. He then returned to West Point to teach Ordnance and Gunnery, like his mentor Benton. He completely revised Benton's text on gunnery instruction, taking into account advances in the field since Benton's work. His obituary in the Association of Graduates Annual Register notes that his book went through three editions, but the work so damaged his eyesight that Metcalfe was compelled to retire.

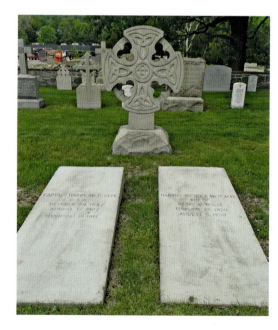

Major General Daniel Butterfield
Congressional Medal of Honor
Section XV, Row D, Grave 50

Daniel Butterfield was not a graduate of West Point, instead beginning his career working for American Express, which his father cofounded. At the beginning of the Civil War, Butterfield served as a first sergeant of the Clay Guards in Washington but was quickly promoted, first to colonel and then to brigadier general of volunteers. He participated in the First Battle of Bull Run and spent time drafting an Army field manual titled *Camp and Outpost Duty for Infantry*.

Butterfield was wounded at the Battle for Gaines Mill in June 1862 and was subsequently awarded the Medal of Honor for his gallantry and heroism in that battle. He continued his rise in the ranks until he commanded a division at Antietam and V Corps at Fredericksburg. He was close to General Hooker and also served as Hooker's chief of staff. After Hooker's ignominious departure from command, Hooker remained as chief of staff under General George Meade and was again wounded, at Gettysburg. After his recovery he again joined Hooker, by now the general commanding the Army of the Cumberland in Tennessee. At war's end, Butterfield was made the assistant secretary of the Treasury in the Grant administration but had to resign that post in disgrace when he was found trying to manipulate the price of gold.

Butterfield is credited with creating "Taps," played now at all military funerals. He edited an existing bugle air called the "Scott Tattoo" by changing the notes and adding text. He did this while convalescing from his wounds at Gaines Mill, and within a short time both the Confederate and Union army buglers were using the new call to signal "lights out" at the end of the day. Tidball, of the horse cavalry, whom we met earlier, was the first to have "Taps" played at military funerals.

Butterfield's monument here at the cemetery is by far the largest and most ornate. It has been derisively referred to as the "cake topper" by some.

Brigadier General (US Volunteers) Egbert L. Viele

Section XXXIV, Row F, Grave 258

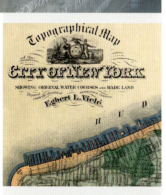

The gravesite of Brigadier General Viele (pronounced *VEE-lee*) is probably unique in the cemetery. Positioned as it is next to Butterfield's ornate memorial, it makes this corner of the cemetery one of the most picturesque.

Viele graduated from West Point in 1847 and, like so many others we have met, became an engineer of note throughout his career. He served briefly in the Mexican War but resigned his commission in 1853 to become a civil engineer. In 1855 he was commissioned to do a topographical survey of the state of New York, and in 1856 he became the engineer in chief of Central Park in New York City. Viele produced a topographical map of Manhattan Island that is so detailed that it is still consulted to this day for geographical features of the island.

He was recalled to active service in the Civil War and again was called upon to serve in engineering roles. Viele was appointed the military governor of Norfolk in 1862 but resigned again in 1863 to resume his civilian career. One wonders about resigning his commission in the middle of an active war; perhaps being military governor was not his style. He served as the chief engineer on the Pittsburgh, Buffalo, and Rochester Railroad, and as the commissioner of parks for New York City. In 1885 he was elected to the US House of Representatives, where he served one term.

Viele and his wife, Juliette, are buried here together in this pyramidal mausoleum. A long-standing West Point story has it that Viele, who had a fear of being buried alive, had a buzzer installed in his coffin that was wired to ring in the house of the superintendent if need arose. There is no recorded incident where it was ever used, and it has now been deinstalled.

Sections XXVIII, XXIV, XIX, XV, and XIII

Professor Dennis Hart Mahan
Section XV, Row C, Grave 28

Professor Mahan is the fourth of our quartet of professors who served West Point together for forty years. Like Professors Church and Bartlett, Professor Mahan attended West Point under Sylvanus Thayer himself, and he graduated first in his class in 1824.

Like the others, he was immediately assigned as an instructor, and in 1826 Mahan was sent by Thayer to Europe to study their advanced engineering techniques, texts, and instruments. He brought back with him four years later a large library of textbooks, maps, and instruments to be used at West Point and resigned his commission to become the chair of the Engineering Department.

In addition to his engineering duties, Mahan also was a professor of military science. He wrote several books on field fortifications, industrial drawing, descriptive geometry, and military engineering. His influence spread across the country, since most engineering schools used the texts used, or developed, at West Point.

Professor Mahan's influence reached a peak during the Civil War, since almost every general officer on either side had studied under his tutelage the art and science of war, as well as civil and mechanical engineering. His writings were also translated and used throughout Europe in the period prior to World War I.

By 1871, Professor Mahan's abilities were in sharp decline, and the West Point Board of Visitors reluctantly decided that he had to retire from his teaching post. Despondent, Mahan took his own life by leaping into the paddle wheel of a steamboat on the Hudson. Mahan Hall, the home of the Engineering Department at West Point, is named after him. His son Alfred Thayer Mahan became America's foremost naval historian and theorist and has his own building named after him at Annapolis.

144   *Stone Tapestry*

Master Sergeant Marty Maher
Section XIII, Row E, Grave 174

Marty Maher was an institution at West Point for fifty years. Maher was born in Ballycrine, Ireland, and came to the United States seeking employment. Beginning as a civilian waiter in the mess hall in 1896, Maher enlisted in the Army two years later. He retired in 1928 at the rank of master sergeant, having spent his entire military career at West Point. Maher then remained at the academy as a civilian instructor in the Physical Education Department until 1946.

Maher was the author of a book about his life and experiences at West Point titled *Bringing Up the Brass*. He collaborated with Colonel Red Reeder, himself an author and longtime resident at West Point, whom we have already met. His boss in the Physical Education Department was Colonel Herman Koehler, another familiar face from our journey. Maher was on close and intimate terms with many of the graduates from this period, including Dwight Eisenhower, Omar Bradley, Reeder, and dozens of others. His primary duty was to teach swimming (although he says in his book that he himself did not know how to swim!), and he also assisted the coaches of the baseball and football teams of this era. He was quite popular with the cadets, and at his retirement the Corps of Cadets gave him a formal review on the Plain.

Maher's book was made into a movie in 1955 directed by John Ford, called *The Long Gray Line*. The movie starred Tyrone Power as Maher and Maureen O'Hara as his beloved Irish wife, Mary. In keeping with Ford's habit as a director, the film was shot entirely at West Point and gives a fairly accurate view of life at the Military Academy during the first half of the 1900s.

Many of Marty Maher's family came to West Point from Ireland after he did, including his brothers and his father. There are more than a dozen Maher graves to be found in the cemetery, all of which are part of Marty's extended family. Sadly, he and Mary never had children of their own.

146 *Stone Tapestry*

Coach Joseph M. Palone
Section XIII, Row G, Grave 242

Coach Palone was the head coach for Army soccer for twenty-nine years, retiring in 1978. He remains the winningest head coach of the soccer team in its history, with a record of 228 wins, 80 losses, and 35 ties.

Palone graduated from the State University of New York at Cortland in the Class of 1931, where he was a star on the baseball field. He began his coaching career at Belmont High School, where he was the coach in soccer, baseball, and basketball. Palone began his association with West Point in 1944, when he joined the Army coaching staff as an assistant in both soccer and baseball. He took over as the head soccer coach in 1947.

Under Coach Palone, Army soccer thrived. The Army team went to the NCAA soccer playoffs ten times and made it to the semifinals four times. His teams were the Eastern Division champions three times. His winning percentage of .715 still ranks as one of the best in the NCAA.

Coach Palone led teams with winning seasons twenty-six times in his twenty-nine years as head coach, and in 1950 and 1951 his teams were unbeaten. In 2020, Coach Palone was voted into the United Soccer Coaches Hall of Fame. Previously he had been voted into the inaugural class of the Army Sports Hall of Fame in 2004.

In addition to his soccer accomplishments, Coach Palone also served as the head coach of the Army baseball team from 1955 to 1957.

Brigadier General John T. Thompson
Section XIII, Row A, Grave 38

General Thompson was famous as the inventor of the "tommy gun," which saw service worldwide both in civilian law enforcement and in military service in multiple countries from 1920 through World War II.

Thompson graduated from West Point in 1882 and initially was commissioned in the field artillery, but he transferred into the Ordnance Corps in 1890. He served in a variety of artillery and ordnance assignments during his early career and was promoted up to the grade of colonel. During the Spanish-American War in 1898, Thompson was made the chief ordnance officer of the US Volunteers and participated in the campaign against Cuba. His service in Cuba convinced him of the need to increase the firepower available to the individual soldier, and he worked incessantly on small-arms designs and improvements. He was instrumental in the development of the Springfield rifle prior to World War I. He retired from active service in 1914 at his own request.

The onset of American involvement in World War I caused the Army to recall Thompson to active service and to promote him to brigadier general. He again served in the Ordnance Corps as chief of the Small Arms Division.

Upon his retirement a second time, General Thompson became the chief engineer at the Remington Arms Corporation in Pennsylvania. He served in subsequent corporations in the development of small arms, including the Warner & Swazey Company and the Auto-Ordnance Corporation. It was during this time that the Thompson submachine gun was developed and patented. In 1921 the Colt Patent Fire Arms Manufacturing Company received an order to build 15,000 Thompsons, and General Thompson became the vice president of sales.

The submachine gun was used by the Marines, the Army, the Navy, and the Coast Guard in World War II. It was in use in foreign countries such as the Belgian Congo Army and was also used by several state police and constabulary organizations, including by penitentiary guards. The gun was used extensively in World War II, although General Thompson had passed away before he could see it.

148   *Stone Tapestry*

Brigadier General George L. Gillespie Jr.
Congressional Medal of Honor
Section XIII, Row A, Grave 59

It is fitting that General Gillespie and his neighbor, Lieutenant Colonel Benyaurd, lie side by side here and their stories are told on sequential pages. Both graduated within a year of one another, both earned the Medal of Honor in the Civil War, during which they served together, and both were engineers of distinction.

General Gillespie graduated second in the Class of 1862 and was commissioned in the Corps of Engineers. He was assigned to the Engineer Battalion in the Army of the Potomac, under General McClellan. He supervised the building of several pontoon bridges and surveyed fords across the Potomac for the Army. He participated in all the major campaigns of the Civil War and was awarded the Medal of Honor for valorous conduct at the Battle of Cold Harbor. Benyaurd was side by side with him in this battle. General Gillespie served with distinction throughout the war and was on the staffs of Generals McClellan, Grant, Meade, and Sheridan.

After the war, Gillespie served as the chief engineer on many projects across the country, including harbors and fortifications in New Hampshire, New Orleans, Chicago, Oregon, and Boston. When the Spanish-American War broke out, Gillespie was made a brigadier general of volunteers and took command of the Department of the East from New York. After the war he was promoted permanently to brigadier and became the chief of engineers.

Interestingly, Gillespie was chosen to redesign the Medal of Honor ribbon in 1904, replacing the red, white, and blue stripes with the now-familiar light-blue field with thirteen stars (both the old and the new designs are shown).

150 *Stone Tapestry*

Lieutenant Colonel William H. H. Benyaurd
Congressional Medal of Honor
Section XIII, Row A, Grave 61

Lieutenant Colonel Benyaurd graduated sixth in the Class of 1862, one year behind Gillespie. He was also commissioned in the Corps of Engineers and immediately joined the staff of the Army of the Potomac. Like his predecessor, Benyaurd served throughout the remainder of the war and was in attendance at Appomattox when Lee surrendered his army. He participated with Gillespie in the construction of the pontoon bridge across the James River during the Petersburg Campaign, at 2,000 feet the longest one ever constructed up to that time.

Lieutenant Colonel Benyaurd earned the Medal of Honor during the Battle of Five Forks in April 1865, almost one year exactly after General Gillespie earned his. Benyaurd, then a lieutenant, rode to the front of the line alongside General Warren when the troops were wavering, grabbed the headquarters flag, and surged forward into heavy enemy fire to rally the formation and resume the attack.

After the war, Benyaurd was assigned as an assistant professor of engineering at West Point. He also served as the supervising engineer on many construction projects across the country, including in Mississippi, Rock Island, the Red River Raft in Louisiana, and San Francisco. During the Spanish-American War he was responsible for the defenses of St. Augustine and Tampa, Florida. By 1899 he was transferred to New York City for duty with the engineer office there. He contracted pneumonia there and died after a brief illness.

Two sterling engineers, two academic achievers, and two Medal of Honor winners lie side by side here.

Sections XXVIII, XXIV, XIX, XV, and XIII   151

CHAPTER 8

Sections I, II, III, and IV

In this chapter we shall begin our stroll through the vast circular area that is the centerpiece of the cemetery. This is an eclectic mix of very old and very new, of famous generals and instructors, of sons and fathers from the Civil War in our own land to the far-distant sand wastes of Afghanistan. The general who developed the potential of the helicopter for land warfare is here, along with his father, who fought in the Indian Wars. We will meet more Medal of Honor recipients, another Army football coach, and more superintendents. Louis Vauthier was a Frenchman and a fencing instructor, who was made an honorary member of the Class of 1923. Come along to meet a most interesting group of people from our history.

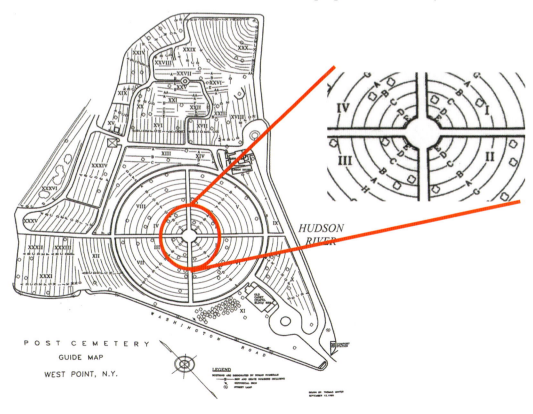

General Hamilton H. Howze
Section I, Row A, Grave 2

Hamilton Howze was born in the commandant's quarters at West Point in 1908. His father, whom we will meet next, was serving as the commandant at the time. General Howze the younger was a fourth-generation member of the Long Gray Line and went on to graduate in the Class of 1930. He was commissioned in the cavalry.

Howze had a series of cavalry assignments, in multiple different regiments, in the pre-WWII years. He married Mary Henry, herself from a third-generation West Point family. In World War II, Howze commanded a tank battalion in the North African and Italian campaigns; his task force was the first to enter Rome in 1944.

After the war, Howze was promoted to brigadier general and began to distinguish himself as a superb trainer of soldiers. First in the 2nd Armored Division and later as the commander of the famed 82nd Airborne Division, General Howze revamped training standards and methods to improve the combat readiness of his soldiers and units. Twice weekly he would publish "Training Notes," which were required reading for the officers in the unit, outlining his views and observations from his training inspections.

Later, during a Pentagon assignment, General Howze began taking private flight lessons in the fixed-wing L-19 aircraft, similar to a Piper Cub. He achieved his private pilot's license and later went on to get both instrument and dual-engine ratings. He then learned to fly helicopters, all while holding down his Pentagon job. He became an enthusiastic proponent of aviation in the Army, clearly seeing the potential for helicopter-borne forces.

In 1962, Howze was named to head up a board that examined Army tactical-mobility requirements. Usually referred to as the "Howze Board," it laid the groundwork for the introduction of helicopters into the force on a massive scale, including the formation of the 1st Cavalry Division as a helicopter-borne force. The First Cavalry would go on to set the standard for air mobility in Vietnam and became the iconic symbol of that war.

154 *Stone Tapestry*

Major General Robert L. Howze
Congressional Medal of Honor
Section I, Row A, Grave 3

General Howze the elder was the consummate soldier during his lifetime. A graduate of the Class of 1888, he was commissioned in the cavalry and immediately participated in a series of campaigns in the Indian Wars. In 1891 he took part in the campaign against the Sioux Indian tribe on the White River and was awarded the Congressional Medal of Honor for gallantry in action.

During the Spanish-American War, then captain Howze was made the adjutant of the cavalry force in Cuba. He was subsequently sent to the Philippines to command an infantry unit during the Philippine Insurrection.

General Howze was then reassigned to West Point to become the commandant, and it was on this tour that young Hamilton was born. In 1907 there occurred a hazing scandal involving the plebe class at West Point, and General Howze threatened to expel the entire class unless the perpetrators could be identified. They were. During World War I, General Howze assumed command of the 38th Infantry Division in France and participated in the Meuse-Argonne Offensive, the major US Army contribution to the ending of that war. After the war he took command of the 3rd Infantry Division in the Occupation Force in Germany.

General Howze's last assignment was in 1925, when he presided over the court-martial trial of Colonel Billy Mitchell. An air accident with the dirigible USS *Shenandoah* caused Mitchell to make some inflammatory comments defaming the senior leadership of the Army for their supposed dereliction of duty in air matters. The Army leadership took a dim view of this, and Mitchell was court-martialed. The court-martial found him guilty of insubordination and sentenced him to be suspended from active duty for five years. Mitchell declined to accept the sentence and instead resigned.

In addition to Hamilton, General Howze's other son, Robert Lee Howze Jr., graduated from West Point in 1925 and became a major general himself. In addition, a transport ship, USS *General R. L. Howze* (AP-134), was named after General Howze the elder.

Sections I, II, III, and IV **155**

General Alexander M. Patch
Section I, Row C, Grave 58

In another example of the Long Gray Line, Alexander Patch, known as Sandy, was the son of an 1877 graduate of West Point. Patch was a member of the Class of 1913 and was commissioned in the infantry.

Patch's first operational experience was in the 1916 Mexican Punitive Expedition, led by General Pershing. The following year, Patch went to France with the 1st Infantry Division, the initial US force to enter World War I. He participated in the Meuse-Argonne Offensive (mentioned with General Howze), and in the battles at the Marne and Saint-Mihiel. He attracted the attention of Colonel George Marshall during the war, who was on the staff of General Pershing (later to become the US Army chief of staff).

In World War II, Marshall saw to it that Patch was promoted to major general and given command of the 23rd Infantry Division (called the Americal Division), then sent to Guadalcanal. General Patch led the division in a vicious and bitter fight on that island against the Japanese, relieving the exhausted 1st Marine Division. Ultimately an additional Army division joined the fight, making it a corps operation, and Patch was promoted to command the corps.

In 1943, Patch's health was failing after several bouts with malaria, and he was recalled to the US to recuperate and command a training corps. By 1944, his health now recovered, Patch was transferred to the European theater and took command of the Seventh Army. He led the invasion of southern France in August 1944 and remained in command of Seventh Army until the end of the war. He was one of only two officers who sequentially commanded a division, corps, and army in World War II (the other being Lucian Truscott).

General Patch returned to the United States after the war to take command of the Fourth Army but died almost immediately, in November 1945.

156 *Stone Tapestry*

Major General Thomas H. Barry
Section I, Row C, Grave 63

General Barry was the superintendent of West Point from 1910 to 1912. A distinguished soldier, he graduated in the Class of 1877, a classmate of Major General William Black, whom we met earlier. His first assignments were with the 7th Cavalry—of Custer fame—in the Dakotas and Montana. He was subsequently transferred to the infantry and served with the 1st Infantry Regiment in Texas, Arizona, and California.

General Barry was widely recognized for his ability, and by 1893 he was appointed as the assistant adjutant general for the Army. During the Spanish-American War, he was a lieutenant colonel and the adjutant general of the 8th Corps. He eventually served as the adjutant general of the Army as a brigadier general.

He participated in combat operations in the China Relief Expedition, and again in the Philippine Insurrection in 1901. President Theodore Roosevelt named General Barry as an observer during the Russo-Japanese War, and he was assigned to the Imperial Russian Army. He must have made an impression on the president because he was subsequently assigned, again by Roosevelt personally, to the Army of Cuban Occupation. Finally, in 1908 he was named the superintendent of the Military Academy.

His career continued after his tour as the supe, and he went on to command the Eastern Division of the Army, which was the largest Army command at the time. When World War I broke out, General Barry was sent to the Philippines again, and then on to China as the commander of all American troops stationed there. At the end of the war, General Barry returned to the United States to command the Central Department until his retirement in 1919. His retirement was short, since he passed away three months later.

Like his classmates General Black and General R. E. Howze, Barry had a troop transport ship named after him, USS *Thomas H. Barry*.

General Joseph W. Stilwell
Section II, Row A, Grave 11

"Vinegar Joe" Stilwell needs little introduction as one of the most famous officers to command in World War II. A member of the Class of 1904, Stilwell was an infantryman through and through. He had an early assignment in the Philippines, then returned to West Point to teach Modern Languages. He repeated this cycle of duty (Philippines to West Point) twice, the last time in 1913. After staff service in France during World War I, Stilwell began his association with the Chinese language and peoples, which was to last the rest of his life.

After studying Chinese, he was assigned to the 15th Infantry in China for three years, followed by four more years as the military attaché. By the time World War II broke out, Stilwell was the most experienced officer in the Army on both the Chinese language and the country.

He continued to rise in the ranks, taking command of the 7th Infantry Division at Fort Ord, California. When the war began, he was personally selected by the secretary of the Army to take command of the China-Burma-India (CBI) theater and represent US interests there. Whole books have been written of his experiences there, and it is impossible to summarize every detail in this tiny space. It is indicative of the man that when Burma fell to the Japanese, Stilwell organized his headquarters group of about 114 men and women and personally led them, on foot, on a long march to safety in India over twenty-four days. He did not lose a single man or woman of his group on the march.

Stilwell then reorganized his Army and, coupled with Chinese and British forces, retook Burma in 1944. A man of true grit, irascible and blunt, without any pomp or ceremony in him, Stilwell was loved by his troops and hated by just about all of his allies. At the end of the war he was given command of the Tenth Army, designated as the invasion force for the invasion of the Japanese homeland, but the war ended before they could be employed.

General Stilwell died in 1946, and his ashes were spread over the Pacific Ocean. This monument was erected by his family.

Major General Frank D. Merrill
Section II, Row B, Grave 37

As with so many other famous duos we have seen in the cemetery, it is fitting that Frank Merrill and Joe Stilwell have monuments so close to one another, given how close they were in life. Merrill headed up the famed guerrilla group "Merrill's Marauders" in Burma during WWII, under Stilwell's command.

Merrill began his military career as an enlisted man, rising to the rank of staff sergeant before gaining an appointment to West Point (on his sixth try). He graduated from West Point in 1929, twenty-five years after Stilwell. By 1938, Merrill was fluent in Japanese and was assigned as the military attaché in Japan. When Pearl Harbor was attacked, Merrill was in Rangoon, Burma. When General Stilwell came to command the CBI theater, he handpicked Merrill to form a regiment of jungle fighters whose missions were to do reconnaissance and raids deep behind Japanese lines.

By 1944, Merrill's Marauders had fought five major battles and thirty smaller engagements and had been victorious in all. Wasted by disease and thirst and hampered by poor supply lines, nonetheless the Marauders carried the fight to the Japanese. The climax of their operations occurred when they crossed an 8,000-foot mountain range in secrecy and overran the vital Myitkyina airfield, opening the Lido Road as a supply line to China.

When General Stilwell took command of the Tenth Army, he brought General Merrill along as his chief of staff, participating in the capture of Okinawa and the Philippines. Merrill was aboard the battleship *Missouri* in Tokyo Bay to receive the surrender of the Japanese nation.

After the war, Merrill became the commissioner of public works and highways in New Hampshire until his death.

Major General Edward L. King
Section I, Row A, Grave 16

General King is another of those soldier-athletes we have met before, as an actively serving officer who was also the head coach of the Army football team. King graduated in the Class of 1896 and was commissioned in the cavalry. He had played football at Army while a cadet, playing halfback on the 1894 and 1895 teams. He was elected as captain of the 1895 team.

Upon graduation, King immediately saw combat service in the Spanish-American War, with service in the Philippines, and was awarded a Distinguished Service Cross for heroism in disarming a Filipino who was about to kill a fellow officer.

In 1903, King returned to West Point and assumed duty as the assistant post quartermaster, with the additional duty of head football coach. In his one year of coaching, he led the Army team to a 6-2-1 record. After his year tour was completed, King was briefly assigned to command a refugee camp near San Francisco, after the disastrous 1906 earthquake in that city. In 1909 he returned to the Philippines for further service.

When World War I arrived, King was promoted to brigadier general and sent to France as the chief of staff of the 28th Division. He saw combat with them in the battle of the Marne. He was subsequently given command of the 68th Infantry Brigade and led them through the Battle of the Somme and the Meuse-Argonne Offensive.

After his return from France at the end of the war, General King became the commandant of the Army's Command and General Staff School at Fort Leavenworth, Kansas. In 1932, General King assumed command of the 4th Corps Area in Fort McPherson, Georgia, and it was here that he passed away from a heart attack while riding on a hunt.

Sections I, II, III, and IV **161**

Brigadier General Edward H. DeArmond
Section I, Row A, Grave 20

Edward DeArmond served with distinction through World Wars I and II. He graduated from West Point in the Class of 1901 and was commissioned in the field artillery. His initial assignment was to the Philippines (as were so many others), where he participated in putting down the Moro Rebellion. He returned to West Point to serve as a tactical officer for the next three years.

As World War I began, Colonel DeArmond then joined the 32nd Infantry Division, serving as the chief of staff under the command of Major General Parker (*seated far left in photo*). DeArmond remained with this division throughout their training and went with them on their deployment to combat in France. By the end of the war, DeArmond had been promoted to brigadier general and moved up to be the assistant chief of artillery of the entire American Expeditionary Force. He earned a Distinguished Service Medal for his performance in France in World War I.

Upon his return to the United States, General DeArmond was assigned to the Office of the Chief of Field Artillery and was instrumental in formulating and teaching the new artillery tactics and methods that came from the Great War. In 1935 he assumed command of the 18th Field Artillery Regiment, then stationed at Fort Sill, Oklahoma. One of his subordinate battery commanders included a young Captain William Westmoreland, mentioned earlier on our walk.

General DeArmond returned to the Philippines in 1938, then became the chief of artillery in the Second Army back in the United States prior to his retirement.

General DeArmond is buried with his son, himself a member of the Class of 1935. The son was a twin but his sister died very young; her gravesite is unknown.

Major General Fred W. Sladen
Section I, Row B, Grave 26

General Fred Sladen was a soldier through and through, and a true son of West Point. He was born into an Army family, and his father, Major Joseph Sladen, won the Medal of Honor during the Civil War. Young Fred spent part of his childhood at West Point when his father was the post adjutant there. Sladen graduated from West Point in 1890, and thus began a long and storied career associated with this place.

Sladen was commissioned in the infantry, and his first assignment was with the 14th Infantry in Vancouver Barracks. In the first ten years of his active service, he was assigned to many posts in the American Northwest and saw combat duty with the 14th Infantry in the Philippines. In 1900, Sladen returned to West Point, where he served as a tactical officer and instructor. He returned to the 14th Infantry after this assignment and, like General Edward King, saw duty in relief of San Francisco during the earthquake and fire in 1906.

In 1911, Sladen returned to West Point to be the commandant of cadets. He served in that role until 1915, when he returned to his regiment for service again in the Philippines, and then in Tientsin, China. During World War I, Sladen, by now a brigadier general, took command of the 5th Infantry Brigade and moved it to France. During the war his brigade saw repeated action in Chateau-Thierry, the Marne, and the Meuse-Argonne Offensive. General Sladen was awarded both the Distinguished Service Cross and the Distinguished Service Medal for his service in France.

At the conclusion of the Great War, General Sladen returned to the US and was appointed as the superintendent of the Military Academy for his fourth and final tour there. He had the fortune to follow General Douglas MacArthur as superintendent and helped cement the sweeping reforms that MacArthur had initiated into the curriculum and training plans.

After his tour as superintendent, General Sladen returned to the Philippines as the commander of all US forces there. His final assignment was back in the US as commander of the 3rd Corps area in Baltimore, Maryland. He retired in 1931 after forty-one years of active service.

164   *Stone Tapestry*

Professor Louis Vauthier
Section I, Row B, Grave 35

Monsieur Vauthier was a French fencing master who came to the United States to teach fencing and ended up at West Point for more than thirty years as fencing coach and French instructor. Revered by many, Vauthier was made an Honorary Member of the Class of 1923 and was also mentioned in the class yearbook by the Class of 1936.

Louis Vauthier was born in France in 1862 and enlisted in the French army. Sent to fencing school, he quickly rose to the rank of first sergeant and obtained a master's degree in fencing. He joined the fencing school of renowned French teacher Monsieur Ayat in 1880. After a few years as M. Ayat's pupil, Vauthier moved to Paris and established his own fencing school.

In 1893 the Fencing Club of New York sought out M. Vauthier to come to the United States and establish his school there. He agreed to come, temporarily, and moved to New York. Within ten years he had established a worldwide reputation as a fencing master. When fencing became an intercollegiate sport at West Point in 1904, the Military Academy offered him the position of fencing coach, and M. Vauthier agreed to take the job. Thus began a relationship with West Point that was to last the remainder of his life.

From 1904 to 1912, while fencing remained a sport, Vauthier's teams dominated, winning several titles and consistently beating archrival Navy. When it was discontinued as a sport, M. Vauthier remained at the academy as a French instructor and continued to teach fencing in the Physical Education Department. In 1922, fencing returned as a sport and M. Vauthier immediately resumed his fencing coach duties and his winning ways. In that year his team won forty-two of forty-five contests. In the class yearbook of 1923, they referred to his "indomitable courage, unfailing spirit, and untiring devotion to all that is noble" when they made him an honorary member of their class.

Brigadier General Elliott C. Cutler Jr.
Section I, Row C, Grave 56

General Cutler is yet another example of the warrior-scholars who are so prevalent in this cemetery. Cutler was both an instructor and the head of the Electrical Engineering Department but was also a highly decorated combat infantryman in not one but two wars. Graduating in the Class of 1942, Cutler was commissioned in the infantry and immediately saw combat in the European theater. There he was awarded the Bronze Star, the Purple Heart for being wounded in action, and the Combat Infantryman's Badge.

After World War II, Cutler went to Japan, where he served in the occupation army. When the Korean War broke out in 1950, he again saw combat in an infantry unit and was awarded a second Bronze Star, as well as a Legion of Merit, and a star on his Combat Infantryman's Badge (denoting earning the badge again in a second war).

After Korea, General Cutler enrolled in the Georgia Institute of Technology, where he earned both a master's and a PhD in electrical engineering. He was then assigned to West Point to teach in the Electrical Engineering Department (affectionately known to generations of cadets as "Juice"). By 1961, then colonel Cutler had risen to be the department chair. He held the chair position until his retirement in 1977.

Cutler was instrumental in bringing the academy into the computer age. Through his efforts, aligned with the Mathematics Department, Cutler established the first computer lab at West Point and introduced computer science into the curriculum for all cadets.

West Point is somewhat rare in placing men and women in leadership positions on their faculty who are both warriors and scholars. Knowing that the faculty members serve as role models for the cadets demands that they be both proficient and have worthy reputations in the profession of arms, as well as the intellectual acumen to teach at the college level. General Cutler is but one example of this.

Sections I, II, III, and IV

Colonel Dean Hudnutt
Section II, Row A, Grave 19

Colonel Hudnutt was a member of the Class of 1916. He was commissioned in the field artillery and served his initial assignment in the 61st Field Artillery Brigade in France in the American Expeditionary Force. The 61st Brigade was formed of three Texas National Guard artillery battalions and was assigned to support the 36th Infantry Division.

At the conclusion of the war, Hudnutt returned to West Point, where he served for the next six years as the assistant quartermaster of the post and an instructor in the Mathematics Department.

In 1925, Hudnutt, by then a major, went to the Field Artillery School at Fort Sill, Oklahoma, where he was assigned to the office of the chief of field artillery and given a secondary assignment of editor for the *Field Artillery Journal*. This journal was the professional magazine for all things field artillery, and during this time it was quite busy in assimilating the lessons learned from the Great War. The increasing mobility of field artillery pieces and the rise of mobile warfare (called *Blitzkrieg* by the Germans) added to the intellectual stimulation in the journal.

In 1936, Colonel Hudnutt competed for and won a spot on the US Olympic team. His sport was 25-meter pistol shooting, specifically in rapid-fire shooting. The US team did not win a medal at this Olympics, being overshadowed by the host nation (Nazi Germany), who took the gold and silver medals, and by Sweden, who took the bronze.

After the Olympic competition, in 1940 Colonel Hudnutt went to Yale University, where he assumed duty as the professor of military science. He served there, overseeing their officer commissioning program, until his death in 1943.

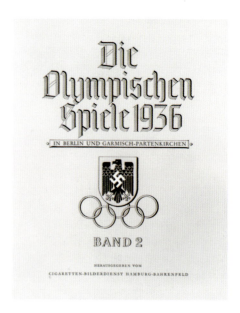

168 *Stone Tapestry*

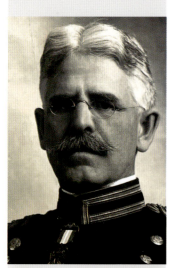

Major General Albert Mills
Congressional Medal of Honor
Section IV, Row E, Grave 77

Albert Leopold Mills graduated in the Class of 1879 and was immediately assigned to the cavalry. He remained at West Point as a member of the staff and faculty, teaching cavalry instruction to the subsequent classes of cadets.

He then joined his regiment, the 1st Cavalry, and spent six years on the plains during the Indian Wars. In 1886, Mills was assigned to be the professor of military science and tactics at the Citadel in South Carolina, but he served there for only a year, after which he rejoined his regiment.

After ten years of active service, Mills was finally promoted to first lieutenant in 1889, and he assumed the duties of regimental adjutant. In 1894, Mills was assigned again to teach, this time at the School of Infantry and Cavalry at Fort Leavenworth, Kansas. While there he wrote a scholarly treatise titled *Campaigns of 1862 in Virginia*. He was at Leavenworth when war was declared against Spain in 1898. Mills was assigned to go to war with the 2nd Brigade of the Cavalry Division.

While in Cuba, Mills distinguished himself in several actions, culminating in the Battle of Santiago, where he was seriously wounded. Shot through the head, Mills was blinded in both eyes but continued to rally his men and form them for the assault. For this action he was awarded the Medal of Honor and was given a brevet promotion to lieutenant colonel.

After the war, Mills regained partial sight in one eye and was assigned to be the superintendent at West Point. He served an astonishing eight years in this position, longer than any other superintendent except for Sylvanus Thayer. Mills helped reform the Military Academy during his tenure, eliminating the worst of the hazing of the underclassmen that had taken place, and giving instructors a year's sabbatical for further study in their fields. He also laid plans to expand the Corps of Cadets to 1,200 strong.

Mills served in other capacities after his tour as superintendent and passed away while serving as chief of the National Guard Bureau in Washington.

Captain Matthew C. Ferrara
Section III, Row D, Grave 71A

Captain Matthew Ferrara graduated in the Class of 2005 and was killed in action in Afghanistan two years later. He had an interesting background, in that he held dual citizenship with the US and New Zealand; his uncle was the defense minister of the New Zealand forces. In another example of the Long Gray Line, Matt's older brother, Marcus, was a member of the Class of 1997.

While at West Point, Matthew distinguished himself in academics and athletics. He was in the top ten of his class academically and was a star on the varsity track and field team. He held a double major in economics and Mandarin Chinese and was offered an opportunity to compete for a Rhodes scholarship, but he turned it down, since he wanted to get to his unit without further academic study.

After graduation, Ferrara was commissioned in the infantry and was assigned to the 2nd Battalion, 503rd Airborne Infantry Regiment, 173rd Airborne Infantry Brigade, in Vicenza, Italy. After his initial entry training, Lt. Ferrara took over an infantry platoon in C Company, 2-503rd, with duty in Combat Outpost Bella, near Aranus, Afghanistan.

On November 9, 2007, Lt. Ferrara was leading a patrol from his platoon on a movement from the combat outpost to the village of Aranus when the platoon was suddenly attacked in a vicious ambush. On a narrow trail, with steep mountain walls on one side and an equally steep drop-off on the other, the initial burst of fire split the patrol into two elements, and the soldiers jumped or scrambled down the steep slope to evade enemy fire.

Lt. Ferrara's radio operator, Specialist Kyle White, was struck in the initial assault but immediately began to return fire while he moved from man to man to determine their injuries and bandage their wounds. White moved several comrades to a more protected position and called for help while under severe fire. He was the first to discover that Lt. Ferrara was dead. For his actions that day, Specialist White was awarded the Congressional Medal of Honor. Lt. Ferrara was awarded the Silver Star and a posthumous promotion to captain.

Sections I, II, III, and IV **171**

Colonel Stuart C. MacDonald
Section IV, Row A, Grave 2

Col. MacDonald was from the Class of 1915, sometimes referred to as the "Class the Stars Fell On" because so many of them achieved general officer rank in World War II. Eisenhower and Bradley were just two of the most famous; a total of 59 out of 164 class members reached the rank of brigadier general or higher. Alas, MacDonald was not one of them, largely because he spent most of the war in a Japanese prisoner-of-war camp.

After graduation, "Shorty" MacDonald was sent to Fort Sill, Oklahoma, where he became an expert of sorts on machine gun operations and tactics. This skill was soon put to use in France in World War I. At the outbreak of World War II, MacDonald was in the Philippines, participating in the defense of the Bataan Peninsula as the chief of staff for the South Luzon Force (as a colonel). Ultimately all the American forces evacuated the peninsula under extreme pressure from the Japanese to the island fortress of Corregidor, and he was captured there when "the Rock" surrendered in 1942.

MacDonald survived the infamous Bataan Death March, where the prisoners from Corregidor were marched across the Philippine Islands under horrendous and barbarous conditions, ultimately to be transported to prisoner-of-war camps. One of his classmates, who was also on the march with MacDonald, referred to their journey after they left the Philippines thus: "We toured the Orient together, including Formosa, Japan, Korea, and Manchuria." MacDonald became known for his iron will in captivity and his scrupulous honesty and fairness in dealing with other prisoners.

In October 1944, MacDonald was on the *Oryoku Maru*, a Japanese troop transport ship being used to transport prisoners of war (POWs). The ship was strafed and bombed by Allied forces (who were not aware there were POWs on board). He remarked at the time that this was "a hell of a way to spend my fifty-third birthday." Fortunately the ship was not sunk, and MacDonald remained in captivity until the end of the war. The ship itself was sunk two months later in another Allied attack, resulting in the loss of more than two hundred POWs at the time.

172 *Stone Tapestry*

Lieutenant General Lemuel Mathewson

Section III, Row A, Grave 24

General Mathewson had a distinguished career, both as an advisor to President Roosevelt and as a senior commander in peace and war. Graduating in the Class of 1922, he was commissioned in the field artillery and served in a wide variety of assignments, including teaching Spanish at West Point.

During World War II, in 1943, Mathewson was named to be the military aide to President Franklin Roosevelt and served as such for over a year. He participated with the president both in the Cairo and Tehran Conferences on the conduct of the war.

He was then assigned to combat duty, first as the deputy commander of VII Corps Artillery, then as the commander of XVIII Airborne Corps Artillery. After the war, Mathewson's language skill in Spanish led him to the Caribbean Defense Command. By 1950 he had returned to Europe to become the commander of the US Berlin Command, an obvious hotspot in our early Cold War relations with the Soviet Union.

Mathewson then went on to serve as the commander of the US V Corps, also in Germany. His final assignment was to command the Sixth Army in San Francisco.

In 1957, Mathewson again drew an interesting assignment, serving as the military aide to Queen Elizabeth II while she went on a tour of the United States. In 1958, Mathewson retired from active service, but he was recalled to active duty in 1960 to serve on the Inter-American Defense Board.

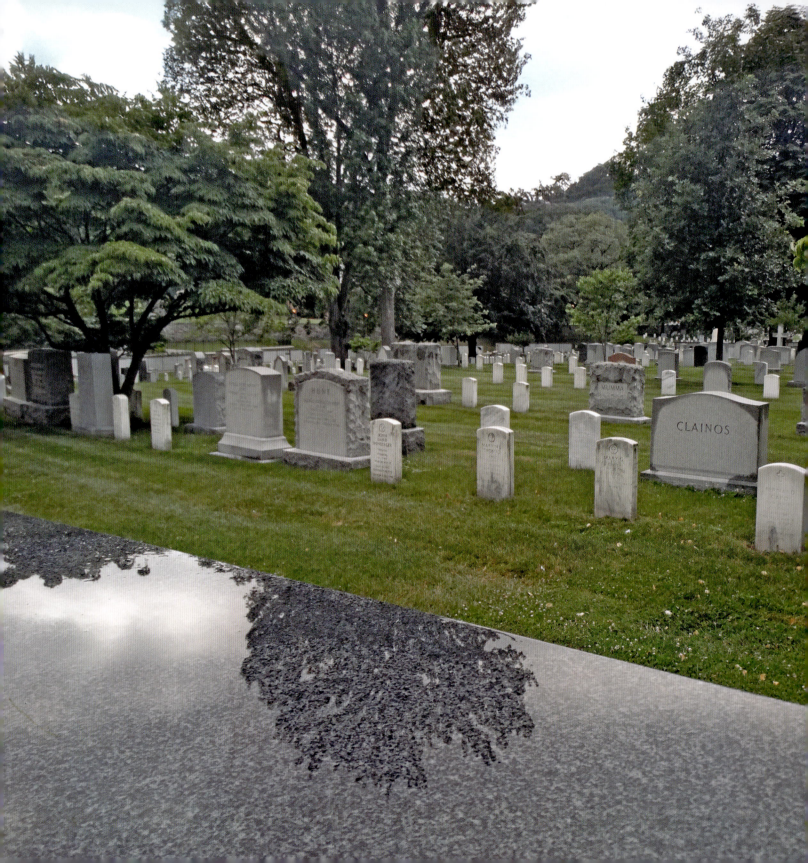

CHAPTER 9

Sections V and VI

In this chapter we will continue our walk through the circular center section of the cemetery, covering the outer, southeastern portion of the circle. And we will continue to meet interesting people on our stroll, covering a very wide swath of American, and West Point, history. We will meet George Anderson, one of the early superintendents of the national park at Yellowstone, along with "Mickey" Marcus, the first general officer in the Israeli Defense Forces. We will find a hotel president here, as well as another of the West Point superintendents. We will also see a dean of the Academic Board here, and a man who was the USMA librarian for many years.

But the major theme of this chapter is the Long Gray Line. Here we will see no fewer than five families where at least two and usually more sons followed in their father's footsteps. Some became generals; some became prisoners of war. Some were killed in combat; some died in accidents. It is a measure of the significance of this institution that so many sons and daughters decided to emulate their parents and attend West Point to serve their nation.

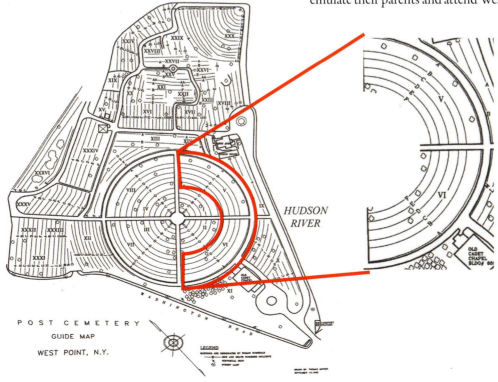

177

Brigadier General George S. Anderson
Section V, Row A, Grave 14

Brigadier General Anderson is another one of those interesting characters who seem to be scattered about the cemetery. A member of the Class of 1871 (along with Major General Frederick Dent Grant, whom we met earlier), Anderson spent most of his career in the West.

Anderson was commissioned in the cavalry, and his initial assignment was to the Sixth Cavalry, engaged in the Indian Wars. From 1871 to 1877, Anderson served continuously in the cavalry in campaigns against the Indians, specifically in fighting against the Cheyenne, Kiowa, and Comanches. His service took him all over the western United States, and he saw action in Kansas, Colorado, Arizona, and New Mexico.

He then returned to West Point to be the assistant professor of natural and experimental philosophy. He served in that capacity until 1881, when he was again ordered to the West, where he took part in suppressing the Indian uprising that took place in Arizona and Colorado.

In 1885 he was promoted to captain (after a mere fourteen years of service!) and was assigned duty as the superintendent at Yellowstone National Park. It was not uncommon in those days for an active-duty Army officer to serve in such a capacity, although it would be highly unorthodox today. In fact, few men were more qualified to superintend the park than a well-worn cavalry soldier who had spent most of his career in the saddle in the West. Captain Anderson is at the left in the picture, taken at Yellowstone.

Anderson continued to serve with the Sixth Cavalry and various other units in the US and the Philippines. He rose to command the Eighth Cavalry as a colonel, then the First Cavalry. He concluded his career as the commander of the Ninth Cavalry and retired in 1912, passing away shortly thereafter.

178 *Stone Tapestry*

General Frank S. Besson Jr.
Section V, Row A, Grave 5

We jump swiftly from a cavalryman at Yellowstone to a transportation logistician in Iran—just another of the interesting juxtapositions we find here. Frank S. Besson was commissioned in the Class of 1932, placing seventh in his class, and immediately went on to graduate school at the Massachusetts Institute of Technology.

During World War II, in 1943, Besson was placed as assistant director of the Third Military Railway District; he was promoted to colonel and director the following year. His primary responsibility in that job was to ensure that railway supplies flowed from Iran into Russia through the Persian Corridor. The railway supply on the southern flank of the Russians was crucial to their war efforts because the sea resupply of Russia was haphazard and sporadic due to the ice and harsh weather at their port of Archangel.

Besson was promoted to brigadier general at age thirty-four; he was the youngest general officer in the Army Ground Forces at the time. He then moved up to command the entire Railway Division of the Army. By the end of World War II, General Besson was the deputy chief transportation officer in the western Pacific, and he assumed full control of all railroads in Japan after their surrender in 1945. He became responsible for the rehabilitation of the Japanese railway system, which the Allies had bombed heavily. He soon had the railways back in operation, moving over 200,000 soldiers and 150,000 tons of supplies in his first two months.

He was an innovator in the design of transportation systems, devising the containerization system used so effectively today, as well as the roll-on, roll-off system for rapid loading and offloading of transport ships.

General Besson went on to command the Army's Transportation School at Fort Eustis, Virginia, then was promoted to the rank of general and became the first commanding general of the Army Material Command in 1962. In 1969, General Besson chaired the Joint Logistics Review Board to review logistical problems reported from the Vietnam War. After his retirement in 1970, General Besson became one of the founding directors of the National Rail Passenger Corporation, which ran Amtrak.

Colonel David H. Barger
Section V, Row A, Grave 38

From cavalrymen in Indian wars and railroads in Iran, we leap ahead to the space age. Colonel David Barger graduated from West Point in January 1943, one of the wartime classes that were accelerated. He served in World War II in the 344th Bomb Group in Europe, earning a Distinguished Flying Cross and eleven Air Medals in combat. Barger had sixty-five combat missions under his belt by the time he was promoted to first lieutenant.

Upon his return to the United States, Barger came back to West Point, where he served on the staff in the Operations Division, then as the aide-de-camp and command pilot for the superintendent.

By 1953, Barger had transferred into the newly minted US Air Force and had served on the Far Eastern Command staff. He became an intelligence specialist for the Air Force and subsequently joined the Air Force Systems Command, where he worked on a communications satellite program. By 1966, Colonel Barger had become the director of the Gemini Support Program for the Air Force, a classified program designed to use Gemini spacecraft in various manned orbital missions for intelligence and reconnaissance.

The program never matured for the Air Force, and in 1968 he became the vice commander of the 6595th Test Wing at Vandenberg Air Force Base, California. Here he was involved in the launch and testing both of military rockets and various satellites. Col Barger then served as the deputy commander of the Space and Missile Systems Organization (SAMSO) in 1969.

In 1973, Colonel Barger retired and went to work with Northrop Corporation (later Northrop Grumman) in the Los Angeles area.

Brigadier General John R. Jannarone
Section V, Row A, Grave 58

General Jannarone graduated in the Class of 1938, just in time for World War II. This was a man accustomed to excellence; he was first in his class in high school, first in his class at West Point, and first in his class in graduate school at Cal Tech. According to his obituary in the Association of Graduates, the head of the civil engineering department at Cal Tech said that Jannarone was the "smartest man I ever taught."

Commissioned in the Corps of Engineers, Jannarone served in combat in the South Pacific theater in World War II. He then was assigned to the Manhattan Engineer District and was the aide-de-camp to General Leslie Groves, the leader of the Manhattan Project, which led to the atomic bomb. In the picture (*right*), Jannarone is at far right, while General Groves discusses uranium with Edgar Sengier, a Belgian who had consolidated much of the world's known uranium supply in the United States before and during the war.

After his graduate studies, Jannarone returned to West Point to teach physics and chemistry and later became the head of that department. In 1965 Jannarone was promoted to brigadier general and became the dean of the Academic Board. He held that position until his retirement in 1973. As dean he oversaw the expansion of the Corps and was instrumental, along with Brigadier General Elliott Cutler, in establishing a computer center and computer science curriculum at West Point.

Jannarone was also an active athlete, and while serving as dean he also served as chairman of the Athletic Board. Jannarone played varsity baseball and basketball at West Point and B-squad football. While in Leyte during World War II, Jannarone played on an all-officer baseball team against an all-enlisted team made up of former pro baseball players. He hit a bases-clearing double off Hugh Mulcahy, a former Philadelphia Phillies pitcher. Jannarone was a colonel at the time. Another story in his obituary was that a long-ball hitter on the Army baseball team decided to flunk chemistry and go home. Dean Jannarone told him, "I never flunk a long-ball hitter," and the man went on to graduate and finally retired as a colonel thirty years later.

In a small personal note, the author has had General Jannarone's signature on his diploma hanging on the wall for the past fifty years and never once realized what a long and distinguished history the dean had behind him.

182   *Stone Tapestry*

Major General Clarence P. Townsley
Section V, Row B, Grave 62

General Townsley graduated fourteenth of fifty-three in the Class of 1881 and was commissioned in the field artillery. After some initial postings in the coast artillery, he returned to West Point, where he taught drawing.

He served in the Spanish-American War as the commander of the Ordnance Office in the 1st Division and was subsequently promoted to take command of the Ordnance Department of Havana. By 1909, Townsley had been promoted to lieutenant colonel and was serving as the commandant of the Coast Artillery School.

In 1912, Colonel Townsley returned to West Point to serve as the superintendent. He was there at the outbreak of World War I and remained at West Point until 1916. As he left West Point, he was promoted to brigadier general and was assigned to the Philippines, where he supervised the coast artillery emplacements at Manila Bay and Subic Bay.

In 1917, Townsley was promoted to major general and returned to the United States, where he took command of the 30th Infantry Division to train it for service in combat in France. He deployed with his division to France but was forced to return home on medical leave due to illness. He was in the hospital at Walter Reed when the war ended.

His final assignment was to command the North Pacific Coast Artillery District before his retirement in late 1918. Townsley was posthumously promoted to major general in 1930. His son also served in the Army and was a brigadier general.

Sections V and VI

The James O. Green Family
Section V, Row B, Graves 95 and 96

The Green family history of services stretches from the Indian Wars through World Wars I and II and into the atomic age. James O. Green graduated in the Class of 1882 (see images of his class ring, *below*) and was immediately sent to the Dakota Territory for service against the Indians. He suffered an illness while on active duty, and after being assigned as the professor of military science at Lawrence University in Wisconsin, he eventually retired in 1897 for disability.

Captain Green was recalled to active duty in 1906 and was sent to Havana, Cuba, where he served on a general court-martial board. He was retired a second time, still for disability, in 1916.

His son, James O. Green Jr., was born in 1894 and graduated from West Point in the Class of April 1917. We have already met some of his classmates, such as Norman Cota and Norman Schwarzkopf Sr.

Like all the members of his family, James Green Jr. was known by the nickname "JOG." He immediately left for France after graduation and served with great distinction in the infantry during World War I. He participated in the Aisne Defensive campaign, and in the battles at Chateau-Thierry and Belleau Woods. In June 1918, Green's unit suffered a gas attack, and while he eventually recovered, it left him with damaged lungs and a persistent cough for the remainder of his life.

During the Chateau-Thierry campaign, Green was awarded the nation's second-highest award for valor, the Distinguished Service Cross. In the citation it says that after two platoons of his command had been destroyed, he continued on to the objective with only two other soldiers and held the position they had taken all through the night against heavy German fire until reinforcements could come up the following day.

JOG continued his education after the war at several Army service schools, including Fort Leavenworth and Fort Benning. He came back to West Point in 1924 to be a tactical officer for a cadet company and was then sent to Lehigh University to serve as the professor of military science and tactics (similar to the job his father held at Lawrence University). In 1937, Green was assigned to the Canal Zone in Panama, but the tropical heat and humidity exacerbated his lung and cardiac issues, and he died suddenly of cardiac arrest.

184 *Stone Tapestry*

James O. Green III graduated from West Point in the Class of 1941. His father had just passed away in the Canal Zone, so his grandfather, the original JOG, came to see him graduate and carry on the family tradition.

Like his father, he was sent directly to war in World War II. Green was commissioned in the field artillery and was assigned to a variety of self-propelled-artillery battalions, ultimately ending up in France in January 1945. After the war ended, Green was assigned in Paris, then Frankfurt, in the Operations Section of the US Forces headquarters there.

JOG went on to get a master's degree in applied physics at UCLA, then went to the Armed Forces Special Weapons Project in Sandia Base, New Mexico. This organization was the follow-on to the Manhattan Project and was primarily concerned with nuclear weapons storage, transport, and assembly training. Green worked with nuclear weapons the remainder of his career. He returned to Europe to be the chief of the Special Weapons Branch in the US Army, Europe, then taught nuclear weapons tactical employment at the Intelligence School in Germany. Ultimately he commanded the 44th Field Artillery battalion.

Green served in many other nuclear assignments, including at the Army Missile Command in Redstone Arsenal, until he commanded the Seneca Army Depot, where Army nuclear munitions were stored.

This family saw continuous active service from 1882 to 1965. It was a long way from the Dakota Territories to a nuclear weapons depot.

Sections V and VI **185**

The Heiberg Family
Section V, Row F, Grave 280

The Heiberg family represents another symbol of the Long Gray Line, with multiple descendants who not only chose to follow in the footsteps of their ancestors but also demonstrated high achievement and character to reflect on the Military Academy.

Elvin R. Heiberg was the first in this family, graduating in the Class of 1896. He was commissioned in the cavalry and spent his early career serving in the Sixth Cavalry and the Third Cavalry. He participated in the Spanish-American War, where his troop, Troop H, Sixth Cavalry, was assigned as the personal escort of General John R. Brooke. Brooke was the commanding general of the Army's I Corps and was stationed in Puerto Rico.

Heiberg participated with his cavalry unit in the suppression of the Boxer Rebellion in China, and in the Philippines during the insurrection there. In 1916, during World War I, Major Heiberg was assigned as the US military attaché in Italy. In February 1917, Major Heiberg dined with the king of Italy, and he later visited the Italian front. While there, with the military attachés of Norway and Argentina, his horse reared and threw him off, causing him to strike his head on a rock. Major Heiberg died there and was buried in Rome with full military honors accorded to him by the Italian government. He was later relocated here to the West Point Cemetery.

Major Heiberg's son Harrison H. D. Heiberg was a cadet at West Point at the time of his father's death, graduating with the Class of 1919. His class graduated just prior to the Armistice at the end of World War I, after having spent only eighteen months at West Point. As a result of their shortened tenure, they returned to West Point for the completion of their education, but as officers instead of cadets. They wore the uniform of Regular Army officers, but with an orange band encircling their caps, and were known forever after as the "Orioles."

Like his father, Harrison Heiberg was commissioned in the cavalry. He had initial assignments at the Virginia Military Institute, Fort Riley, and Fort Leavenworth, then came to serve at Fort Knox under General Adna Chaffee. Chaffee was determined to transform the cavalry into an armor branch, and Heiberg spent his time testing concepts and equipment in US Army armor systems that would later prove decisive in World War II. During that war, Heiberg served in armor units in progressively higher staff and command responsibilities until he was the plans officer for Omar Bradley's Twelfth Army Group.

After the war, Colonel Heiberg continued to develop and test armor concepts and ultimately became the president of the Army Field Forces Board at Fort Knox, then the research and development chief at Fort Monroe. Much of the Army's success in Desert Storm in 1990 came as a result of the armor concepts and equipment developed under Colonel Heiberg's tutelage.

The next Heiberg we find here is Elvin R. Heiberg II, who was the youngest son of the original. This officer graduated from West Point in the Class of 1926 and, contrary to the family history, was commissioned in the Corps of Engineers. Heiberg II also attended Cornell University, where he received a master's degree in engineering. His wife, Evelyn, had the distinction of being the women's singles tennis champion in West Virginia.

Colonel Heiberg commanded the 808th Airborne Engineer Battalion at March Field, California, at the time of Pearl Harbor. He went on to serve with distinction in the Pacific as the engineer on General MacArthur's staff. He was largely responsible for the planning and building of the airfields that enabled the "island hopping" strategy. After the war he went to Fort Leavenworth to serve on the faculty at the Command and General Staff College. From there he was selected by President Truman to serve as the head of the Mechanics Department at West Point, a post where he served from 1949 to 1968. He retired as a brigadier general.

188 *Stone Tapestry*

General Heiberg had two sons who graduated from West Point: E. R. Heiberg III (Class of 1953) and William L. Heiberg (Class of 1961). Heiberg III deserves mention in these pages, although he is not buried here at West Point. Like his forebears, he served with great distinction in the Army, retiring as a lieutenant general and chief of engineers. His service included a tour in Vietnam, where he won a Silver Star for valor, and a tour serving as the executive officer for the secretary of the Army. Heiberg III was elected to the National Academy of Engineering in 1995.

His brother is the fourth member of the Heiberg family to be buried at West Point. William L. Heiberg graduated in the Class of 1961, after having attended Princeton for one year. In a stroke of coincidence, he, his wife (the former Louise O'Meara), and both of their sons all were born at West Point.

This Heiberg, like his predecessors, was a high academic achiever, as can be seen by the star on his collar in the cadet photo, indicating his position in the top 10 percent of his class academically. He was commissioned in the field artillery, apparently believing that he could not add any further Heiberg luster to either the cavalry branch or the engineer branch.

After serving a year in Vietnam, where he was awarded a Bronze Star for valor, he returned to West Point, where he was a professor in the Social Sciences Department.

His last tour of duty was at Fort Sill, Oklahoma, where he served as the systems manager for the development of the M109A6 Paladin howitzer, a redesigned and improved 155 mm artillery piece. As such, he represented the user community during the howitzer's development and was instrumental in turning out a solid product that served with great distinction during Operation Desert Storm. The author was privileged to serve with Colonel Heiberg during this assignment.

The Heiberg family is not unique in this cemetery. There are many other examples of whole families devoted to the service of the nation who had many members of character and competence. When one includes their spouses, and in-laws of such families, the numbers grow even further. This nation owes a debt of gratitude to families such as the Heibergs and their achievements merit attention.

Sections V and VI **189**

Colonel Elbert E. Farman Jr.
Section V, Row B, Grave 85

Colonel Farman came from accomplished stock; his father served as the consul general to Egypt under General Grant's presidency, and he authored two books about Egypt as a result.

Young Elbert graduated from West Point in the Class of 1909, the same class that produced General George S. Patton. One of his classmates was the father of General Besson, whom we met just a few short pages ago. Farman was commissioned in the cavalry and served in the West for several tours in the 8th Cavalry and the 2nd Cavalry.

From 1914 to 1918, Farman served as a professor of foreign languages at West Point. Farman then went to Texas and served with the 16th Cavalry at Fort Sam Houston. When World War I arrived, then-major Farman went overseas with the 4th Infantry Division. He served briefly as an exchange officer with a British division in France, then was assigned to the General Headquarters of the Allied Expeditionary Force (AEF). It is interesting how he served with many different forces in his early career; after his tour at the AEF General Headquarters, he was assigned to the headquarters of a French division.

After the Armistice, Major Farman was promoted to lieutenant colonel and assigned as the military attaché to Poland. After this assignment, Farman returned to the 1st Cavalry until he was retired medically in 1924. By 1928, Farman had returned to West Point to serve as the librarian, following in the footsteps of Edward Holden (chapter 5). He spent the next fourteen years at West Point, revamping and improving the library. One of the changes he initiated was to make the school library into the post library, and he added a children's section of more than four hundred books to open the facility up to the families of the instructors who resided here.

In 1942, Farman requested to return to active duty to support World War II; he was reinstated as a lieutenant colonel and served in North Africa and Europe, serving in the 9th Air Force and the European theater of operations headquarters. He was awarded a Bronze Star for his service in World War II.

190 *Stone Tapestry*

The Benedict Family
Section V, Row B, Grave 121

The Benedict family is yet another example of the Long Gray Line in action. Charles Calvert Benedict is the first we shall see who is buried here at West Point, but he is not the first of his line. His brother, Jay L. Benedict, graduated with the Class of 1904 and ultimately became the superintendent at the Military Academy, but he is buried in Arlington National Cemetery.

Charles Calvert Benedict graduated with the Class of 1915, known forever after as the "Class the Stars Fell On" because of the high number of general officers in World War II. Some of his famous classmates include Dwight Eisenhower and Omar Bradley, and we met his classmate MacDonald earlier in our walk.

Alas, stars were not to be in Benedict's fate. He became one of the Army's earliest fliers and served in several airdromes in France in World War I but was killed in an aircraft accident in Langley, Virginia, in 1925.

Charles Calvert had three children: Patricia, Charles Jr., and Calvert. Charles C. Benedict Jr. graduated from West Point in January 1943, while Calvert P. graduated in 1946. Patricia married Harrison Lobdell, a classmate of Calvert P.'s in the Class of 1946.

Charles Calvert Benedict Jr., like his father, went into the Army Air Corps. Graduating third in his class, and first among the Air Corps cadets, he chose to fly bombers. Soon he was flying the massive, new B-29 Superfortress, the largest and fastest bomber in the US fleet, based out of Karagphur, India. In December 1944, less than two years out of West Point, he and all his crew were killed in combat in a raid over Mukden, Manchuria. Their aircraft was hit by a Japanese fighter, itself already mortally wounded, which detonated their entire bombload upon impact.

His brother, Calvert P. Benedict, was still a cadet himself at that time, and so he graduated sorrowfully in the Class of 1946, having lost both his father and his brother. Calvert chose not to go into the Army Air Corps but instead was commissioned in the infantry.

Calvert began his career in an infantry regiment in the occupation forces in Germany until 1950, then began the usual cycle of Army schools, including the Command and General Staff College at Fort Leavenworth. Benedict then spent a tour in Iran in the office of the Army attaché. This was followed by an assignment to the 82nd Airborne Division, where he served as the G-2 (intelligence officer) and commanded the 1st Battalion, 505th Parachute Infantry Regiment.

Benedict then went off to the University of Oklahoma, where he earned a master's degree in history. He then returned to West Point, where he taught military history. After his tour as a professor, Benedict was assigned to Vietnam, where he commanded a second infantry battalion, the 1st Battalion, 16th Infantry, in the 1st Infantry Division.

After another tour in the 82nd, where he was promoted to brigadier general and served as the assistant division commander, Benedict was sent to be the deputy commandant at the Army War College in Carlisle, Pennsylvania. Upon his promotion, Major General Benedict returned to the 1st Infantry Division at Fort Riley, this time as the division commander. General Benedict then retired, having been awarded a Distinguished Service Medal, three Silver Stars for valor, a Distinguished Flying Cross, and five Bronze Star Medals.

Harrison Lobdell, one of his classmates from '46, married Calvert's sister, Patricia. Lobdell came to West Point after attending the New Mexico Military Institute for five years. Such background and exposure to discipline certainly made his West Point experience more palatable! Lobdell chose to be commissioned in the Army Air Corps upon graduation.

Lobdell originally began as a fighter pilot but soon was transferred into reconnaissance. In 1948 he was assigned to the 8th Tactical Reconnaissance Squadron in Japan. Within a year he was reassigned into bombers and joined the 13th Bombardment Squadron, also in Japan. When the Korean War broke out, he was flying the B-26 Invader aircraft, and he personally led the first US Air Force mission over North Korea in that aircraft. Ultimately he completed more than sixty missions over Korea.

Lobdell then had several assignments in Washington on the Air Staff and served as the deputy director for physical training at the brand-new Air Force Academy. Major Lobdell returned to his Army roots in 1958 when he was sent to the Army Command and General Staff College at Fort Leavenworth, Kansas, as an exchange student.

He then returned overseas, first to Germany and later to England, where he served in staff and command positions in reconnaissance squadrons, including commanding the 1st Tactical Reconnaissance Squadron. After a brief stint at the Air War College, Colonel Lobdell went to Southeast Asia for the war in Vietnam. Based out of Thailand, he first commanded the reconnaissance section and later became the deputy for operations/reconnaissance for the 355th Tactical Fighter Wing. He flew a total of 105 missions, of which sixty-six were reconnaissance missions over North Vietnam.

Lobdell commanded two different training wings in Texas until he received his first star and served as deputy chief of staff for plans of the US Air Force in Europe. In 1976, General Lobdell assumed command of the National War College in Washington, DC.

Like his brother-in-law Calvert, Lobdell was awarded the Distinguished Service medal (in Lobdell's case twice), and the Legion of Merit twice.

From Charles's untimely death in a biplane at Langley, to Charles Jr.'s fiery end in a B-29, to Harrison Lobdell's sixty-six combat reconnaissance missions over North Vietnam, much of the history of Army, and Air Force, aviation can be seen in the lives of this family.

194 *Stone Tapestry*

The Bunker Family
Section VI, Row A, Graves 11 and 12

The family of Paul Bunker exhibits a more melancholy side of the Long Gray Line. Bunker was a member of the Class of 1903, along with Douglas MacArthur and U. S. Grant III. A stellar football player while a cadet, Bunker was selected twice on Walter Chase's All-American team, once as a tackle and the following year as a halfback, only the second person to be selected twice for two different positions.

Commissioned in the coast artillery, Bunker had several assignments up and down the East Coast, including command at Fort Amador in Panama. He served with the 59th Coast Artillery at Corregidor, in the Philippines, several times, ultimately commanding the base during World War II.

Bunker's son, Paul Jr., graduated with the Class of 1932. He chose infantry as his branch but went on to flying school and became an Army aviator in the Air Corps. As World War II approached, Paul Jr. was serving in Hawaii, while his father served as the commander of a coast artillery unit at Fort MacArthur in Los Angeles (named after General Arthur MacArthur, Douglas's father). In 1937, Paul Jr. was killed in a freak mishap during a practice bombing run in Hawaii. The bomb his aircraft released accidentally armed itself, and when it struck his landing gear it detonated, destroying the aircraft instantly. Paul Sr. escorted his son's remains here to the cemetery for burial.

As World War II began, Bunker found himself again on Corregidor, now serving with his classmate MacArthur, who was the supreme commander. Under siege by the Japanese, MacArthur was ordered to leave the island and organize further defenses in Australia. Ultimately, when General Jonathan Wainwright surrendered the island to the Japanese, Bunker was ordered to strike the American flag and burn it. Instead he cut off a small piece and saved it in his shirt. Bunker died in captivity on Formosa, Japan, before the war ended. Before he died, he gave the flag remnant to another officer for safekeeping, with instructions to return it to the secretary of the Army. It now can be seen in the West Point Museum.

The Long Gray Line is about more than honors and glory. Sometimes it is about sacrifice and heartache.

Brigadier General William B. Kunzig
Section V, Row C, Grave 172

Thirty ranks in front of Paul Bunker Jr., on graduation day in 1932, stood William Kunzig. Like Bunker, Kunzig's father had also graduated from West Point. Louis A. Kunzig was an infantryman from the Class of 1905 and rests here in the cemetery as well, in Section V, Row E, Grave 257.

William Kunzig did not suffer Paul Bunker Jr.'s fate of dying early; on the contrary, he lived to become the oldest living member of his class when he passed away in 2008. Like his father, Kunzig was an infantryman, and by 1942 he had been promoted to major and was the chief of the Commando and Ranger Division at the Amphibious Training Command in Maine. The Army by then had realized that it was going to have to conduct many amphibious landings in World War II and established the school to train the specialty troops who would go ashore in the first wave.

From Maine he was sent to Woolacomb, England, to run all the battalion and regimental landing exercises for the units to go ashore on D-day. For those who saw the movie *Saving Private Ryan*, the units depicted in the opening scene would have all been trained by Colonel Kunzig on the difficult tasks of getting ashore, consolidating, and moving inland under intense enemy fire.

After D-day, Lieutenant Colonel Kunzig joined the staff of the First Army and remained with them for the remainder of the war. He played a significant role in the Battle of the Bulge, directing and coordinating the transfer of forces and movements as Patton's Third Army relieved Bastogne. In Korea, Kunzig served in the Eighth Army Headquarters in the G-3 section, and later in the IX Corps. Ultimately he returned to Germany as the chief of staff for VII Corps. Promoted to brigadier general, Kunzig ended his career by serving as the chief of staff of the Sixth Army at the Presidio of San Francisco.

He then began a second career as a hotelier in San Francisco, leasing several hotels and establishing the Residential Hotel Owners Association. He continued an active role in the hotel business until he finally retired at age ninety-six.

196 *Stone Tapestry*

Colonel David "Mickey" Marcus
Section VI, Row B, Grave 125

David "Mickey" Marcus was a legend in his own time in two countries. Graduating with the Class of 1924, Marcus was commissioned in the infantry but attended law school on his own at night. In 1926 he resigned from the Army and went to law school full time, obtaining his JD degree in 1928 from the Brooklyn Law School.

A single short page is not enough to mention all of Mickey's exploits in a very full life. In 1939 he served again in the Army, now in the Judge Advocate General Corps in the 27th Infantry Division, New York National Guard. In addition to his lawyer duties, Marcus also served as the headquarters commandant and provost marshal and established the Division's Ranger School for training in jungle combat during World War II.

He also served during the war in Europe, accompanying the 101st Airborne Division into Normandy on D-day (seemingly on his own volition), and was personally involved, as a lawyer, in drafting and negotiating the surrender instruments both for the Italian and German fronts. He attended the Dumbarton Oaks Conference, which framed the charter of the United Nations. He participated in the war crimes trials in Nuremberg and Marcus set up and led the War Crimes Branch of the Civil Affairs Division in the War Department at the conclusion of World War II.

After the war, he again resigned his commission and resumed the practice of law in Brooklyn. In 1947 the fledgling Israeli government sought out Marcus and asked him to come to Israel and help them establish an officer corps and a general staff for the newborn Israeli army. He agreed to come for a year and worked tirelessly to organize and train the officers and general staff of the Israeli army, including drafting their training manuals. When the Arab nations attacked Israel in May 1948, Marcus returned to Israel, was given a commission as an *aluf*, or brigadier general, and organized the defenses of Jerusalem. On June 10, while inspecting a portion of his lines around Jerusalem, a mere hours before a ceasefire was to go into effect, Marcus was accidentally shot by one of his own sentries and died. He is the only man in this cemetery to have fought under two different flags.

Stone Tapestry

The Hayes Family
Section VI, Row C, Grave 172

Here we stop to meet the Hayes family. Thomas J. Hayes Jr. is the first member of the Long Gray Line to be buried here, a member of the Class of 1912. He served in World War I, in the American Expeditionary Force in the ordnance branch, and all his assignments were in ordnance, procurement, maintenance, or supply. In World War II, Major General Hayes served as the director of procurement in the Office of the Secretary of War. Later in the war he became the chief of Industrial Service in the ordnance branch and oversaw the procurement and production of $30 billion of weapons and ammunition. (General Hayes's son, Theodore, who was not a West Point graduate, is buried next to him.)

His namesake, Thomas J. Hayes III, is also buried alongside. This generation of the Hayes family graduated from West Point in 1936 and was commissioned in the Corps of Engineers. He received a master's degree in engineering at the Massachusetts Institute of Technology, then attended the Engineer School. While his father ran procurement from the Pentagon, the younger Hayes served in engineer regiments overseas. At the opening of the war, he was serving in Greenland constructing Sondre Stromord Air Base under Arctic conditions.

After his Greenland tour, Hayes was sent to Nassau to warm up, and to construct two further air bases for the Royal Air Force. He and his wife were married in the cathedral there. Having resumed reasonable temperatures, Hayes was promptly sent to Alaska for further construction work.

After the war, Hayes became the military attaché in London, and from there he went on to increasing responsibilities in engineer districts throughout the United States. In 1960 he was placed in command of construction for the US intercontinental ballistic missile (ICBM) bases nationwide. In 1962, Hayes was sent to NASA, where he supervised construction of their facilities at Cape Canaveral, Huntsville, and the Manned Spaceflight Center in Houston. When Ed White, whom we met earlier, flew on Gemini missions it was controlled from facilities that Tom Hayes III built.

After his retirement, General Hayes became the president and CEO of International Engineering, overseeing construction of projects worldwide, including Egypt, Iran, Afghanistan, and Zaire. In 1975 he was elected to the National Academy of Engineering.

General Hayes's son, Thomas J. Hayes IV, graduated from West Point in 1966 as the ninth man in his class in academic standing. He had attended Duke University for his freshman year prior to entering West Point.

The youngest Hayes was commissioned in the Corps of Engineers like his father and, because of his academic standing, was chosen to attend graduate schooling at a civilian university of his choice. Hayes chose to defer this honor, instead volunteering for service in Vietnam. He attended some basic Army schooling, including Ranger School, Airborne School, and Pathfinder School, then went to Vietnam.

While overseas, he served with valor and was promoted to first lieutenant. Hayes volunteered for duty with the 1st Infantry Division's Long Range Reconnaissance Patrol unit and was awarded the Combat Infantryman's Badge and the Bronze Star for valor while with them. He then was tapped to lead the Division Aero Rifle Platoon, a part of the 1st Squadron, 4th Cavalry. He participated in more than a hundred air assault operations, and on his last one, going in to rescue two of his wounded soldiers, he was killed by enemy fire.

Hayes, in his short but brilliant career, was awarded two Silver Stars for valor in combat, four Bronze Stars with V device (for valor), an Air Medal with V device, and a Purple Heart. Hayes Gym at West Point is named after him, as is Hayes Hall at the Engineer School at Fort Leonard Wood, Missouri.

200 *Stone Tapestry*

Brigadier General Douglas Kinnard
Section VI, Row B, Grave 116

Next we will meet two classmates, both authors, from the Class of 1944. We have already met John Eisenhower from that class, another distinguished author.

Douglas Kinnard was initially selected to attend the Coast Guard Academy in New London, Connecticut, and spent his first year there. A vacancy arose for a West Point appointment in his home district, and Kinnard competed for it, winning the appointment. He then entered West Point in 1941. Recall that the curriculum was shortened during the war, so he graduated on D-day, June 6, 1944, and was commissioned in field artillery.

He immediately went off to war, joining Patton's Third Army, and was assigned to the 71st Infantry Division. Upon war's end, he returned to the United States and attended one year at Princeton, in the Department of Politics. During the Korean War, he served as the intelligence/operations officer of IX Corps Artillery. He continued his Army assignments, graduating from the Command and General Staff College and the Army War College.

He served as the chief of operations analysis in the J3 of the Military Assistance Command, Vietnam, making that his third wartime assignment. In 1968, Kinnard decided to retire and was accepted at Princeton for a fellowship, but he came down on orders from the Army to return to Vietnam. Princeton graciously permitted a yearlong delay, and Kinnard returned to Vietnam for his fourth combat tour.

Upon his return home, now Brigadier General Kinnard retired and completed his PhD at Princeton. He accepted a position at the University of Vermont and taught political science there. The author of eight books (two of which are shown), he took a two-year leave of absence to return to the Army as the chief of military history. He also served on the American Battle Monument Commission and helped in the design of the World War II Memorial on the National Mall.

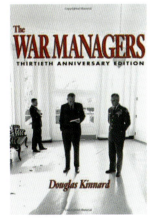
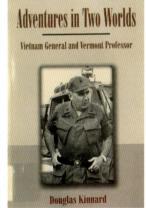

Sections V and VI   201

Colonel George "Ike" Pappas
Section VI, Row D, Grave 211

Colonel Pappas (not to be confused with the CBS reporter of the same name) graduated in the Class of 1944 along with Douglas Kinnard and John Eisenhower, our other distinguished authors from that class. He was commissioned in the coast artillery, and his initial assignments included a variety of staff and command assignments in Hawaii, New Jersey, and Maryland.

Pappas attended the Command and General Staff College at Fort Leavenworth, then went on to the assignment that defined his future: attendance at the Army War College in Carlisle Barracks, Pennsylvania. After graduating from the War College, he remained on the faculty there as the assistant chief of research and publications. There he published his first book, *Prudens Futuri: The US Army War College, 1901–1967*.

Pappas remained at the War College for the remainder of his career, until he retired. He organized and ran the Army Military Research Collection, which grew to become the current Army Heritage and Education Center. Under his leadership the organization grew from two rooms in Upton Hall into eventually taking over the entire building, then two more, to its current location on a 56-acre campus in Carlisle. The holdings of this research collection contain more than 15 million items, including 400,000 books and 1.7 million photographs. This collection is available not only to the staff and faculty of the War College but also to academic researchers and the public.

After retirement, Colonel Pappas went on to found Presidio Press, a military history publishing company, and he also continued to write. He published *To the Point: The United States Military Academy, 1802–1902*, with a second volume titled *More to the Point: The United States Military Academy, 1902–2002* (in progress at the time of his death). He also published a scholarly work on the chapel at West Point: *The Cadet Chapel, United States Military Academy*.

Lieutenant Colonel William Rice King
Section V, Row C, Grave 130

In most of our meetings with members of the Long Gray Line in this stroll, we have seen them buried side by side. Here, in William Rice King, Class of 1863, we have an example of the tip of the iceberg. The connections with this family to West Point run very deep and very far but are not visible to the naked eye as we stroll among the quiet. One of his descendants has graciously furnished me with the details of those connections.

King's father-in-law was also a West Point graduate: Israel C. Woodruff, Class of 1836 (chapter 7). One of King's daughters (Blossom) married Raymond's son (Robert). Indeed, King had only one son, who tragically died at age two and is buried here next to his parents. His other five children all were girls, three of whom married West Point graduates.

King's lineage continues, with four grandchildren attending West Point, seven great-grandchildren, and three great-great grandchildren, including two women.

When one considers the connection to the Raymond family, the list is even longer. In the Register of Graduates there is a section dealing with genealogical succession, through birth or marriage, for graduates. King shows a total of fourteen descendants; Raymond, as we have mentioned before, seventeen.

There is not an inkling of this long string of relationships in the physical surroundings here, but they exist nonetheless. This is another example, seen so many times before in these pages, that there is more here than meets the eye.

If the reader would indulge the author briefly for a personal aside. In 1998 the author came to his son's graduation at the Military Academy. He noticed that there was a woman graduate, a classmate of his son, whose father was a classmate of the author. His daughter, Katherine King Miller, is the latest in the William Rice King line, a seven-generation West Point family.

And with the King family we shall take our leave and depart this section of the cemetery. Indeed, the Long Gray Line is much in evidence here and, as the King family shows, is very much here even if not in physical evidence.

CHAPTER 10

Sections VII and VIII

If the theme of the last chapter was the Long Gray Line, then the theme of this chapter is valor in combat. Here we will meet twenty-one honored dead, twelve of whom lost their life prematurely in combat and four of whom were awarded the Medal of Honor. We shall also meet a former director of the USMA Band, which has such a central role in cadet life: waking the cadets up each morning, putting them to bed at night, and almost everything in between. We will meet a couple of professors, a chaplain, more authors, and even one soldier who served in the Egyptian army after his graduation.

But the overwhelming feeling as one strolls past these headstones is the vast number who were killed in combat. We will see war dead along the way from many of our nation's wars. We will meet the last officer killed in World War I and the first officer killed in World War II. There are many Korean War names here in this section, and we will meet a few of them. Several of these men were cadets, while Maj. Gen. Bryant Moore was the superintendent during the late 1940s and early 1950s. They went off to war as lieutenants and were killed in action; Gen. Moore followed them to Korea after his superintendency and died there. It is fitting that they lie here together.

Several of these pages remain partially empty. This is not laziness on my part, nor is it because there is nothing to write about in their earlier lives. Instead, it is to cause the reader to reflect on what deeds and honors these men and women might have achieved had they not died so early in their lives, instead living to fulfill their potential. When you see the half-empty page, ponder.

We will find Medal of Honor recipients from Cuba, World War II, and Korea.

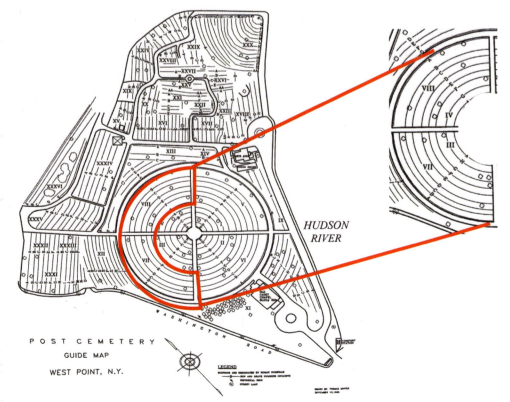

205

Brigadier General William H. Wilbur
Congressional Medal of Honor
Section VII, Row C, Grave 147

General William Wilbur is the first of those honored men we shall see. We just met one of his classmates from the Class of 1912, Major General Thomas J. Hayes, who lies nearby with his sons and grandson. Wilbur's son also lies here, himself killed in combat in Korea, and was awarded the Distinguished Service Cross (our second-highest award for valor). Reflect for a moment on a father-and-son combination who both were awarded such lofty medals for valor.

General Wilbur was not killed in combat, and he won his Medal of Honor for his intrepid action in seizing a French gun emplacement on the shores of Morocco during the invasion of North Africa in 1942, during Operation TORCH. His earlier career had led him to France twice: once for a year at the French military academy, St. Cyr, and a second tour at the French War College. His knowledge of French and all things French military made him a valuable member of Major General George Patton's staff during the invasion of French Morocco in TORCH. Wilbur was given the delicate mission of carrying a letter to the senior French commander, seeking their support against the Germans. His mission rebuffed, he was on his way back to his lines when he saw a French gun emplacement firing on the American beachhead. Taking charge of some approaching American tanks and an infantry battalion, Colonel Wilbur led the assault on the gun emplacement and eventually overran it. It was reported that at their surrender, Wilbur had but five tanks and fifteen men left standing. Wilbur was promoted to brigadier general the following month, in December 1942.

The picture (*below*) shows General Wilbur being awarded his Medal of Honor in January 1943 in Casablanca by President Franklin Roosevelt, with Major General George Patton assisting and General George C. Marshall looking on.

Wilbur also authored several books in his life, most notably *The Making of George Washington* in 1970.

General Michael S. Davison
Section VII, Row C, Grave 159

General Davison was a member of the Class of 1939, a classmate of General Frank Kobes, whom we met earlier. Davison was commissioned in the cavalry and was sent to Fort Brown, Texas, in the 12th Cavalry.

About a year after Pearl Harbor, Davison was assigned to the Operations Division of the War Department, and from there he went to North Africa as the assistant G-2 (intelligence) of an infantry division. He remained with the division through the invasion of Sicily, then Italy. He took command of an infantry battalion at the Anzio beachhead and remained with them through their invasion of southern France. By the end of World War II, Davison was a corps G-3 (operations).

After the war, Davison took command of a mechanized cavalry squadron based in Puerto Rico, then obtained a master's degree in public administration from Harvard. After a brief time back at West Point, where he commanded the cadet 1st Regiment, Davison took command of a brigade in the 3rd Armored Division and later became chief of staff to V Corps. By now he was a brigadier general.

In 1963, Brigadier General Davison returned to West Point to become the commandant of cadets. From there he went on to command the Command and General Staff College at Fort Leavenworth, then on to Vietnam. General Davison commanded the US Army, Pacific, and finally II Field Force on the ground in Vietnam. In 1971 he was given his fourth star and assigned as the commander in chief, US Army Europe. The assignment also included commanding the Central Army Group within NATO.

After his retirement, General Davison became the president of the United Services Organization (USO) and was named the president of the Association of Graduates in 1983. He was awarded the USMA Distinguished Graduate Award in 1997.

Lieutenant Colonel Andre C. Lucas
Congressional Medal of Honor
Section VII, Row C, Grave 160

Lieutenant Colonel Andre Lucas graduated in 1954 from West Point, after first serving in an infantry regiment as an enlisted soldier. His father had commanded the same regiment in World War I. Lucas's mother was French, and she insisted that he begin his education in France. Throughout his entire life, he had a dual loyalty to America and France.

Lucas was commissioned in the infantry and attended the usual group of Army schools, including Airborne School and Ranger School. He also led a special-forces A team while assigned in Germany.

Lucas went to Vietnam for the first time as an advisor to a Vietnamese battalion, earning a Silver Star for valor in combat while there. He then returned to the United States to complete the Command and General Staff College and from there returned to his mother's homeland to attend the French War College in Paris and stay on the staff of the European Command, also in Paris. After a battalion command of an infantry battalion in Germany, Lieutenant Colonel Lucas returned to the US and volunteered to return to the war in Vietnam. In fall 1969 he joined the 101st Airborne Division in Vietnam.

In July 1970, Lucas was commanding the 506th Parachute Infantry Regiment, based at Fire Base Ripcord, and had already been awarded a second Silver Star for valor in combat. His battalion fought the last major combat operation of the US involvement in the war. Surrounded by a much-larger force of North Vietnamese regulars, Lucas organized the defense of Ripcord and fought it tenaciously for three weeks. Finally ordered to abandon the base, Lucas was hit by mortar fire as he was preparing to board the last helicopter to depart the base, losing his leg. He quickly bled to death.

For his actions at Ripcord, Lucas was awarded the Medal of Honor, the last one awarded in the Vietnam War. Note the gilt lettering on his headstone, a distinguishing characteristic of Medal of Honor recipients.

208 *Stone Tapestry*

Lieutenant Colonel Mortimer L. O'Connor
Section VII, Row D, Grave 221

One of the sad things to see while creating this book is those pages where the young and old photos I have chosen are so similar, indicating that a young soldier died before he could age. Lieutenant Colonel Lucas is one example of that, as is Lieutenant Colonel O'Connor.

O'Connor's family was not unfamiliar with West Point; he had five relatives who graduated: one in 1924, two in 1926, one in 1935, and one in 1941. O'Connor graduated in the Class of 1953, one year before Colonel Lucas. He was commissioned in the infantry and attended the usual Airborne and Ranger Schools before his first assignment.

His father, Brigadier General William O'Connor, had commanded one of the infantry regiments in the 1st Infantry Division, and his uncle was killed in action in the same division. O'Connor sought assignment to the Big Red One, as the 1st Infantry Division is known, in Germany in 1954. After his initial assignment there he moved, with the division, to Fort Riley, Kansas. After attending the Infantry Advanced Course, O'Connor attended the University of Pennsylvania to obtain a master's degree in English, followed by a three-year teaching assignment in that department at West Point. This assignment was followed by a three-year tour at Temple University as the chief of its Reserve Officer Training Corps (ROTC) program. While at Temple, O'Connor completed the coursework for a PhD and had begun a draft of his dissertation. He planned to complete his PhD after his return from Vietnam.

By 1967, O'Connor had been promoted to lieutenant colonel and taken command of the 1st Battalion, 2nd Infantry, again with the Big Red One in Vietnam. Lieutenant Colonel O'Connor served with valor; he was awarded two Silver Stars, two Bronze Stars (with V device), a Purple Heart, and the Combat Infantryman's Badge. He was an infantryman who led from the front.

After the Tet Offensive was over, O'Connor's battalion led an effort to clear the road networks north of Saigon. During this operation, his forward company encountered enemy fire while clearing the jungle. O'Connor moved up to the head of the column to investigate, and a Vietcong soldier rose out of the ground from a "spider hole" and shot him in the chest with a burst of automatic-weapons fire. O'Connor died instantly.

210 *Stone Tapestry*

First Lieutenant John L. Weaver
Section VII, Row E, Grave 229

Lieutenant John Weaver is another of those who died too young. Graduating in the Class of 1950, he was killed in action in Korea less than two years later. It is easy to draft pages of accomplishments for those who lived to their seventies or eighties and had full careers—usually two careers. It is a much more difficult proposition when the young man lived to be only twenty-five years old. One must look at potential lost, rather than fame gained.

In his obituary in the Association of Graduates, a high school friend wrote that the single most memorable thing about Weaver was his sense of personal responsibility and duty. Like Mort O'Connor, whom we just met, the Weaver family was familiar with West Point. Both his brothers attended the academy, one graduating in 1945 and one in 1955.

Weaver went on to Airborne School after graduation, and in 1952 he went to Korea, where he served as a platoon leader in the 27th Infantry Regiment, known as the "Wolfhounds." The Chinese Communist forces assaulted his position, known as "Sandbag Castle," on the night of September 6 with vicious, hand-to-hand fighting. Lieutenant Weaver was killed along with many of his platoon defending the ridgeline.

The remainder of this page is left blank, leaving to the reader's imagination the deeds and heights to which Lieutenant Weaver might have risen had he not died so young.

Sections VII and VIII   **211**

First Lieutenant Samuel S. Coursen
Congressional Medal of Honor
Section VII, Row E, Grave 230

Young Samuel Coursen, killed at age twenty-four after only a year and four months of service. Graduating in the Class of 1949, Coursen was another infantryman—as was John Weaver—assigned to the 1st Cavalry Division as a platoon leader. Sent to Korea, he participated in the Eighth Army's first offensive into North Korea. His Medal of Honor citation describes his final day:

"While Company C was attacking Hill 174 under heavy small[-]arms fire, his platoon received enemy fire from close range. The platoon returned the fire and continued to advance. During this phase, his men moved into a well[-]camouflaged emplacement, which was thought to be unoccupied, and [one of his men] was wounded by the enemy who were hidden in the emplacement. Seeing the soldier in difficulty he rushed to the man's aid and, without regard for his personal safety, engaged the enemy in hand-to-hand combat in an effort to protect his wounded comrade until he himself was killed. When his body was recovered after the battle, 7 enemy dead were found in the emplacement. As a result of 1st Lieutenant Coursen's violent struggle several of the enemies' heads had been crushed with his rifle. His aggressive and intrepid actions saved the life of the wounded man, eliminated the main position of the enemy roadblock, and greatly inspired the men of his command."

Coursen has been memorialized in many ways since his death, including the naming of one of the passenger ferries operating in New York Harbor between Manhattan and Governor's Island (the *Lt. Samuel S. Coursen*, *left*). His high school, the Newark Academy, named its athletic grounds Coursen Memorial Field, and a bronze plaque was placed in Cullum Hall at West Point as a Medal of Honor recipient.

A man we have already met in these pages, General Phillip A. Feir, was a classmate and roommate of Coursen while they were cadets. In Coursen's obituary, Feir wrote, "I have felt the strength of his loyalty, and to this day I have drawn inspiration from it." Recall that Feir went on to be the commandant of cadets at West Point. What might Coursen have achieved had he lived?

Second Lieutenant Courtenay C. Davis Jr.
Section VII, Row F, Grave 305

"Court" Davis served even less time than Sam Coursen before he lost his life in Korea. Commissioned from West Point in June 1949, by September 1950 he was dead, killed just thirteen days after entering combat. Davis died valiantly and was awarded the Distinguished Service Cross, our second-highest award for valor. He was killed leading his platoon on an assault on Hill 188, cut down by a North Korean machine gunner.

Like for Lieutenant Weaver's entry, the remainder of this page is left blank, like the blank canvas of Lieutenant Davis's life, a reminder to all of us about what potential was lost that day in Korea.

Second Lieutenant George W. Tow
Section VII, Row F, Grave 270

We just met Lieutenant Court Davis; his classmate Lieutenant George Tow died in the same battalion in the same fight as Court Davis, a mere four days later. Another platoon leader in the 5th Cavalry, Tow was a part of the same operation and commanded a weapons platoon supporting Davis. Tow saw a better position for his machine gun section, scouted it out, and was on his way back to move his men forward when he was killed by a sniper's bullet.

A poignant fact about George Tow: he had already been awarded a Purple Heart in Korea and was in the hospital in Pusan a month before he died. He wrote home, "I have had a good rest and naturally am not anxious to go back but pangs of conscience won't let me 'goldbrick' anymore. I know what my men are going through up at the front . . . I will check out tonight and probably be there by tomorrow morning." He did, he was, and he died leading those men not quite three weeks later.

Sections VII and VIII **215**

Major General Bryant E. Moore
Section VII, Row G, Grave 334

It is entirely fitting that General Moore lies here in this section, and it leads to yet another of those interesting and startling realizations one can have while walking through this hallowed ground. Moore was the superintendent at West Point from 1949 to 1951. Davis, Weaver, Coursen, and Tow all were cadets here under his leadership, then left for Korea to perish. Moore, when his tour was completed as superintendent, also left for Korea and perished as well.

Bryant Moore was a member of the class of 1917 and was commissioned in the infantry. He had one tour back at West Point as a French instructor, but his star really began to rise in World War II. In 1942 he commanded the 164th Infantry Regiment, which fought in Guadalcanal alongside the US Marine Corps. After that, he was promoted to brigadier general and assigned as the assistant division commander of the 104th Infantry Division under the leadership of Major General Terry De La Mesa Allen, one of America's finest warriors.

General Moore was given a second star and command of the 8th Infantry Division in Europe. At war's end, he was commanding the 88th Infantry Division in Austria. That division was deactivated in 1947, and General Moore then stayed on in Yugoslavia for an additional year. He came back to West Point and assumed his duties as the superintendent in 1949.

After his tour at West Point, where he saw hundreds of his graduates go off to Korea, he was assigned to Korea. General Matthew Ridgway was the US commander there, and he assigned General Moore to command IX Corps in Operation Ripper, which was the Eighth Army's offensive back into North Korea. During a flight back to his headquarters after a review of the front lines, General Moore's helicopter lost power and crashed into the Han River. Although he survived the crash and made it to shore, he died suddenly afterward, apparently from heart failure.

General Moore was awarded three Distinguished Service Medals in his career and two Silver Stars for valor in combat. He belongs here, in this section among the men who were his students, having all perished in the same noble pursuit.

216 *Stone Tapestry*

Colonel William H. Schempf
Section VII, Row H, Grave 349

Leaving aside for the moment the dull, cold, muddy fields of Korea and the tired and dirty infantrymen there, next we meet Colonel William Schempf, a musician. Colonel Schempf was not a graduate of West Point, instead studying the clarinet at the University of Wisconsin. After his graduation, he went on to the Eastman School of Music and earned a master of music degree. He joined the Army in 1942 and was trained as a meteorologist in the Eighth Army Air Force in Europe.

After the war, Schempf returned to music and was named the chairman of the music department at Lehigh University. By 1952 he had been granted a Fulbright scholarship to study in Vienna, and by 1957 he was named the teacher of music at West Point (Sylvanus Thayer had created the position of teacher of music at West Point when he was the superintendent).

Colonel Schempf retained his position in the US Army Reserve and ultimately was promoted to colonel. He earned a PhD in musicology from the Eastman School in 1960. He remained the music director until 1974, when he retired from the Army. He then went on to become the chairman of the music department at Central Michigan University for another seven years.

I particularly enjoyed the aphorism at the bottom of his headstone: "No fun without music; no music without fun."

Major Chancellor Martin
Section VIII, Row A, Grave 12

Major Martin defies description. His large and irregular headstone perhaps perfectly describes this man of many talents but irregular in manner. Martin graduated in 1868 from West Point and was commissioned in the infantry. Lieutenant Martin was assigned to the Third Infantry on the frontier and participated in the Indian Wars under General Sheridan. When the Army decided it had too many officers and created an incentive for easy departure, Lieutenant Martin decided that perhaps his best career choice lay outside the infantry, so he requested to be honorably discharged in 1870.

Martin decided to take up a business profession and became a merchant (a profession for which, his obituary says, he had "no natural inclination"). After three years of this purgatory, Martin decided to change careers again.

In an unusual move, he moved his family to Cairo, Egypt, and became a major in the Egyptian army service. Major Martin served on the staff of the khedive, the chief of the Egyptian army (normally a British officer). He served in Cairo, enjoying the social scene for four years. By all accounts he served with distinction and was very thorough in his performance of his duties. His obituary (written by one of his classmates) notes that he had plenty of time to tour Europe while in the service of the khedive and had a son born in Geneva.

The Martins returned to the United States in 1874, and in another bold career change, he decided to take up the study of medicine. By 1879, Martin had graduated with a doctor of medicine degree (although he never took up practice).

Apparently bored with medicine too, he instead took a position in the civil service and joined the New York Customs House. By 1890 he was the deputy collector of customs in the Port of New York and chairman of the board of examiners of the Port of New York.

Finally retiring from public service in 1908, Martin then purchased a mansion on the banks of the Hudson in Cornwall, New York, just north of West Point, and lived comfortably there for the remainder of his life.

This has to be one of the more unusual careers of anyone in this cemetery!

Stone Tapestry

Major General John Biddle
Section VIII, Row B, Grave 126

Major General Biddle graduated in the Class of 1881, second of fifty-three in academic rank. He was commissioned in the Corps of Engineers and spent most of his early assignments in engineering duties. In 1887 he returned to West Point, where he taught Practical Military Engineering. During this assignment he was detached for duty at Johnstown, Pennsylvania, during the recovery efforts from the Johnstown flood.

During the Spanish-American War, he became the chief engineer of the volunteer forces and served in Cuba. Biddle was assigned as the chief engineer of the 6th Corps, and later in the same capacity in 1st Corps; he earned a Silver Star for valor in Cuba.

After the war, General Biddle was transferred to the Philippines, where he served as the chief engineer officer. During this assignment he was sent to Guam to survey a dam there and make improvements to the harbor there.

Upon his return to the United States, General Biddle was appointed as the engineer commissioner of the District of Columbia, and later in California. From 1909 to 1911 he assumed command of the fortifications in the port of San Francisco. In 1914 he was sent to Europe as an observer with the Austro-Hungarian army in Galicia and Poland, a common occurrence during World War I. Recall that we met Major Elvin R. Heiberg on similar duty in Italy in the last chapter.

In June 1916, General Biddle assumed his duties as superintendent at West Point, where he oversaw the rapid compression of the course of instruction to furnish officers for World War I. The war cut short his own tour as superintendent, and within one year he was sent to France, where he commanded a brigade of American engineers. In October 1917 he returned to the United States and took over as the acting chief of staff of the Army until March 1918. He then returned to Europe, where he commanded all US forces in Great Britain. After the war, General Biddle returned to the United States and retired after more than forty years of service.

The Reverend H. Percy Silver
Section VIII, Row B, Grave 123

Next in our stroll we find a man of the cloth, the Reverend H. Percy Silver. Silver served as the chaplain of the Military Academy from 1913 to 1918, while General Biddle was the superintendent.

Horace Percy Silver was born in Philadelphia in 1871 and was a graduate of the General Theological Seminary in New York. Silver was made a deacon in 1894 and in the following year gained the priesthood. From 1894 to 1901 he served in churches in Omaha and Lincoln, Nebraska.

In 1901, Silver left his ministry in Lincoln to become an Army chaplain. He was named chaplain of the Thirtieth Infantry Regiment and served for two years with the regiment in the Philippines. In 1910, Silver left the Army and became the secretary to the Episcopalian Mission in the American Southwest territories. By 1913 he became reacquainted with the Army by being named the chaplain here at West Point.

He served here as chaplain during the tumultuous war years of the First World War. He saw the curriculum here shortened and shortened again, until the Class of 1918 graduated with so little time at the academy that they were brought back after the war to complete their training.

Silver was very active in establishing at West Point a branch of the Young Men's Christian Association (YMCA). There were YMCA groups for each class of cadets here, with Sunday meetings, music, and reading rooms established. Also during Silver's tenure was the famous Class of 1915 (the "Class the Stars Fell On"), including both Eisenhower and Omar Bradley among many others, some of whom we have met.

After he left West Point, Silver went to the Church of the Incarnation in Manhattan and served as rector there until his death in 1934. The church rectory there is now named the H. Percy Silver House and has been designated as a New York City Landmark.

220 *Stone Tapestry*

First Lieutenant Todd W. Lambka
Section VIII, Row B, Grave 115

Sadly, graduating and hastening off to an early death in combat was not confined to the war in Korea. Lieutenant Todd Lambka graduated in the Class of 2010 and was killed twenty-six months later in Afghanistan by an improvised explosive device (IED). Lambka was an infantry officer and was assigned to the 1st Battalion, 28th Infantry Regiment, in the 1st Infantry Division, at the time of his death.

While Lambka was a cadet, his mother passed away. Prior to his graduation, he was awarded the Robert Foley Scholarship of Honor, which is named for a Medal of Honor winner from Vietnam and is awarded to the cadet who successfully overcomes personal hardships during his years at West Point.

Lieutenant Lambka has a twin brother who was also serving in Afghanistan at the time of his death. His brother accompanied his body home. Lambka was awarded the Combat Infantryman Badge, the Bronze Star, and a Purple Heart after his death.

Brigadier General John W. Heard
Congressional Medal of Honor
Section VIII, Row A, Grave 12

General Heard has an unusual headstone, somewhat reminiscent of George Goethal's stone, which we saw many pages ago. One of the curious features about the stone is his middle name. Whereas "Wilkinson" is clearly etched in the stone, his obituary by his classmates set down his middle name as "William."

Heard graduated with the Class of 1883. He was assigned to the 3rd Cavalry on frontier duty, fought against the Apache Indians, and participated in the campaign against Geronimo.

When the war with Spain arrived, Heard was still with the 3rd Cavalry and had been assigned to the steamer *Wanderer*, responsible for supplying ammunition and rations to Cuban insurgents fighting the Spaniards. When he was attempting to land his cargo in Cuba, the ship was taken under accurate fire by Spanish marksmen. Half the men on the deck of the ship were wounded or killed immediately, and the controls to the engine room of the ship were disabled. Heard immediately sent two men to relay commands to the engine room, but both were killed. Heard then exposed himself in the open to relay commands to the engine room while a hot fire sprang up around him, with bullets passing through his clothing but leaving him miraculously uninjured. Through his efforts they were able to regain control of the ship, and it was able to move out of danger. For his coolness and bravery, Heard won the Medal of Honor.

In his obituary it notes that during his long career, Heard served in "every state, territory and insular possession of the United States." He participated in the Punitive Expedition against Pancho Villa in Mexico and was serving in Hawaii as the head of the Hawaiian Department when the US entered World War I. Upon his retirement from the Department of Hawaii, the Hawaiian Legislature voted to award him a saber and a vote of thanks, something never done in that department.

222   *Stone Tapestry*

General Cortlandt V. R. Schuyler
Section VIII, Row C, Grave 172

General Schuyler graduated from West Point in 1922. We have already met two of his classmates: Generals Lemuel Mathewson and Blackshear Bryan. Schuyler graduated in the top 10 percent of his class and was commissioned in the coast artillery, where he specialized in the early development of antiaircraft artillery techniques. While working at the Coast Artillery Board—the research-and-development arm of the branch—he developed the first multiple, power-operated machine gun mount, known as the "Quad .50."

Interestingly, General Schuyler had no combat assignments during World War II. Instead he was assigned to Romania as the US military representative to the Allied Control Commission. After the war, he returned to Washington and became involved in the newly developing organization NATO (North Atlantic Treaty Organization). When General Eisenhower was named as the first supreme commander of NATO, General Schuyler went with him as a special assistant to the chief of staff.

In 1953, General Schuyler assumed command of the 28th Infantry Division in Germany, but he quickly returned to Paris to become the new chief of staff at NATO. In 1956, General Schuyler was promoted to four-star rank and remained as the NATO chief of staff.

General Schuyler retired in 1959. He then joined the staff of Nelson Rockefeller, who was the governor of New York at the time. His first assignment with Rockefeller was as a special assistant, but he was later named the commissioner of general services for the State of New York, where he remained for ten years.

An interesting note about General Schuyler's second wife, Helen Stillman, from his obituary: she had the same middle name as Schuyler, which was Van Rensselaer, even though they were not related.

From 1965 to 1968, General Schuyler served as the president of the West Point Association of Graduates.

224 *Stone Tapestry*

Brigadier General Joseph E. McCarthy

Section VIII, Row C, Grave 156

Our next two soldiers both were members of the Class of 1945. Both were commissioned in the infantry and went on to command infantry units in peace and war. General McCarthy lived a long and full life, while George Eyster was cut down by a sniper's bullet in Vietnam.

General McCarthy began his career in Japan as part of the occupation force. He was sailing to his first assignment, most likely as a platoon leader in the assaulting force, when the atomic bomb was dropped on Japan and the war ended.

His obituary says that McCarthy commanded at the brigade (full colonel) level three times in his career, in six different Army divisions. His final field command assignment was in the 4th Infantry Division in Vietnam in 1969.

General McCarthy's greatest contributions to the Army came in the field of education and history. He attended the University of Maryland for his postgraduate education, completing both a master's degree and a PhD in political science. He then remained at the school to teach. He converted his doctoral dissertation into a book, *Illusion of Power: American Policy toward Viet-Nam, 1954–1966*.

After his retirement from the Army, McCarthy settled in Carlisle, Pennsylvania. He worked for three different Pennsylvania governors on the base development committee, advising them on which military bases in the state should remain open and which should be closed for cost savings.

His legacy is in the establishment of the Army Heritage and Education Center in Carlisle. The center is a combination museum and training center, and McCarthy worked with Ike Pappas, whom we met, to establish this facility in Carlisle and make its material available to the public. Lectures, a scholarship program, manuscripts, and photographs, along with artifacts from the Army, make up the AHEC portfolio, a research treasure in central Pennsylvania dedicated to the Army and its history.

Sections VII and VIII   225

Lieutenant Colonel George S. Eyster Jr.

Section VIII, Row D, Grave 206

George Eyster was commissioned in the infantry upon graduation in 1945. He was born into an Army family (his father was Brigadier General George Eyster Sr., of the Class of August 1917).

Like McCarthy, after graduation Eyster headed west, but he did not go as far as Japan. After an initial assignment at the Tank Destroyer School, Lieutenant Eyster went to the Philippines, to the 86th Infantry Division. While there, he served as the aide to the commanding general, then had a short tour with the Philippine Scouts.

He went on to Japan, serving there again as an aide to the chief of staff of the Far Eastern Command, then two infantry assignments again: one with the 15th Infantry Regiment and one with the 3rd Infantry Regiment.

After some advanced schooling at Fort Benning, Georgia, Eyster headed back west again, serving in Task Force Seven at Eniwetok Atoll as an observer to several atomic bomb tests. Returning to the United States, Eyster went to the Command and General Staff College at Fort Leavenworth. In July 1965, Lieutenant Colonel Eyster assumed command of the 1st Battalion, 28th Infantry, in the 1st Infantry Division and took the unit to Vietnam. It was during an operation here, near Cu Chi, that Eyster was shot and killed. A Vietnamese soldier secured in a tunnel complex under his feet rose out of a spider hole and shot LTC Eyster in the chest. He was immediately given first aid but, two days later, succumbed to a pulmonary embolism and died in Saigon.

The circumstances of Eyster's death were eerily familiar to those of Mort O'Connor, whom we met earlier. He was also shot and killed by a Vietnamese rising out of a spider hole. Eyster's death sparked a manhunt and careful search of the area, and an enormous tunnel complex was found underground near Cu Chi, including a hospital.

226 *Stone Tapestry*

Captain Robert M. Losey
Section VIII, Row E, Grave 265

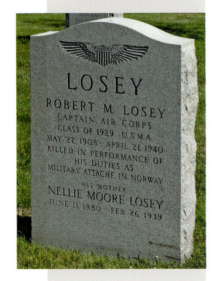

The next two men we shall meet are ironic, and tragic, bookends. Captain Robert Losey is the first American officer to be killed in World War II, and Lieutenant Walter Schulze is the last American officer to die in World War I. It is just one more of the strange juxtapositions we find here in the cemetery.

Robert Losey was a graduate of the Class of 1929 from West Point and was commissioned in the field artillery. Within his first year of active service, he transferred to the fledgling US Army Air Corps and learned to fly. He gained his wings in San Antonio in 1930.

Losey then reported to Mather Field in California, where he took up the routine duties of a junior Army aviator (and got married). Lieutenant Losey was part of the 77th Pursuit Squadron, and when Mather Field closed he moved with the squadron to Barksdale Field. He was selected for attendance at the Advanced Navigation Training Unit.

In 1934, Losey was sent to the California Institute of Technology to obtain a master's degree in meteorology, an essential science for an aviator. After he received his degree, he requested and got permission to return to Caltech for a second master's degree, this time in aeronautical engineering. After his second graduation, Losey was sent to Washington to be the chief of the weather section in the office of the chief, Air Corps.

In 1939, Losey was assigned to Scandinavia, first as the assistant military attaché for Finland and later as the assistant military attaché for Norway. In April 1940, during the German invasion of Norway, Losey was killed by a German bomb fragment. He was assisting in the evacuation of other US citizens from the war at the time he was killed. This unfortunate timing caused Captain Losey to be the first US officer killed in World War II, even though the US was not yet engaged in the war.

228   *Stone Tapestry*

Lieutenant Walter H. Schulze
Section VIII, Row F, Grave 279

Lieutenant Walter Schulze graduated from West Point in the Class of 1917. He was commissioned in the cavalry branch and was assigned to the 3rd Cavalry in Texas, and later in France during World War I. In June 1918 he transferred to the Air Corps and underwent pilot training. He joined the 185th Aero Squadron in France just prior to the Armistice in November 1918. He was seen as a natural aviator and was selected to perform some exhibition flying in the First Army Horse Show.

After the Armistice, Schulze was transferred to the 138th Aero Squadron in the Army of Occupation. Many do not recall that the American army remained in France for almost a year after the Armistice as one of the armies of occupation, until the peace treaty was signed between the warring parties in World War I. When the peace treaty was signed in June 1919, Lieutenant Schulze was assigned to fly copies of the newspapers declaring peace to all the units in the Army of Occupation, to get the word out quickly. While engaged in this mission, his aircraft engine failed and he crashed near Montabour, Germany. The picture (*left*) shows a small memorial erected at the crash site by the citizens of Montabour to memorialize the death of the last American officer to die in the war. In 1935 the Nazi Party took over the government in Germany, and they tore down the monument.

Lieutenant Schulze lived just two years after his graduation. Dying young in the service of your country is not a recent development.

Sections VII and VIII 229

Colonel Charles P. Echols
Section VIII, Row E, Grave 249

Taking a break from the tragedy of untimely deaths of young men in combat, we now turn to Colonel Charles P. Echols, a professor of mathematics at West Point for many decades.

Echols graduated in the Class of 1891 as the third man in his class in academic standing. While a cadet, Echols was given the delightful nickname "Puckles."

Commissioned in the Corps of Engineers, as so many have done who had earned high class standing, he first served in engineer assignments in New York before he was brought back to West Point for the first time as a professor of mathematics. He was known to the cadets then and forevermore as "P" Echols, an abbreviation of his title as "Professor." That tradition still stands at West Point, and instructors are universally referred to as "Ps."

Around 1897, Echols returned to his engineering duties and served an overseas tour in the Philippines. By 1898 he had been assigned for the second time to West Point; he remained there in the Mathematics Department until 1931. During the First World War, Echols took a short sabbatical from the Math Department to go to France and serve as a military observer with the French army.

Echols never married; he played a very active role at West Point in much more than just chairing the Mathematics Department. He served as the secretary of the Army Athletic Association for years and served as the treasurer of the Association of Graduates.

Echols was brutally murdered in New York City by a group of thugs while he was out for an evening stroll one night in 1940.

The then chief of staff of the US Army, General George C. Marshall, wrote:

> Professor Echols' Army career was noteworthy for the highly efficient manner in which he performed every duty. Most of his service of more than forty years active duty was in the Department of Mathematics at the United States Military Academy, where his exceptional service and brilliant scholastic attainments contributed to a marked degree to the maintenance of the high standards of the institution.

Stone Tapestry

RGE·WILLIAM·

CHAPTER 11

Sections XII, XXXI, XXXII, and XXXIII

The people we shall meet in these sections are among the most eclectic of the cemetery. There is no overarching theme for those lying here, just service to their nation and duty well performed. We shall meet an Olympic boxing coach who was a noncommissioned officer, a librarian, and several generals. One served his country honorably on active duty, only to be killed while a civilian in Croatia. We will see another member of the USMA Band, one of the iconic drum majors. We will see a couple of soldiers who spent their career in the shadows of classified programs, denied public acclaim and recognition but honorable and faithful nonetheless. One led a raid on a prisoner-of-war (POW) camp in the Philippines in World War II, the precursor and model for the Son Tay POW rescue attempt in Vietnam, and even more recently the Desert One debacle trying to rescue US hostages in Tehran in 1980. We will meet Major General Bruce Staser and his wife, Betty, who composed a poem to be engraved on her monument, one of the more unusual in the cemetery.

And we shall see a heartbreaking row of infants who died here at West Point, most after only a day or two of life. If the death of young men killed in combat shortly after graduation is a tragedy, surely the death of an infant after twenty-four hours is doubly so. One can only imagine the grief surrounding these tiny graves.

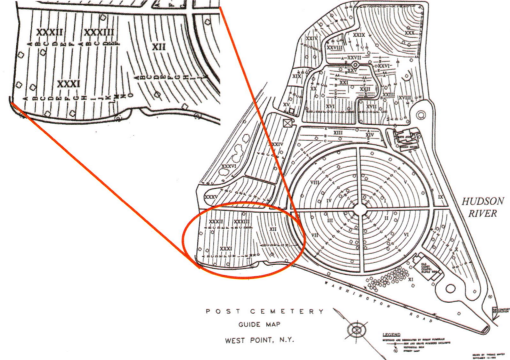

Master Sergeant Pasquale "Pat" Nappi
Section XII, Row K, Grave 485

Master Sergeant Pat Nappi served as a boxing coach for the All-Army Teams from 1940 through 1977, an incredible thirty-seven years. After enlisting in the Army, he rose to the rank of master sergeant and served overseas both in World War II and the Korean War.

Nappi served as the coach of the Army boxing team from 1953 to 1977.

Nappi achieved international acclaim when he served as the coach of the US Olympic boxing team in 1976, 1980, and 1984. The Olympics in 1976 were held in Montreal, Canada, and the US team won five gold medals, one silver medal, and one bronze medal. During this Olympics, some of the US boxers who were coached by Nappi who won gold medals included both Leon and Michael Spinks, Sugar Ray Leonard, Leo Randolph, and Howard Davis.

In 1980 the United States led sixty-six other nations in a boycott of the Summer Olympics in Moscow, in protest over the Soviet Union's invasion of Afghanistan. Nappi had been named as the United States coach and had the team in training when the boycott ended their hopes for more golds.

In 1984, Nappi returned as the coach of the boxing team. This team won seven gold medals, two silver medals, and one bronze medal. The boxing gold medals in these Olympics were won by Paul Gonzales, Steve McCrory, Meldrick Taylor, Pernell Whitaker, Jerry Page, Mark Breland, Frank Tate, Henry Tillman, and Tyrell Biggs.

Nappi was from Syracuse, New York, and in 1998 was inducted into the Greater Syracuse Sports Hall of Fame. In their memorial article, they describe Pat Nappi as the first boxing coach ever to be chosen as coach of the year.

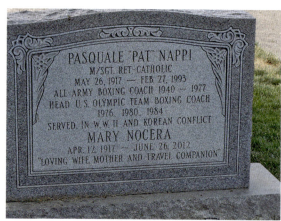

The Infants
Section XII, Row K, Multiple Graves

This heartbreaking row, right alongside the walking path, is a series of infants, two of whom passed away within a day of being born. They are not related to one another (that I can tell), and it is a mystery why they all lie here alongside one another. Like the tragedy of the unknown graves that we saw earlier, they represent one of the saddest sections of the cemetery.

Most of these poor children were not given names, just recorded as the parents' last name and the term "child." One of the tiny graves is marked as an unknown infant, a mysterious entry in a category all its own.

Sections XII, XXXI, XXXII, and XXXIII **235**

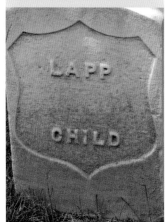

It is sobering to reflect on this tiny little row and to understand the grief that accompanies these cold stones. All others in this cemetery had at least a chance to make their mark upon the world, to achieve the potential they had at birth, and, as we have seen, many did so very well. These poor children fall into a different category, and one could easily ask themselves why, indeed, were they born at all, if only to depart again so soon? Such mysteries are imponderable.

Nearby lies another set of headstones touching each other. In this entire cemetery, I have seen only two examples of headstones touching one another. One case was a woman who had married a second time after her first husband had passed away, and all three were in the same grave with headstones touching. The other is here: poor Irene Kulebokeon, who died in childbirth, and her son Walter, who preceded her by a single day. I do not know who Irene's husband was, but my heart is full of sympathy for him.

Major General Norman B. Edwards
Section XII, Row H, Grave 295

Major General Edwards is another of those typical residents here, a man who made his way through the Army and life, excelling at his work, honorable, but not destined to be famous except within his own circle. Edwards graduated from West Point in 1935, but our story does not begin there. Edwards was a stellar athlete in high school, and in New River State College, where he went prior to his appointment. He joined the US Army Reserve in 1929, and two years later he was granted an appointment to West Point after the principal selectee failed to qualify for admission.

Edwards was never a star student, but he did have perseverance. At Christmas in his plebe year, he failed both mathematics and English. He was "turned out," in cadet slang. After making up the deficiency, he was again turned out in his yearling Christmas, but this time only in English. For the second time he succeeded in passing his reexamination, and Edwards returned to graduate with his class. His obituary noted, dryly, that his class standing improved every year, until at graduation he was fiftieth from the bottom of the class.

Apparently, class standing at graduation is a poor predictor of future success. Edwards went on to have a brilliant career, working on the staffs first of General Patton, and then General Eisenhower in World War II. He participated in the invasion of North Africa, and in Europe he was part of the campaigns that captured Metz, the Ardennes, and the Remagen Bridge. He was awarded the Silver Star for his actions at Remagen and finally joined General Patton again in the Third Army at the end of the war.

After the war, Edwards commanded all the US forces that participated in a joint US-Canadian exercise in the Canadian Arctic called "Musk Ox." During the Korean War he was sent to the Pacific, where he joined General MacArthur's staff. In 1951 he took command of the 27th Infantry Regiment (we have already met Lieutenant John Weaver of the Wolfhounds earlier) in the 25th Infantry Division. He returned to Korea as a major general in 1962 and commanded the US Military Assistance Advisory Group, Korea. General Edwards ended his career in 1968 as the chief of staff, Sixth Army, in San Francisco.

Technical Sergeant William S. Lewis and Frances W. Lewis

Section XII, Row K, Grave 469

Frances Lewis is not a graduate, nor was her husband a graduate. He was an enlisted soldier—eventually a noncommissioned officer—who spent his career at West Point on the staff here. Frances was the assistant librarian and labored here in the Cadet Library for thirty years.

Both people represent something much larger than themselves in the pages of this book. They were not famous, or flashy, and are not remembered by any but their families. Yet, they, and many who lie around them here in this section, formed the fabric of the Military Academy and helped it, in their own way, shape the lives of the great men and women who achieved fame and fortune.

William Lewis was an immigrant, born in modern-day Lithuania and brought to this country in 1891. He enlisted in the Army in 1902 and married Frances (a local Highland Falls girl) in 1917. He spent his career here at West Point. His records show he was promoted to private first class in June 1919, was busted back to private forty days later, and was repromoted six months after that. He must have learned his lesson, because he showed no disciplinary action after that, was a staff sergeant by 1930, and retired as a technical sergeant in 1933. He and Frances had three children. The third, Robert, died twenty-four days after he was born in 1925 and is buried here with them.

Frances worked in the Cadet Library in positions of ever-increasing responsibility for thirty years until she was the assistant librarian in 1958. We have seen two other Cadet Library people in our pages: Edward Holden in chapter 5 and Colonel Elbert Farman in chapter 9. Frances Lewis joined the library at the same time Colonel Farman did (1928), and she was instrumental in helping him create a children's library of more than four hundred books during his tenure. Recall that Colonel Farman expanded the library to be the post library and did not focus just on the cadets. During the time that Mrs. Lewis was in the Cadet Library, they saw the collections grow from 118,000 volumes to over 152,000 volumes.

238 *Stone Tapestry*

Sometimes when I walk through the cemetery, I feel a quiet sort of reproach coming from people such as Sergeant Lewis and Frances. Very few who visit here will recognize their names, or their contributions. They are certainly not as famous as the Medal of Honor awardees, or as a high-ranking general, but they are very much a part and parcel both of West Point and the cemetery's sacred ground.

Lieutenant Colonel Robert E. Donovan
Section XXXIII, Row F, Grave 102

Lieutenant Colonel Donovan graduated from West Point in 1963. He was commissioned in the Corps of Engineers and began his active duty career in Thailand, serving in the 809th Engineer Battalion doing construction work in building airfields there. In 1966 he went back to school, earning a master's degree in physics from the Massachusetts Institute of Technology.

The war in Vietnam was escalating by the time he graduated from MIT in 1968, so he went off to serve as an advisor to a Vietnamese unit for a year. Upon his return to the States, Donovan was assigned to the US Army Engineers Reactor Group (USAERG). A project run by the Army Nuclear Power Program, it focused its efforts on developing small, pressurized-water and boiling-water nuclear power reactors that could generate electrical and heating power in remote sites.

After his tour at Fort Belvoir with the USAERG, Donovan returned to West Point, where he was an instructor in the Physics Department. He also returned to school, studying at night for a master's in business administration at Farleigh Dickinson University. In 1972 he graduated from Farleigh Dickinson, and the following year he resigned from the active Army, becoming a member of the Army Reserves.

Donovan had a brilliant career in the business world, rising to be the president at Babcock & Wilcox Canada, an engineering firm. By 1990 he had moved to the Foster Wheeler Corporation, where he was the vice president. Within two years he was president of the Power Plant Systems Division of the Swiss power development firm ABB, and in two more he was the president of all ABB operations in the Americas.

On April 3, 1996, Donovan and thirty-four others were killed instantly when the transport plane carrying them and US Secretary of Commerce Ron Brown slammed into a mountain peak in bad weather while on a trip to Dubrovnik, Croatia. The delegation was made up of Brown and industrial CEOs who were going to establish trade relations with the Croatians after their long civil war with Bosnia-Herzegovina.

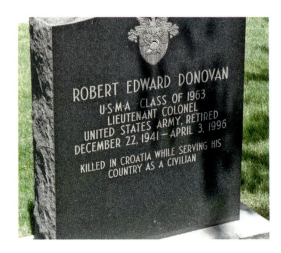

Brigadier General Charles H. Schilling
Section XXXIII, Row F, Grave 100

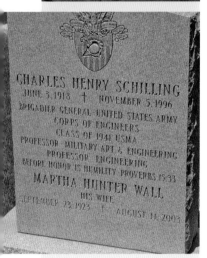

Near Lieutenant Colonel Donovan we find another engineer, Charles H. Schilling. Schilling graduated from West Point in 1941, but he first began his association with military schooling by spending a year at the Citadel in South Carolina. He was a stellar basketball player, playing all four years at West Point and lettering in the sport. He remained a basketball athlete his entire life.

Schilling, like Donovan, was commissioned in the Corps of Engineers, and he immediately went to the 23rd Armored Engineer Battalion in the 3rd Armored Division. He rapidly rose during World War II and soon was commanding the 165th Combat Engineer Battalion, which he led across France and Germany after D-day.

When the war ended, Schilling went back to school and obtained a master's degree in civil engineering from the University of California at Berkeley. He returned to Germany, where he supervised the expansion and upgrades to Rhein-Main Air Base. During the period 1951 to 1955, Schilling was back at West Point, teaching in the Department of Military Art and Engineering. He was then assigned to be the Army's engineer who supervised all military construction in Iceland.

After his Icelandic tour, General Schilling returned to West Point in 1956 and did not leave again. He was assigned as an instructor in the Engineering Department until he took a sabbatical in 1959 to earn a PhD in civil engineering from Rensselaer Polytechnic Institute. He then returned to West Point to be a permanent professor in the department.

In 1963, Colonel Schilling was named the head of the Department of Military Art and Engineering, and he held that post until the department changed its name to the Department of Engineering in 1969. Schilling finally retired as a brigadier general in 1980. General Schilling's obituary says that he was the last man in the Class of 1941 to retire from active duty, thirty-nine years after graduation.

General Schilling loved to play basketball and continued to do so after he retired. He was playing a game in a men's church league at the time of his death at age seventy-eight.

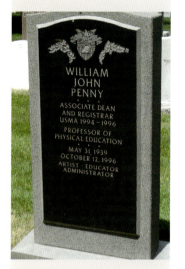

William J. Penny
Section XXXIII, Row F, Grave 99

William Penny is in yet another class of individuals whom we find here in this cemetery. Penny was not a graduate of West Point or an Army officer at all but instead was a visiting professor who came here to teach cadets, remained as an administrator, and chose to be buried here when he passed away.

Penny graduated from Brooklyn College in 1961 with a bachelor of science degree in physical education. He went immediately to graduate school, attending the University of Illinois, where he received his master's degree in physical education.

Penny then began his career as an instructor and simultaneously began to work on his doctorate, still at the University of Illinois. In 1968 he obtained his PhD. His dissertation is titled "An Analysis of the Meanings Attached to Selective Concepts in Administrative Theory," indicating not only his interest in physical education, but in administration and management of teaching physical education. By 1971, Professor Penny was the head of the department of professional physical education at East Stroudsburg State College in Pennsylvania. It was noted in his obituary that he headed up a regional conference titled "Curriculum Improvements in Secondary School Physical Education," covering thirteen states in the mid-Atlantic region. By 1986 we find Professor Penny named the director of the office of administrative services at East Stroudsburg, now re-named East Stroudsburg University.

Shortly after that, Professor Penny was asked to come to West Point as a visiting professor in physical education. Physical education is a major portion of the curriculum at West Point, and we have seen two Masters of the Sword in these pages: Brigadier General Frank Kobe and Colonel Herman Koehler. Penny came to West Point in 1989 and never departed. By 1994 he had moved up into the Dean's Office as the associate dean and registrar for West Point, a remarkable position for a nongraduate.

William Penny represents a group of visiting professors who brought their own unique experiences in history, foreign languages, and physical education to West Point and blended them with the ideals of the institution.

Sections XII, XXXI, XXXII, and XXXIII   **243**

Major General Bruce I. Staser
Section XXXI, Row L, Grave 231

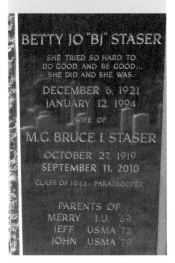

The next monument in our stroll is that for Bruce and Betty Jo Staser. It is unique because the stone has a full poem engraved on the back, written by Betty Jo before her death, titled "To Those I Love."

Major General Staser was a member of the Class of 1944 and was commissioned in the infantry. He was known as "Rock" to his classmates and friends and was an exceptional athlete while at West Point, earning his Army "A" on the varsity boxing team as a heavyweight. Staser was a classmate of John Eisenhower's, whom we met earlier, and graduated on D-day, June 6, 1944. He married Betty Jo the same day.

Staser immediately went to parachute school and joined the 515th Parachute Infantry Regiment North Carolina. The unit deployed to Europe but did not see combat, and after the war ended, he returned to the United States and was transferred to the 505th Parachute Infantry Regiment. Staser was an Alaskan native, and his tour with the 505th PIR took him back home, to participate in cold-weather maneuvers called Task Force Frigid.

Staser had several assignments in Austria and Germany, then was sent to be the professor of military science in the ROTC unit at the University of California at Berkeley. He then went on a short tour to Korea, and finally back to the 505th at Fort Bragg in 1957. He continued his infantry assignments, commanding the 1st Battalion, 13th Infantry, in Germany, and had several Pentagon tours until he retired as a colonel in 1973.

The same day of his retirement from active duty, Staser was appointed a major general in the Alaska National Guard. General Staser served in that capacity for two years, until the governor's office changed hands. He then became the executive assistant to the mayor of the City of Anchorage, Alaska. Staser also authored a book, *Cold War Soldier*, about his experiences while on active duty, especially in Alaska.

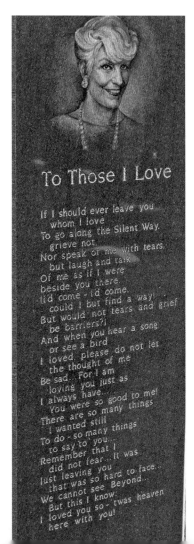

244 *Stone Tapestry*

Master Sergeant James B. Mahan
Section XXXIII, Row D, Grave 365

Sergeant Mahan (*below, seated at far right*) is another unique individual here in the cemetery. Like several others in this chapter, he is not a graduate of West Point, but Mahan served his entire military career here as a musician with the West Point Band. He completed his active-duty career as the drum major of the band sometime in the early 1940s.

The West Point Band is the oldest band in the US Army and is the oldest unit stationed at West Point. It has served continuously here since the Revolutionary War. It was officially named the West Point Band in 1817.

Mahan was born in Highland Falls. His father was an immigrant from Ireland, while his mother was a New York native. He joined the Army, and the West Point Band, in 1917 at age twenty-six as a "Musician, 2nd Class." He was promoted to sergeant by 1930 and ultimately retired as master sergeant, having not served anywhere but here. Mahan's wife, Lucille, was born in nearby Newburgh.

During his service as drum major of the band, Master Sergeant Mahan participated in all parades and public appearances of the band. It is noteworthy that during his tenure, the band was awarded a Meritorious Unit Citation by President Franklin D. Roosevelt. The mace carried by the drum major is inscribed with the Military Academy crest circled by oak leaves, symbolizing the unit citation. The sash worn by the drum major (*see below for the current example*) has red piping reflecting the Engineer Corps, which was stationed here in its earliest days, and the drum major is the only soldier on the parade ground who wears white feathers on his uniform cap (commonly called a "tar bucket"). He also carries a cadet saber in his uniform.

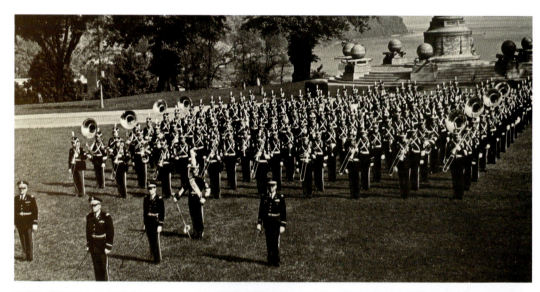

Colonel Henry A. Mucci
Section XXXII, Row F, Grave 102

Colonel Mucci graduated from West Point in 1936. A passion for lacrosse, and a disdain for academics, helped him place 246th out of 275 in his class. He was commissioned in the infantry and was the provost marshal at Pearl Harbor on December 7, 1941. He survived that experience and ended up in New Guinea in 1942 as the commanding officer of a group of artillerymen called the 98th Field Artillery Battalion (Pack), a mule-drawn outfit.

It is interesting enough that an infantryman ended up commanding an artillery battalion in New Guinea in 1942, but it soon became apparent why. Mucci was directed to disband his battalion, reduce it in strength, and reconstitute it as the 6th Ranger Battalion. This he did with great vigor.

After a year of arduous Ranger training in the New Guinea jungle, Colonel Mucci's 6th Rangers took part in the invasion of Leyte, during the recapture of the Philippine Islands. In January 1943, Mucci was notified that his unit was tasked to conduct a rescue mission on a POW camp called Cabanatuan. There were approximately five hundred American POWs there who had been captured during the battle for Bataan long before, and the US advance was nearing the camp. Fearing that the Japanese would massacre all the prisoners if they felt they were threatened by the US Army advance, General Walter Krueger, Sixth Army commander, ordered the 6th Ranger battalion to conduct a raid to seize the camp, kill the guards, and bring all the prisoners out to safety.

The mission went almost like clockwork. After some very brief planning, and no rehearsal, the Rangers moved to the camp without detection and attacked it on the night of January 28, 1943. Every prisoner was evacuated safely, with only two of the Rangers killed in action. One POW died of his injuries just minutes before they reached the safety of American lines. Mucci was awarded the Distinguished Service Cross for his leadership and heroism in leading the raid and became a national hero in the United States.

In 2005, a movie was made about the raid titled *The Great Raid*, with Benjamin Bratt playing the role of Colonel Mucci.

248 *Stone Tapestry*

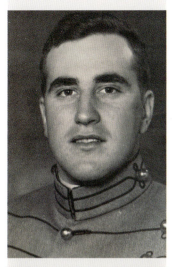

Major Timothy E. Krebs
Section XXXII, Row D, Grave 62

Major Tim Krebs represents one example of another sort of soldier buried here in the cemetery. There are many men and women who served in the shadows who were active in the Central Intelligence Agency or other shadowy organizations, going all the way back to the Office of Strategic Services (OSS) in World War II. Their service necessarily remains quiet and out of sight, especially to those in the "real Army," who rarely knew what these men and women were doing. Their accomplishments must remain behind a veil of secrecy.

Colonel Mucci, whom we just met, was reputed to have worked in such an assignment later in his life while living in Bangkok. We have already met General Wayne Downing of USSOCOM, who spent most of his career in such assignments. We will meet another, Red White, in the next chapter. Tim Krebs is another example.

Major Krebs graduated from West Point in the Class of 1970 and was commissioned in the infantry. He began his career with a series of infantry assignments, first in Germany with the 3rd Infantry Division, then at the Infantry Center at Fort Benning. He commanded a combat support company in the 3rd Battalion, 70th Armor, then was assigned to Fort Carson, Colorado. He was sent to a joint tour with the Air Force when he became the ground liaison officer at Hill Air Force Base. He then disappeared from the larger Army's view and spent the next nineteen years working in a classified organization, first as an active-duty officer until his retirement, then as a contractor.

Major Krebs worked on programs focusing on exploiting the current and future tactical potential of national systems and integrating the capabilities into the Army's tactical-decision-making process. For his efforts he was awarded the Legion of Merit, a rare award for an officer in the grade of major. It is symbolic of his contributions to national defense.

Such officers are not common and usually remain unnoticed. Their work is done behind a veil of secrecy, and their efficiency reports and award citations are often classified. The public never hears of them, and in most cases even their spouses do not know precisely what they are doing. Yet, their work is crucial to the defense of the nation. I included Major Krebs in these pages as a representative of the others, to help rectify that omission.

Colonel Roger H. Nye
Section XXXII, Row A, Grave 1

Colonel Roger Nye was a member of the West Point Class of 1946. We have seen two of his classmates already: General Sam Walker and Calvert P. Benedict. Nye was commissioned in the armor branch and served in the Korean War, earning two Bronze Star medals with "V" device for valor.

After the war, Nye attended Princeton for a master's degree, then came back to West Point for a tour as an instructor in the Social Sciences Department. Major Nye then attended the Command and General Staff College at Fort Leavenworth. He returned to West Point for a second tour as a professor, again in the Social Science Department.

Nye then attended Columbia University, where he earned a PhD in American history. In 1971, Nye returned to West Point for a third time as professor and deputy head of the History Department. He remained here until 1975, when he retired from active duty. Colonel Nye was recalled again to active duty in 1977 to serve in the Office of the Chief of Staff to review the education and training program for all officers. That assignment lasted for a year, when he again retired.

In his retirement, Colonel Nye became an author of two superb books: *The Challenge of Command* in 1986 and a second on General Patton (*The Patton Mind: The Professional Development of an Extraordinary Leader*) in 1991. In addition to his books, Colonel Nye served as the editor of the Art of Command series of essays, and he served as the chairman of the Friends of the West Point Library organization.

Colonel Nye's books are used in the curriculum at West Point and other Army service schools and reflect his wisdom and scholarly approach to leadership and command.

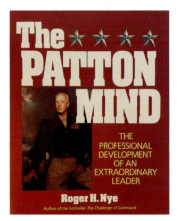

CHAPTER 12

Sections XXXVI and XXXIV

In this, the final chapter of our stroll through the cemetery, we will find a microcosm of the earlier decedents in the book. We will find a superintendent, an athlete, several generals, a Rhodes scholar, and a chaplain. We will also find something we have not previously encountered. In this section of the cemetery, we will find several women graduates and a female command sergeant major. The first woman graduate who was killed in action lies here. We also will find foreign-exchange students, including the first Asian graduate of the Military Academy. This section of the cemetery has many who fell during the Vietnam War and the global war on terror, mainly from Iraq and Afghanistan.

We will end our tour at the grave of one of the earliest graduates, General René De Russy, who was a member of the Class of 1812, only ten years after the founding of the Military Academy. In a sense we have come full circle, having begun in the Old Cadet Chapel honoring men who had fought for this country before it became a country. Now, after a lengthy tour around the grounds and seeing distinguished men and women from all classes and all conflicts, as well as much peacetime development, we will end with a man who graduated just in time for the War of 1812.

It is also fitting that we end our tour next to the most recognizable monument in the whole cemetery, that of Egbert Viele, whom we met in chapter 7. It is a good place, and a good time, to reflect on what we have seen on the tour. This is a place of serene beauty and exemplifies many of the higher human virtues, such as loyalty, honor, mercy, duty, and, most of all, love.

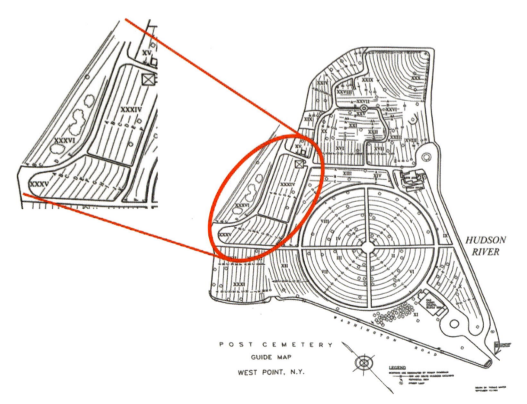

253

Colonel Lawrence K. "Red" White
Section XXXVI, Row A, Grave 40

"Red" White is another soldier who, like Major Tim Krebs, labored in secrecy, although not for his whole career. White graduated with the Class of 1933 and served in the Pacific theater during World War II. He was decorated several times for valor in combat, earning a Distinguished Service Cross, two Silver Stars, three Bronze Stars (valor), and two Legions of Merit. Unfortunately he also was awarded the Purple Heart and was wounded so severely in the Philippines in 1945 that he spent two years recovering in Army hospitals.

After Colonel White was released from the hospital, he was medically retired from the Army and immediately went to work in the Central Intelligence Agency. His first assignments there were in the Operations Branch. Within his first two years there, he became the chief of the Foreign Broadcast Information Branch within the Office of Operations, where he directed all overt collection functions on foreign countries. According to an interview with White conducted in 2000, the Foreign Broadcast branch had a reputation as being a rather "unruly and troublesome organization," and Colonel White was successful in tamping it down.

Because of his success, White was promoted to be the deputy assistant director of the Office of Operations in late 1950. Two more years and he was further promoted to be the assistant to the deputy director for administration. In 1954, White was promoted to be the deputy director for administration by Allen Dulles, who was the director of central intelligence (DCI), and he held that post until 1965.

In 1965 the new DCI, Admiral William Raborn, appointed Colonel White to be the executive director–comptroller, where he was responsible for all the agency's budget proposals and outlays. He finally retired from that position in 1972.

A sharp-eyed viewer in the cemetery might notice that White's award of the CIA's Distinguished Intelligence Medal was misspelled on the headstone as "distinquished." A stone mason's mistake does not diminish the achievements of a man who spent twenty-five years working in the shadows.

254 *Stone Tapestry*

General Theodore W. Parker
Section XXXVI, Row B, Grave 90

General Theodore Parker is one of those graduates who served with distinction both in the military sphere and in the policy sphere. He graduated from the Military Academy in 1931 and was commissioned in the field artillery. He returned to West Point in 1935 to teach in the Philosophy Department and remained there for three years. Following that tour, he went to Iceland for two years, where he served as an aide to Major General Charles Bonesteel.

During World War II, Parker was on the staff of the Ninth Army in Europe, where he served as the G-3 (operations officer). At the conclusion of the war, Parker wrote the official history of the Ninth Army, titled *Conquer: The Official History of the Ninth Army in World War II*.

Between the wars, Parker served as the chief of staff of the 10th Infantry Division (Training) at Fort Riley, Kansas. When the Korean War broke out, Colonel Parker was sent to the peninsula, where he commanded first a division artillery and then a corps artillery. After the war he was promoted to major general and commanded the 1st Infantry Division, again at Fort Riley. General Parker returned to Washington as the deputy chief of staff operations (DCSOPS) in 1962 and served in that capacity during the Cuban Missile Crisis.

From a policy standpoint, he had several assignments, including a year in the executive office of the president and a three-year tour in Paris on the staff of the North Atlantic Council. When he returned from Paris, General Parker worked as a special assistant to the chairman of the Joint Chiefs of Staff. When he was promoted to four-star rank, he was transferred back to Europe, where he served as the chief of staff of the Supreme Headquarters Allied Powers Europe (SHAPE).

When General Parker retired from active duty, he went to work for the then governor of New York, Nelson Rockefeller, where he served as the New York State commissioner of transportation.

Major General Henry R. McKenzie
Section XXXVI, Row B, Grave 75

Logisticians are a special breed of men. Most people who think about military operations tend to think about battles, maneuvers, and the Pattons or Schwarzkopfs of the Army. But there is an old Army saying that is more representative of the truth: "Amateurs talk tactics; professionals talk logistics." Without logistic support, tactical maneuvers mean nothing and frequently can't even be attempted.

Major General Henry McKenzie was a logistician's logistician during the most difficult war of all, World War II. Commissioned in the Class of 1929, he first joined the coast artillery. Bored with their peacetime inactivity, he quickly transferred to the Quartermaster Corps, convinced that the Army would always need supplies, even in peacetime, and so he expected more-interesting assignments. He certainly found them!

Graduating from Harvard in 1939 with a master's degree in business administration, he was soon caught up in the enormous expansion of the Army, and the subsequent logistics problems associated with that. In 1939 the Army had about 170,000 men on active duty; Portugal had a larger army than the United States did at the time. By 1945 that army had expanded to over eight million men, in ninety divisions, which had to be fed, equipped, organized, trained, and shipped across two oceans to the farthest theaters of war... and be expected to win when they got there. McKenzie played a leading role in this, both in the United States and later in the Pacific theater. He first went to work in Chicago, organizing the new Market Centers Program, which was responsible for controlling thirty-six different purchasing and distribution centers across the US for all fresh produce used by the Army. Later, this program was expanded to include dairy products and finally added meat and fish. More than fourteen million people were being served by these distribution centers.

He then went to the Pacific theater, where he was the quartermaster of the US Army, Middle Pacific, under General MacArthur. He was responsible for all quartermaster activities, including ammunition, food, petroleum products, clothing and equipment, and everything else an Army needs to survive.

After his retirement, General McKenzie became a professor of business administration at both San Francisco State College and the University of San Francisco.

First Lieutenant Laura M. Walker
Section XXXVI, Row B, Grave 64C

Lieutenant Walker was born to a military family and, as such, moved frequently. Her obituary says she lived in eighteen different cities and three countries before she graduated from high school, which, fittingly enough, was the Supreme Headquarters Allied Powers Europe (SHAPE) American High School in Belgium. She joined the Long Gray Line in the Class of 2003. She was an athlete while a cadet, was captain of the women's handball team, and led that team to a national championship.

Walker was commissioned in the Corps of Engineers, and her first duty assignment was with the 555th Engineer Brigade at Fort Lewis. They soon went to Iraq in the first deployment of Operation Iraqi Freedom, and she worked in support of the 4th Infantry Division. She earned the right to wear the 4th Division patch as a combat patch during that deployment, something both of her grandfathers experienced, having served with the 4th Infantry in World War II and in Vietnam.

She returned safely from her deployment to Iraq, and the following year Lieutenant Walker deployed again, this time with the 864th Engineer Combat Battalion (Heavy), to Afghanistan. Five months into her second combat tour, Lieutenant Walker was killed in action in an improvised explosive device (IED) attack. She was awarded the Bronze Star and Purple Heart for her final combat tour, as well as the Combat Action Badge.

There have been women graduates from West Point since the Class of 1980, but Laura Walker was the first to give her life for her country in combat.

Second Lieutenant Emily J. T. Perez
Section XXXVI, Row B, Grave 64F

Lieutenant Perez lies almost next to Lieutenant Walker. Perez was a graduate in the Class of 2005, referred to as the "9-11 Class" because they were plebes when the horrific attacks were made on the World Trade Center and Pentagon. We have already met young Matthew Ferrara, another member of the Class of 2005.

Lieutenant Perez was a stellar cadet and was the command sergeant major of the corps in her senior year. She was in the top 10 percent of her class in academics as well and was a star performer on the women's track team, competing in the triple jump.

After graduation, Lieutenant Perez was commissioned in the Medical Service Corps and, like Lieutenant Walker before her, went to the 4th Infantry Division. In November 2005, a mere six months after graduation, Lieutenant Perez deployed to Iraq as a Medical Service Corps officer. On September 12, 2006, she was killed by an IED explosion in her vehicle at Al Kifl, Iraq.

258 *Stone Tapestry*

Command Sergeant Major Mary E. Sutherland

Section XXXVI, Row C, Grave 97

We now meet another superb woman soldier and leader, Command Sergeant Major Mary Sutherland. Sutherland enlisted in the Women's Army Corps in June 1969 at age eighteen as a clerk/typist. At that time, that was one of a very few military occupational specialties open to women.

Sutherland served as an enlisted soldier and noncommissioned officer throughout her career. She was stationed in Germany, Bosnia, Honduras, and Italy during her rise through the enlisted ranks in increasing positions of responsibility. She served as the command sergeant major at Fort Ord, California, and again in the division support command in the 1st Armored Division.

During her last seven years on active duty, CSM Sutherland served as the sergeant major of all three of the major commands here at West Point. She first was appointed the CSM of the US Corps of Cadets (USCC) on the commandant's staff. She then served as the CSM of the garrison command here at West Point, and finally she was appointed as the CSM of the United States Military Academy on the superintendent's staff, the most senior enlisted position at West Point. She was the first woman appointed to all three of these positions.

By the time she retired, CSM Sutherland had served on active duty in the Army for thirty-five years. She was the most senior female enlisted soldier ever to serve in the Army. After she hit the thirty-year mark, it took a special authorization from the secretary of the Army for her to continue for her final five years. Of her thirty-five years of service, sixteen years were spent in overseas assignments.

In 2015, the garrison command at West Point dedicated the new community center to the memory of CSM Sutherland.

Chaplain James D. Ford
Section XXXVI, Row C, Grave 102

James Ford is another chaplain we meet along our stroll. Ford was ordained as a Lutheran priest after graduating from Gustavus Adolphus College in Minnesota and the Augustana Theological Seminary. Both his father and his grandfather were Lutheran priests. In 1961 he came to West Point to serve as a Lutheran priest, and in 1965 he was named by President Lyndon Johnson as the West Point chaplain, becoming the youngest chaplain to be so named.

Chaplain Ford served in that capacity until 1979. In 1976, Chaplain Ford, along with two other people, sailed across the Atlantic in a 31-foot sailboat named *Yankee Doodle* to honor the American Bicentennial. The crew of three departed Plymouth, England, and fifty-one days later sailed up the Hudson River to dock at West Point.

In 1979, Chaplain Ford departed West Point and went to Washington, where he became the chaplain of the US House of Representatives. He served in that capacity for twenty years before retiring. As the House chaplain, Ford presided over the opening and closing of all sessions of the Congress and served as the spiritual advisor to House members and their families.

During the impeachment debate in the House during President Clinton's administration, Chaplain Ford came to the podium to offer a prayer before the final vote was taken. He chose to recite the Prayer of Saint Francis:

> Let us pray, using the words of St. Francis: "Lord, make us instruments of your peace. Where there is hatred, let us sow love; where there is injury, pardon; where there is discord, union; where there is doubt, faith; where there is despair, hope."

Ford said he chose the prayer, and the timing, carefully.

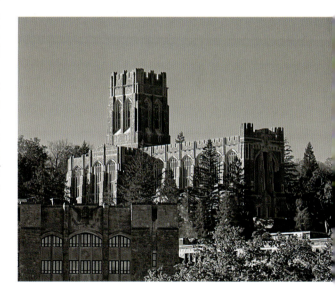

Lieutenant General John A. Heintges
Section XXXVI, Row D, Grave 146

John Heintges was born in Germany, the son of a German army officer who was killed in action in World War I. His family immigrated to the United States and became US citizens. Heintges graduated in the Class of 1936, along with General Westmoreland, whom we have already met. He was commissioned in the infantry and during World War II commanded a battalion in the 7th Infantry Regiment, and then the regiment itself. During his combat tour in Sicily, Italy, southern France, and Germany, Heintges was awarded three Silver Stars for valor in combat, a Purple Heart, and five Bronze Star medals. His regiment had the distinction of capturing the Berghof, Hitler's retreat in Berchtesgaden, Germany.

After the war ended, Heintges returned to the United States and attended the War College. Upon graduation from there, he returned to Germany and was appointed the chief of the US Army group on the military assistance mission to West Germany. In this tour he was responsible for devising the training plans for the newly created West German army. This must have been a most interesting assignment for a man whose father had fought in the old German army, who himself had fought the Wehrmacht and was now responsible for training the new German army.

After a short assignment training US soldiers at Fort Dix, New Jersey, Heintges assumed command of the Program Evaluation Office in Laos, where he drafted plans for improving the performance of the Royal Lao Army. During this assignment, he separated from the Army for the duration of the tour so he could serve as a "civilian," returning to active duty upon the completion of the assignment.

General Heintges then commanded the 5th Infantry Division, followed by command of the Infantry School at Fort Benning, Georgia. Upon promotion to three stars, he took command of the I Corps in South Korea. He then went to Vietnam as deputy in the MACV headquarters until he was relieved by General Creighton Abrams. He returned to Europe, where he assumed duty as the deputy commander, Seventh US Army. He finally retired as the deputy commander in chief, US Army, Europe.

262 *Stone Tapestry*

Major General Chih Wang
Section XXXVI, Row D, Grave 132B

Major General Chih Wang is not the first Chinese student at West Point; that distinction belongs to Ying Hsing Wen of the Class of 1926. We will meet Wen shortly on our stroll. Wang graduated with the Class of 1932 after first graduating from the Norwich Academy with a degree in history.

Wang then returned to China and became an English teacher at Hunan University. The conflict between the Chinese Communist Party and the Chinese Nationalist government was already beginning, and local paramilitary forces were raised to protect road and rail shipments of salt and other commodities to the countryside. Wang served in this force. When World War II began in China (in 1937, after the Japanese invaded Manchuria), Wang took command of an engineer battalion.

By 1941, upon American entrance into the war, Wang was a colonel and was appointed to General MacArthur's staff as a liaison officer to the Chinese forces. This assignment took him to the Philippines, and when they fell, to Australia with General MacArthur.

In 1943, Wang was sent by General MacArthur to present his (MacArthur's) plan of the campaign to Generalissimo Chiang Kai Shek in Chungking, China. Wang remained with MacArthur throughout the war and was promoted several times until he was a major general in the Chinese army. At the Japanese surrender on the battleship *Missouri* in 1945, Wang was successful in persuading MacArthur that the Chinese representative should be the second person to sign the instrument of surrender after Fleet Admiral Chester Nimitz of the United States because China had been in the war the longest.

After the war ended, Wang continued in his role as the Chinese army liaison officer with MacArthur from his Tokyo headquarters. Eventually he returned to China and headed up the Chinese Military Academy at Hankou.

When China fell to the Communists in 1949, General Wang fled to Taiwan with the Nationalist government. From 1965 to 1983, he served as the academic dean and dean of Chinese studies at Soochow University in Taiwan. In 1976 he immigrated to the United States to take a teaching post at Michigan State University.

Brigadier General Charles R. "Monk" Meyer
Section XXXVI, Row D, Grave 132A

Charles R. "Monk" Meyer was an unlikely football hero, and an equally unlikely war hero. At West Point he stood 5 feet 9 and weighed 150 pounds but was their star quarterback in 1936 and 1937. He was the runner-up to the first Heisman trophy ever awarded and was selected as an All-American.

Meyer's father was an Army officer, and he was born at West Point in 1911. He graduated with the Class of 1937 and was commissioned in the infantry. He began World War II in Pearl Harbor and served throughout the Pacific theater. He commanded the 2nd Battalion, 127th Infantry Regiment, in Luzon and earned a Distinguished Service Cross for single-handedly destroying two Japanese pillboxes that were blocking the advance of his battalion.

During his World War II combat service, in addition to his DSC, Meyer was awarded two Silver Stars, two Bronze Stars, and two Purple Hearts. After the war, Meyer became the operations officer for the Sixth Army in Japan and further served in the Korean War. After a short stint as the assistant division commander of the 1st Infantry Division, General Meyer went to Vietnam and commanded the Area Support Command for the Military Assistance Command, Vietnam. Meyer was also awarded two Distinguished Service Medals for his meritorious performance of duty at the Sixth Army Headquarters, making him one of the most decorated senior officers of his time.

In addition to his awards for valor, he was also elected to the College Football Hall of Fame and was awarded the Gold Medal Award by the National Football Foundation. In that honor he was following in the footsteps of both General Dwight Eisenhower and General Douglas MacArthur. From college football all-star to combat infantryman in three wars is quite a legacy. It is unlikely that many members of the College Football Hall of Fame have such a sterling combat record.

In addition he left a legacy in the Long Gray Line when his son, Charles R. Meyer II, graduated in the Class of 1967.

Congressman Benjamin A. Gilman
Section XXXIV, Row AA, Grave 29

Congressman Benjamin Gilman is the first member of the House of Representatives that we meet on our tour, and the only one buried in the cemetery. A contemporary of Chaplain Ford, whom we just left, they would have surely known each other from their days together in the House. Gilman represented the 26th District of New York in the House for thirty years (1973–2003).

Mr. Gilman entered the Army Air Corps in 1942 and served until the end of the war in the Pacific theater. He was an aircrew member serving on B-29 bombers and participated in the bombing raids over Japan. Gilman was awarded the Distinguished Flying Cross and several Air Medals during his combat time and attained the rank of staff sergeant.

After the war, Gilman graduated from the University of Pennsylvania's Wharton School of Business in 1946 and went on to graduate from the New York Law School four years later. He served as the assistant attorney general for New York briefly and practiced law in his home district until 1967. He was elected that year to the New York State Assembly and served several terms there until 1972. In 1973 he was elected to the US House of Representatives.

During his time in Washington, Mr. Gilman served on several committees and was the chair of the House Committee on International Relations. He was awarded the Secretary's Distinguished Service Medal, the highest honor a secretary of state can bestow on a civilian. He chaired the House Committee on Foreign Affairs from 1995 to 2002.

The congressman was a strong supporter of India and was very involved in Indian affairs in the House. In 2001 he was awarded the Padma Vibhushan, the second-highest civilian award from the Indian government.

The Benjamin A. Gilman International Scholarship Award is established in his name, a Pell Grant award to further study abroad for deserving and meritorious students. When he retired, Representative Gilman was the oldest sitting member of the House. The Gilman Center at Orange County Community College is named for him.

Colonel Seth F. Hudgins Jr.
Section XXXIV, Row AA, Grave 9

Colonel Seth Hudgins was a member of the Class of 1964. He was another member of the Long Gray Line; his father and namesake graduated in the Class of 1939. Hudgins was commissioned in the armor branch and was an aviator. In his first Vietnam tour (1965–66), he served with the 17th Cavalry in the 101st Airborne Division. He flew Cobra gunships and was an aviation company commander. During this tour he earned three Bronze Stars, two of which were for valorous conduct, and a Combat Infantryman's Badge.

He served for a year as aide-de-camp for the commander of the Armor Center at Fort Knox, then returned to Vietnam. In this second tour he earned a Distinguished Flying Cross, another Bronze Star, and two Air Medals for valor.

Upon his return from his second Vietnam tour, Hudgins attended Syracuse University for a master's degree, then returned to West Point, where he joined the Tactical Department. At the completion of that tour, he went to Germany, where he served in a second company command assignment, then was named as aide-de-camp of the supreme Allied commander, Europe (SACEUR). He came back to West Point for another tour on the staff, commanded an aviation battalion, and did a tour in the Pentagon. In 1986, Colonel Hudgins returned to West Point for the third time and did not leave again. He was the chief of staff of the Corps of Cadets and then the deputy commandant before he retired.

Colonel Hudgins then joined the Association of Graduates and remained there until his retirement in 2007. He began as the executive vice president of the association from 1990 to 1993 and served as the association president from 1993 to 2007.

During his time at the AOG, Colonel Hudgins oversaw the Military Academy's bicentennial celebration in 2002, raising more than $200 million for the academy.

Lieutenant Colonel Jaimie E. Leonard
Section XXXIV, Row AA, Grave 6

Jaimie Leonard was destined for a military life even before she entered West Point. She entered Marion Military Academy on a merit-based scholarship prior to entering the Military Academy with the Class of 1997. She was commissioned in the military intelligence branch and was assigned to Fort Bragg, North Carolina, for her first tour.

She was no stranger to war; in her first assignment she was deployed to Bosnia and served with the International Force (IFOR). Her next assignment took her to Korea, where she served as an intelligence officer on the staff of the 2nd Infantry Division.

Next, then captain Leonard served in the Iraq War in Operation Iraqi Freedom (OIF), where she was awarded a Bronze Star medal. In 2007, Captain Leonard served a tour in the Pentagon on the Joint Staff and, while there, earned a master's degree in public policy from Georgetown University.

In 2011, Captain Leonard was deployed to Afghanistan, where she served as the intelligence officer on the staff of the Regional Command (South).

In 2013, Major Leonard joined the 2nd Brigade Combat Team of the 10th Mountain Division at Fort Drum, New York. The unit immediately deployed to Afghanistan, marking her fourth tour in a combat zone since graduation. While she was training an Afghan army unit in small-arms training at Zarghun Shahr, an insurgent dressed as an Afghan soldier turned his weapon on the instructors, killing Major Leonard, LTC Todd Clark, and civilian Joseph Morabito. After her death, Leonard was promoted to lieutenant colonel. Her awards included two Bronze Stars, the Purple Heart, two Meritorious Service Medals, the Joint Commendation Medal, and three Army Commendation Medals.

In her sixteen-year Army career, LTC Leonard spent five tours overseas: four in active combat zones and another in Korea.

268 *Stone Tapestry*

Major John A. Hottell III
Section XXXIV, Row C, Grave 116

As we come near to the end of our stroll, we meet Major John Hottell III, the last of our friends of the modern era in our walk. Hottell graduated in the Class of 1964, a classmate of Seth Hudgins's, whom we have just met. Hottell was the tenth man in his class and was awarded a Rhodes scholarship as a result. He was commissioned in the infantry, but after his Infantry Basic Course he went off to Oxford University, Magdalen College, to study until 1968. Hottell was an athlete, and while he was at Oxford he won the British National Diving Championship—not once, but twice in consecutive years.

Upon taking his degree at Oxford, Captain Hottell was assigned to Vietnam and assumed command of a rifle company in the 1st Battalion, 8th Infantry. He extended his combat tour in Vietnam so he could be brought up to the division staff of the 1st Cavalry Division. Captain Hottell served there as aide-de-camp to Major General George Casey, the division commander. In 1970, both Casey and Hottell, and four others, perished in a helicopter crash in the mountains of Vietnam. Hottell was awarded two Silver Stars for valor in combat in his short life, as well as three Bronze Stars.

Major Hottell (he was posthumously promoted) drafted his own obituary shortly before his death, and it has been widely publicized since then. A short excerpt reads thus:

I loved the Army: it reared me, it nurtured me, and it gave me the most satisfying years of my life. Thanks to it I have lived an entire lifetime in 26 years. It is only fitting that I should die in its service. We all have but one death to spend, and insofar as it can have any meaning it finds it in the service of comrades-in-arms. And yet, I deny that I died FOR anything – not my Country, not my Army, not my fellow man, none of these things. I LIVED for these things, and the manner in which I chose to do it involved the very real chance that I would die in the execution of my duties.

Each year a silver saber is presented in Hottell's memory to select students who excel in history at West Point.

Lieutenant General Ying-Hsing Wen
Section XXXIV, Row F, Grave 218

We pause here at the grave of the first Chinese—indeed, Asian—graduate of West Point. Ying-Hsing Wen first attended Pieyang College in Tientsin, China, and subsequently the Virginia Military Institute in Lexington, Virginia. After a special act of Congress, he and one other Chinese cadet were admitted to West Point in 1905 and graduated in the Class of 1909 (the second Chinese cadet, Ting Chia Chen, graduated as well but was the last man in his class). Another famous member of the Class of 1909, General George Patton, also attended VMI for a year before he came to West Point, but unlike Wen, Patton took five years to graduate. So while they were classmates here, they were not at VMI.

After graduation, Wen returned to China and participated in the revolution that overthrew the Manchu dynasty and set China on a path to becoming a republic. He served in the Chinese army, becoming a brigadier general by 1920. Ultimately he rose to the grade of lieutenant general in World War II. He fought both the Communists and the Japanese as a general under Generalissimo Chiang Kai-Shek and served alongside Major General Chih Wang, whom we met.

At the end of the war, General Wen retired from the Chinese army. From 1946 to 1951, Wen served as a senator in the Chinese national government.

In 1951 he immigrated to the United States. He moved to Silver Spring, Maryland, where he opened a laundry business.

Every year, two cadets are chosen by the Foreign Languages Department for the Lieutenant General Ying Hsing Wen Memorial Award. The award funds research trips overseas for the chosen winners.

In 2018, General Wen was posthumously awarded the Generational Legacy Award by the Museum of Chinese in America for his contributions to improving relations between the Chinese and Americans.

First Lieutenant Thomas E. Selfridge
Section XXXIV, Row F, Grave 232

We should note here that Lieutenant Selfridge is not, in fact, buried under this monument. Instead, he is buried in Arlington National Cemetery. This stone was erected here by his classmates in his memory.

Selfridge graduated from the Military Academy in the Class of 1903, along with perhaps his most famous classmate, General of the Army Douglas MacArthur. Selfridge was commissioned in the field artillery and was assigned to the Presidio of San Francisco during the great earthquake of 1906. He participated in the recovery and cleanup operations there. Afterward he was assigned to Fort Myer, Virginia, in the US Army Aeronautical Division of the Signal Corps, where he was to learn to fly. He was slated to fly one of the Army dirigibles and was training toward that objective.

Selfridge was named the US government's representative to the fledgling Aerial Experiment Association, directed by Alexander Graham Bell. He began to fly, first in kites and later in an experimental aircraft he helped design. In May 1908, Selfridge became the first military officer to fly an aircraft in Hammondsport, New York. He flew several times at ever-increasing distances in this aircraft, *White Wing*, in summer 1908.

In August 1908, Selfridge was designated as one of three pilots to fly the Army's first dirigible, imaginatively named Army Dirigible Number One, from Fort Omaha, Nebraska, to the Missouri State Fair in Sedalia, Missouri. But before that epic event could take place, Selfridge returned to Fort Myer to go through the acceptance trials of the Army's first winged aircraft. The Army had agreed to buy the aircraft from the Wright brothers, and the acceptance trials were set to begin in September 1908.

Orville Wright brought the first Wright Military Flyer to Fort Myer, and he was to fly it while Selfridge was the passenger. In his fifth circuit around Fort Meyer, the propeller broke and slashed the control wires to the rudder. Selfridge was mortally injured in the crash, while Orville sustained serious injuries.

272 *Stone Tapestry*

Brigadier General René E. De Russy
Section XXXIV, Row F, Grave 255

And so we arrive at our final monument on our stroll. Here we find Brigadier General René De Russy, who graduated (at the bottom of his class!) in the Class of 1812. De Russy was commissioned in the Corps of Engineers, despite his low academic standing, and immediately went to war.

After the War of 1812 was settled, De Russy went to New York Harbor and became the superintending engineer of the construction of the forts there. That became his forte, and in his subsequent assignments he oversaw building or repairing harbor forts in coastal cities all around the United States. After New York he went to the Gulf of Mexico and worked on coastal fortifications there for several years.

He then returned to New York and supervised the building of Fort Hamilton in New York Harbor. Fort Hamilton served as an Army headquarters for many years after; General of the Army George Marshall served there as an aide to a division commander just prior to our entry into World War I.

In 1833, De Russy returned to West Point, where he became the superintendent immediately following Sylvanus Thayer. De Russy served as the superintendent for a period of five years, during which he solidified and built upon the reforms that Thayer had made during his own tenure.

After his time at West Point, De Russy again went back to his business of constructing harbor defenses. He worked both in Virginia in the Hampton Roads area and in Delaware and was named to the Atlantic Coastal Defense Board. In 1854 he went west and served in the San Francisco area on their harbor defenses. He was also named to the Pacific Coastal Defense Board while he served in San Francisco. He continued to bounce back and forth, returning to the Washington area in 1857, then back to San Francisco in 1861.

De Russy died in San Francisco in 1865. He is credited with inventing the barbette depressing gun carriage for use in coastal artillery forts, to enable gun carriages to swing down under cover when not actually firing.

Sections XXXVI and XXXIV 273

Epilogue

And thus we finish next to the most obvious of all the memorials here in the cemetery, the pyramidal mausoleum of Brigadier General Viele. As we stroll down the gravel path back to the Chapel, I would like for the reader to indulge your tour guide in one final point, and one final grave.

I came to realize, while drafting this book, the terrible injustice I was doing to all the men and women buried here who were not included as part of the famous gravesites. As I walked through the cemetery, I could almost feel their silent rebuke: "What of us? Was our life not noteworthy? Were we not important enough to include?" Yet, the tyranny of space prevented me from including everyone, lest the book be too heavy to lift.

But in a very real sense, those who lie silent between the famous are the very material of the tapestry of the Long Gray Line and reflect a deeper meaning of "service to the country." They are the ones who toiled in the shadows, who tried their best in their own lives to live up to the ideals of the Military Academy, who never achieved lasting fame or public celebrity but nonetheless carried on the tradition of faithful adherence to duty, honor, and country. They represent the continuity, the background fabric, without which the famous would be merely isolated, unconnected, bright examples instead of the highlights of a continuous whole. If one uses the cadet full-dress gray coat as a metaphor, the Westmorelands, the Schwarzkopfs, and the Custers are the gilt buttons, while the remainder make up the whole gray cloth of the coat.

They served as living examples of the West Point ideals within their own families, and for their friends and neighbors. In their own way they are even more important than the famous because they touched many more lives, and much more intimately, than the gilded historical figures of the famous. I urge the reader to stop and consider them carefully during the walk through the stone tapestry of the cemetery. Reflect on why there are so many children who followed their parents' footsteps along the Long Gray Line. It was because they wanted to be like their parent, and there can be no higher compliment than that.

And what of the wives? Those who kept hearth and home safe, who raised children and managed households while their husbands were off at war gaining glory? Many worked themselves, in addition to their family duties, and many indeed were noteworthy in their own right. A whole separate book should be authored about the Army wives who kept their families together while the men were off serving their nation. Alas, it cannot be this book.

So when walking through the cemetery or perusing the photos in this book, reflect a bit on the people "in between," not mentioned, but who are intimately connected to West Point. They are the real substance of the values this place represents.

For example, on our way back to the road leading to the Chapel, stop briefly in Section XXX, Row AA, at Grave 5. The name should be familiar: it is Lieutenant Colonel James F. Holcomb, along with his wife, Ann. Holcomb graduated from West

275

Point in 1945, along with Larry Jones, Joe McCarthy, and George Eyster, all of whom we have met. He was an infantry officer who served for twenty-two years and three wars, earning a Legion of Merit, Bronze Star, and Purple Heart along the way, along with a coveted Combat Infantryman Badge. He went to graduate school at Georgia Tech, majoring in electrical engineering, and taught at West Point. He retired from the Army in 1966 but voluntarily asked to return to active duty in 1969 so he could go to the Vietnam War; the Army agreed and he did. Before he arrived, his classmate George Eyster was killed. Holcomb was there commanding a brigade in the 1st Cavalry Division when the helicopter crash that took young John Hottell's life also killed another classmate, his friend and division commander, Major General George Casey. He and Ann raised a strong and loving family of five children, two of whom went to West Point themselves, as did one of his grandsons. He embodied the very concept of duty to his children.

Cemeteries are, of necessity, a place of death, but if human life is to have any meaning at all, it resides in the memory of the people, the deeds, and the societies that have gone before. The culture of the Military Academy is embedded within these 14 acres; its motto, the words "Duty, Honor, Country," are carved in stone on many of the monuments. One can't help but marvel at the wide and varied contributions of the men and women buried here, in the field of war but also in engineering, railways, flight, city planning, astronautics, music, sports, and many others. These men and women were special through their lives, and our nation is enriched because they lived, studied, competed, and worked here in America.

They were mostly soldiers, of course. They fought British tyranny in the Revolutionary War, defeated Britain again in 1815, subdued Mexico, preserved the fragile and precious Union, and saved Europe from German domination not once, but twice. They fought and lost, then returned and won in the jungles in Burma, in Indochina, in the islands of the Pacific, and on the Korean Peninsula. They developed land warfare in the age of the telegraph and the railroad, amphibious warfare across the globe in World War II, and helicopter warfare in Vietnam. They developed our Air Force from its very birth, swept the skies clear of Communist aircraft in Korea and Vietnam, and maintained that superiority in the air ever since. They turned the Iraqi army from the fourth-largest army in the world to the second-largest army in Iraq in one hundred hours. They fought terrorism in Afghanistan and brought security to Iraq, even if it was thrown away afterward. They fought the Cold War and kept the Soviet empire at bay for four decades. They are still fighting global Islamic terrorism.

They also were civil servants. They developed Central Park and mapped Manhattan. They built the railroads that entwined the states of the fledgling Union and bound it together from coast to coast. They perfected and accomplished probably the two finest engineering achievements in the twentieth century: the Panama Canal and the Apollo moon landing. They governed a defeated Germany and Japan with a magnanimous spirit and did the same in Iraq and Afghanistan in conjunction with their new civil governments. They were spies—some of them—who toiled in the dark. They wrote music, coached sports teams, and taught religious devotions. There is more to the story of this cemetery than mere excellence in war; it touches all of the human experience.

The achievements of the men and women gathered in this serene and peaceful 14 acres tell the story of the development, maturation, and dominance of the United States over more than two hundred years in world affairs, from thirteen separate British colonies to a global force representing freedom and democracy everywhere on the globe. This is truly a place sacred to the memory of the men and women who rest here, but also a place sacred to our country and the ideals of liberty wherever found.

In Rick Atkinson's book *The Long Gray Line*, when mentioning the cemetery he quotes the poet Shelley, who was describing the Protestant cemetery in Rome. Shelley had written, "It might make one in love with death, to think that one should be buried in so sweet a place." Just so.

APPENDIX

Men of the Class of 1973 in the Cemetery

Gaylyn F. Jones was admitted to West Point from Oklahoma. He was commissioned in the Transportation Corps. He was medically retired with disability in 1976 as a first lieutenant and passed away in El Paso, Texas, on December 28, 1976.

George S. Perkins came to West Point from New York. He was commissioned in the armor branch and his first assignment was with the 1st Battalion, 70th Armor, in Germany, 1974–76. He was awarded an Army Commendation Medal after this assignment. He then was assigned to the 4th Brigade of the 4th Infantry Division from 1976 to 1980. Perkins attended Boston University for a master's degree, then returned to West Point in 1983, where he was an instructor in the Behavioral Sciences and Leadership Department. Major Perkins died on July 23, 1984.

Robert E. Morris came to West Point from Alaska. He was commissioned in the Corps of Engineers and was a company commander in the 864th Combat Engineer Battalion from 1973 to 1977. He attended Cornell University for a master's degree and from 1980 to 1982 was a project engineer in the US Engineer District (USED), Saudi Arabia. He returned to Alaska to be the resident engineer in the USED Alaska. After a tour as the operations officer for the 15th Engineer Battalion, he attended the College of Naval Command and Staff. He returned to the 15th Engineers as the executive officer, then took command of the 84th Engineer Battalion in Hawaii. Morris attended the Army War College in 1993 and passed away on May 21, 1998.

Patrick A. Putignano came to West Point from New Jersey. Commissioned in the armor branch, his first assignment was in the 4th Infantry Division as a platoon leader, then as aide-de-camp to the assistant division commander. He held troop command in the 1st Squadron, 10th Cavalry, then served on the 8th Infantry Division staff. He obtained a master's degree from Princeton University and returned to West Point, where he taught in the Social Sciences Department. Putignano served next as a White House Fellow, then attended the Command and General Staff College. He became the legislative assistant to the US Senate from 1987 to 1988, then was appointed the special assistant to the secretary of the Air Force from 1988 to 1989. Pat then went to work for General Dynamics, then SAIC, and finally the American Legion. He was serving as the vice president of Omega Tech when he passed away on September 13, 2003.

Daniel L. Edelstein came from New York. He was commissioned in the infantry and spent 1973–78 in the 1st Battalion, 28th Infantry, at Fort Riley, Kansas. He resigned his commission in 1979 and went to work for Proctor & Gamble. He rose in responsibilities there, beginning as a department manager and then rising to operations group manager and associate director, and in 1992 became a plant manager. He became a director in 1996. Dan died in Phoenix, Maryland, on March 18, 2005.

Robert S. Mair came to West Point from Pennsylvania. He was commissioned in the armor branch and served in the 2nd Squadron, 2nd Armored Cavalry Regiment, in Germany from 1974 to 1977. He then went to Flight School. After graduation he joined the 4th Squadron, 9th Cavalry, and then the 2nd Aviation Battalion. He attended the Naval Postgraduate School, where he earned a master's degree in aeronautical engineering. Mair then went to Edwards Air Force Base to serve as a test pilot, and he remained at Edwards at the Army Aviation Technical Test Center. Mair became the chief of the Airworthiness Quality Test Directorate. He retired in 1993 and returned to Pennsylvania, where he joined Swoyer Plumbing and Heating, Inc. Robert died on April 3, 2006.

Men of the Class of 1973 in the Cemetery   279

Robert V. Kurrus came to West Point from Illinois. Commissioned in the Finance Corps, his first assignment was with the 172nd Infantry Brigade in Alaska from 1974 to 1977. He then went to Rock Island Arsenal, where he served in the finance office. After earning a master's degree from the Florida Institute of Technology, he returned to West Point to serve in the Office of the Director of Intercollegiate Athletics. In 1984 he was sent to serve in the finance office in Sinops, Turkey, and then to Saint Louis, Missouri. Kurrus graduated from the Command and General Staff College in 1987 and participated in Operation Desert Storm in 1990–91. He commanded the 39th Finance Battalion in Germany from 1993 to 1995. He served in the Defense Finance and Accounting Service in Indianapolis until his retirement in 2001, then rejoined them as a civilian. Kurrus died on September 28, 2007.

Richard M. Johnson came to West Point from Virginia. He was commissioned in the infantry branch and was assigned to the Infantry School in 1977. He resigned his commission in 1979 and passed away in St. Joseph, Michigan, on November 6, 2007.

David C. Blackerby came from North Carolina and was commissioned in the field artillery. He served with the 3rd Squadron, 3rd Armored Cavalry Regiment, from 1974 to 1977. He resigned his commission in 1979. Dave joined the firm Southworth Machinery, where he served as a manager. He passed away in Shrewbury, Massachusetts, on October 2, 2008.

Herbert R. Mills Jr. was born in Virginia. He was commissioned in the infantry, with his first assignment the 1st Battalion, 23rd Infantry, in Korea in 1974–75. His next assignment was the 1st Battalion, 3rd Infantry, from 1975 to 1977. He was then assigned to the 3rd Battalion, 10th Special Forces Group, in 1977–78. He resigned his commission in 1978. Mills joined the Ohio National Guard as a chief warrant officer 2. From 1981 to 1987 he was assigned to the JFK Center for Special Warfare. In 1987–88, he was assigned to the Special Operations Command, Europe, and then the 2nd Battalion, 11th Special Forces Group, from 1988 to 1994. He was transferred to the 2nd Battalion, 19th Special Forces Group, serving there from 1994 to 2008. He was then assigned as the operations officer of the 73rd Troop Command. After his retirement he became the plant manager for Wayne-Dalton Plastics in 2000, remaining there until 2004. He became the support project engineer for the Gossen Corporation in 2005. Mills died on October 24, 2010.

George W. Everett Jr. came to West Point from Massachusetts. He was commissioned in the field artillery and served in the 1st Battalion, 84th Field Artillery, in the 9th Infantry Division. He then went to serve on the faculty at the Field Artillery School until he resigned his commission in 1978. George went to work for Citibank Corporation. In 1981 he earned a master's degree in business administration from Pace University. He then joined Kidder Peabody until 1982, when he returned to Citibank as a vice president. In 1987 he moved over to the American Express Company as a vice president, and in 1990 he returned to Citibank as a vice president. George then went to t he Northwestern Mutual Life Insurance Company, the IOF Foresters company in 2000, and the New York Live Insurance Company in 2006. Everett passed away in Lake Tapps, Washington, on June 22, 2014.

Harry F. J. Campbell Jr. came to West Point from Virginia. He was commissioned in the infantry, and his first duty assignment was with the Headquarters Detachment, the Infantry Center. He resigned his commission in 1979. He joined the firm of Standard Register as an account executive. From 1982 to 1986 he worked for ITT as a communication executive. In 1986, Franklin joined Goldome Bank. In 1988 he joined DDI and worked as a program manager. Harry passed away in Northport, New York, on November 17, 2014.

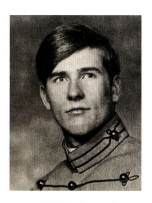

Richard E. Dakin came to West Point from Connecticut. He was commissioned in the field artillery and served with the 1st Battalion, 81st Field Artillery, in Germany from 1974 to 1977, then with the faculty of the Artillery School at Fort Sill, Oklahoma. He resigned his commission in 1979 and earned a master's degree in business administration from the University of Oklahoma in 1979. He joined the Homebuilding Company as an engineering sales manager, ultimately rising to be the vice president of the company. Dakin died in Colorado Springs, Colorado, on June 20, 2015.

David B. Kimball came to West Point from Michigan. He was commissioned in the field artillery. His first duty station was at Fort Carson, Colorado, from 1974 to 1977. He then went to Germany and served in the US Army, Europe, in 1977. Kimball commanded the 560th Medical Company in Korea from 1978 to 1979. He resigned his commission in 1979 and became the vice president of the Operations Medical Center in 1986. He passed away in Cedar Springs, Michigan, on August 28, 2016.

And when our work is done
Our course on earth is run
May it be said, "Well Done;
Be Thou At Peace."
E'er may that line of gray
Increase from day to day,
Live, serve, and die, we pray,
West Point, for thee

Men of the Class of 1973 in the Cemetery 283

Bibliography

The most common reference work I used in preparing this book was *The Register of Graduates and Former Cadets*, 2020 edition, prepared by the West Point Association of Graduates. The history of every graduate is recorded in this volume, along with assignments and decorations awarded, and a wealth of other information about West Point as well. I was also able to use the *Annual Reunion of the Association of Graduates of the United States Military Academy*, also published by the Association of Graduates, for obituaries in the early years, and the *Assembly* magazine obituaries published in later years.

The listed books, websites, and documents are the sources I used in preparing the manuscript of the book. I found Wikipedia to be a useful guide as well, and helpful to point to original sources. I have arranged these documents by chapter, and they include sources that are useful for background reading for those interested in the Military Academy and its graduates.

Chapter 1

Alvord, George B. "Building and Maintaining West Point." Unpublished manuscript by the Directorate of Public Works, US Army Garrison West Point, 2007.

Ambrose, Stephen E. *Duty, Honor, Country: A History of West Point*. Baltimore: Johns Hopkins Press, 1966.

Betros, Lance. *Carved from Granite: West Point since 1902*. College Station: Texas A&M University Press, 2016.

Capps, Marie T. "The Old Cadet Chapel and Cemetery at West Point." *Friends of the West Point Library Newsletter* 30 (April 1997)

Maish, A. M. "West Point Cemetery." *The Pointer*, January 30, 1942.

Palka, Eugene J., and Jon C. Malinkowski. *Historic Photos of West Point*. Nashville: Turner, 2008.

Palmer, Dave Richard. *The River and the Rock*. New York: Greenwood, 1969.

USMA Memorial Affairs. *West Point Cemetery: American Heroes, Military Leaders, Army Legends*. New York: US Military Academy.

USMA Memorial Affairs. *Trees of the West Point Cemetery . . . A Self-Guided Walking Tour*. New York: US Military Academy.

Chapter 2

"Charles C. Pinkerton Jr., Jan 1943." West Point Association of Graduates website. https://www.westpointaog.org/memorial-article?id=1592d745-0403-4058-9ca8-ad12c4dcf208.

"The Collected Works of Ducrot Pepys." University of Chicago website. https://penelope.uchicago.edu/Thayer/E/Gazetteer/Places/America/United_States/Army/USMA/Collected_Works_of_Ducrot_Pepys/home.html.

"Earl H. Blaik 1920." West Point Association of Graduates website. https://www.westpointaog.org/memorial-article?id=c21dcbec-9811-47d8-919d-a09c26038606.

"Frederick G. Terry 1930." West Point Association of Graduates website. https://www.westpointaog.org/memorial-article?id=cf3a106f-b1f3-43bf-a842-85174f1b5bfa.

"Frederick G. Terry 1960." West Point Association of Graduates website. https://www.westpointaog.org/memorial-article?id=00ccbc18-35de-446e-86a8-5a9791fa5568.

"Glenn Davis 1946." Heisman Trophy website. http://www.heisman.com/heisman-winners/glenn-davis/.

"Glenn W. Davis 1947." West Point Association of Graduates website. https://www.westpointaog.org/memorial-article?id=c9533322-ee6c-4527-9d8b-47bcca7102ad.

"Hall of Fame." GoArmyWestPoint website. https://goarmywestpoint.com/hof.aspx?hof=75.

"Herbert N. Schwarzkopf Apr 1917." West Point Association of Graduates website. https://www.westpointaog.org/memorial-article?id=126c29ec-48d7-411b-897c-fe3f82326b55.

"Historical Vignette 037—the Relationship between the Corps of Engineers and College Football." US Army Corps of Engineers website. https://www.usace.army.mil/About/History/Historical-Vignettes/Sports-Entertainment/037-College-Football/.

"James M. Gavin 1929." West Point Association of Graduates website. https://www.westpointaog.org/memorial-article?id=e84374a2-e368-4558-a827-a1a005c82021.

"John F. Buyers Jun 1943." West Point Association of Graduates website. https://www.westpointaog.org/memorial-article?id=a2d1c0d2-25d9-46ac-9dcc-72a35fceace9.

"Lawrence (Biff) Jones, 84, Football Star, Coach, Dies." *Washington Post*, February 13, 1980. https://www.washingtonpost.com/archive/local/1980/02/13/lawrence-biff-jones-84-football-star-coach-dies/9d462d4a-d748-47fb-9da7-60d1cad6e4a5/?utm_term=.5f924cb16774.

"Lawrence M. Jones Aug 1917." West Point Association of Graduates website. https://www.westpointaog.org/memorial-article?id=4281800b-518b-435d-85e2-9ecdb72053de.

"Maggie Dixon." GoArmySports website. http://goarmysports.cstv.com/sports/w-baskbl/mtt/dixon_maggie00.html.

"The Maggie Dixon Story: An Inspiring Legacy." DePaul Women's Basketball website. http://www.depaulbluedemons.com/sports/w-baskbl/spec-rel/112009aaa.html.

"'Manners Are an Outward Expression of Character': The Cadet Hostess at West Point." West Point Center for Oral History website. https://www.westpointcoh.org/interviews/manners-are-an-outward-expression-of-character-the-cadet-hostess-at-west-point.

"Norman D. Cota Apr 1917." West Point Association of Graduates website. https://www.westpointaog.org/memorial-article?id=0ebf3620-0569-4665-98c8-4e106196254b.

"Norton, John, LTG." Army Together We Served website. https://army.togetherweserved.com/army/servlet/tws.webapp.WebApp?cmd=ShadowBoxProfile&type=Person&ID=280846.

"Paul D. Harkins 1929." West Point Association of Graduates website. https://www.westpointaog.org/memorial-article?id=45dbb9fd-5291-40f1-bd08-23d90d1fcd51.

"The Red Blaik Coaching Tree." 247Sports website. https://247sports.com/college/army/Article/The-Red-Blaik-Coaching-Tree-105226170/.

Reeder, Russell Potter, Jr. *Born at Reveille: The Memoirs of an American Soldier.* Quechee, VT: Vermont Heritage Press, 1966.

"Russell Reeder, 95, Leader in Invasion on D-day, Dies." *New York Times*, March 1, 1998. https://www.nytimes.com/1998/03/01/us/russell-reeder-95-leader-in-invasion-on-d-day-dies.html.

Schwarzkopf, H. Norman, Jr., with Peter Petre. *It Doesn't Take a Hero.* New York: Linda Gray Bantam Books, 1992.

"Veterans History Project—John Norton Collection." Library of Congress website. https://memory.loc.gov/diglib/vhp/bib/loc.natlib.afc2001001.31599.

Chapter 3

Historic American Buildings Survey / Historic American Engineering Record (HABS/HAER) Inventory Sheet. US Department of the Interior, National Park Service. Building No. 329, Groundskeeper's Cottage, dated September 1981.

Historical Record of Buildings at West Point, New York.

Historical Structures Inventory, USMA, West Point, New York. Vol. 2.

Chapter 4

"Aubrey S. Newman 1925." West Point Association of Graduates website. https://www.westpointaog.org/memorial-article?id=6434d8b9-8a63-4a08-8c3a-c3d30d3aa8e3.

Bernard W. Rogers entry, Class of 1949. In *The Register of Graduates and Former Cadets.* New York: West Point Association of Graduates, 2020.

Blackshear W. Bryan entry, Class of 1922. In *The Register of Graduates and Former Cadets*, Edition, New York: West Point Association of Graduates, 2020.

Donald V. Bennett entry, Class of 1940. In *The Register of Graduates and Former Cadets.* New York: West Point Association of Graduates, 2020.

"Edward H. White 1924." West Point Association of Graduates website. https://www.westpointaog.org/memorial-article?id=054bae5f-b6d5-4bee-9546-dfd4fb762fb3.

Edward H. White Jr., Class of 1952. In *The Register of Graduates and Former Cadets.* New York: West Point Association of Graduates, 2020.

Frederick Grant obituary. In *43rd Annual Reunion of the Association of Graduates of the United States Military Academy at West Point, New York, June 11th, 1912.* Saginaw, MI: Seeman & Peters.

"Garrison H. Davidson 1927." West Point Association of Graduates website. https://www.westpointaog.org/memorial-article?id=f1df1f94-10c8-41ec-a969-59fdde93d4ce.

"General Lucius D. Clay, USMA June 1918." *Assembly* (magazine) 37, no. 1 (June 1978).

"General Wayne A. Downing—Passing of an American Hero." The Small Wars Journal website. https://smallwarsjournal.com/blog/general-wayne-a-downing-passing-of-an-american-hero.

George W. Goethals entry, Class of 1908. In *The Register of Graduates and Former Cadets.* New York: West Point Association of Graduates, 2020.

"Howard D. Graves." USMA Class of 1961 website. http://www.usma1961.org/Graves.htm.

John Buford Jr. entry, Class of 1848. In *The Register of Graduates and Former Cadets*. New York: West Point Association of Graduates, 2020.

Judson Kilpatrick obituary. In *13th Annual Reunion of the Association of Graduates of the United States Military Academy at West Point, New York, June 12, 1882*. Philadelphia: Times Printing House.

"Major General Edward H. White." US Air Force website. https://www.af.mil/About-Us/Biographies/Display/Article/105237/major-general-edward-h-white/.

"Obama Awards Officer Medal of Honor for Civil War Heroism." Reuters website. https://www.reuters.com/article/us-usa-medalofhonor-cushing-idUSKBN0IQ24P20141106/.

"Philip R. Feir 1949." West Point Association of Graduates website. https://www.westpointaog.org/memorial-article?id=a08a8165-be2a-4eca-88af-1da056d18d13.

"Philip R. Feir Obituary." *Washington Post*, August 11, 2011. entry; https://www.washingtonpost.com/local/obituaries/2011/08/11/gIQA6h0TQJ_story.html?_=ddid-4-1641594540.

Richard J. Tallman entry, Class of 1949. In *The Register of Graduates and Former Cadets*. New York: West Point Association of Graduates, 2020.

Sam S. Walker entry, Class of 1946. In *The Register of Graduates and Former Cadets*. New York: West Point Association of Graduates, 2020.

Samuel W. Koster entry, Class of 1942. In *The Register of Graduates and Former Cadets*. New York: West Point Association of Graduates, 2020.

"Vincent J. Esposito 1925." West Point Association of Graduates website. https://www.westpointaog.org/memorial-article?id=53f2664f-b959-4c9d-9f6e-410b0b993313.

"Wayne Downing." For What They Gave on Saturday Afternoon website. https://forwhattheygave.com/2007/10/21/wayne-downing/.

William Westmoreland entry, Class of 1936. In *The Register of Graduates and Former Cadets*. New York: West Point Association of Graduates, 2020.

Chapter 5

Cassidy, T. E. "Appendix III: Ensign Dominic Trant: Irish-American Hero." In *The Trant Family*. Extract of manuscript from USMA Library Archives, n.d.

"Edward Holden." In *1914 Annual Report of the Superintendent–United States Military Academy*. West Point, NY: United States Military Academy Printing Office.

"Edward S. Holden, Class of 1870." In *The Register of Graduates and Former Cadets*. New York: West Point Association of Graduates, 2020.

"Eleazer Derby Wood" For What They Gave on Saturday Afternoon website. https://forwhattheygave.com/2012/06/10/eleazer-derby-wood/.

"Louis Benz (Bentz)—West Point Bugler." Taps Bugler website. https://www.tapsbugler.com/louis-benz-bentz-west-point-bugler/.

"Major John Lillie, 1755–1801: The Lillie Family of Boston 1663–1896." Internet Archive. https://archive.org/stream/majorjohnlillie00piergoog/majorjohnlillie00piergoog_djvu.txt.

"Susan Bogert Warner and Anna Bartlett Warner." *Britannica Online Encyclopedia*. https://www.britannica.com/biography/Susan-Bogert-Warner-and-Anna-Bartlett-Warner.

Chapter 6

Alexander S. Webb obituary. In *42nd Annual Reunion of the Association of Graduates of the United States Military Academy at West Point, New York June 12th, 1911*. Saginaw, MI: Seeman & Peters.

"Black, William Murray, MG." Together We Served website. https://army.togetherweserved.com/army/servlet/tws.webapp.WebApp?cmd=ShadowBoxProfile&type=Person&ID=338505.

"Clarence S. Ridley 1905." West Point Association of Graduates website. https://www.westpointaog.org/memorial-article?id=e7a4fa6f-387f-4d48-86eb-52c8422fd60f.

"Dennis M. Michie, Class of 1892." In *The Register of Graduates and Former Cadets*. New York: West Point Association of Graduates, 2020.

Edward Settle Godfrey obituary. In *63rd Annual Report of the Association of Graduates of the United States Military Academy at West Point, New York, June 9th, 1932*. Newburgh, NY: Moore.

"Ethan A. Hitchcock, Class of 1817." In *The Register of Graduates and Former Cadets*. New York: West Point Association of Graduates, 2020.

"Frank J. Kobes Jr. 1939." West Point Association of Graduates website. https://www.westpointaog.org/memorial-article?id=64484058-1bd9-44a2-9a7e-52e793078874.

"George A. Custer, Class of 1861." In *The Register of Graduates and Former Cadets*. New York: West Point Association of Graduates, 2020.

"George Derby, Class of 1846." In *The Register of Graduates and Former Cadets*. New York: West Point Association of Graduates, 2020.

"Herman Koehler." Wikipedia. https://en.wikipedia.org/wiki/Herman_Koehler.

"John C. Tidball, Class of 1848." In *The Register of Graduates and Former Cadets*. New York: West Point Association of Graduates, 2020.

"John Sheldon D. Eisenhower 1944." West Point Association of Graduates website. https://www.westpointaog.org/memorial-article?id=f1ffcf39-ef1d-4110-99d6-b00302ce716c.

"Ora E. Hunt 1894." West Point Association of Graduates website. https://www.westpointaog.org/memorial-article?id=522a1beb-7510-4ac0-aed5-848ea877a0fe.

"Ora E. Hunt, Class of 1894." In *The Register of Graduates and Former Cadets*. New York: West Point Association of Graduates, 2020.

"Paul Kendall's War": A Wyoming Soldier Serves in Siberia." Wyoming History website. https://www.wyohistory.org/encyclopedia/paul-kendalls-war-wyoming-soldier-serves-siberia.

"Paul W. Kendall Nov 1918." West Point Association of Graduates website. https://www.westpointaog.org/memorial-article?id=a60b09ca-c15e-4f71-ae7e-011f79274656.

"Peter Smith Michie." Wikipedia. https://en.wikipedia.org/wiki/Peter_Smith_Michie.

"Robert Anderson, Class of 1825." In *The Register of Graduates and Former Cadets*. New York: West Point Association of Graduates, 2020.

Stiles, T. J. *Custer's Trials: A Life on the Frontier of a New America*. New York: Alfred A. Knopf, 2015.

"Sylvanus Thayer, Class of 1808." In *The Register of Graduates and Former Cadets*. New York: West Point Association of Graduates, 2020.

"Thomas Devin." Wikipedia. https://en.wikipedia.org/wiki/Thomas_Devin.

William Murray Black obituary. In *65th Annual Report of the Association of Graduates of the United States Military Academy at West Point, New York, June 11th, 1934*. Newburgh, NY: Moore.

William S. Beebe obituary. In *30th Annual Reunion of the Association of Graduates of the United States Military Academy at West Point, New York, June 7th, 1899*. Saginaw, MI: Seeman & Peters.

"Winfield Scott." Wikipedia. https://en.wikipedia.org/wiki/Winfield_Scott.

Chapter 7

"Bernard J. D. Irwin." Wikipedia. https://en.wikipedia.org/wiki/Bernard_J._D._Irwin.

"BG Charles Walker Raymond." Find a Grave website. https://www.findagrave.com/mcmorial/34195960/charlcs-walkcr-raymond.

"Book Review—*Sea Miner: Major E. B. Hunt's Civil War Rocket Torpedo, 1862–1863*. Naval Historical Foundation website. https://www.navyhistory.org/2016/06/book-review-sea-miner-major-e-b-hunts-civil-war-rocket-torpedo-1862-1863/.

Charles Walker Raymond obituary. In *44th Annual Reunion of the Association of Graduates of the United States Military Academy, June 11th, 1913*. Saginaw, MI: Seeman & Peters, 1913.

Cyrus Ballou Comstock obituary. In *43rd Annual Reunion of the Association of Graduates of the United States Military Academy, June 11th, 1912*. Saginaw, MI: Seeman & Peters, 1912.

"Daniel Butterfield." Wikipedia. https://en.wikipedia.org/wiki/Daniel_Butterfield.

"Dennis H. Mahan, Class of 1824." In *The Register of Graduates and Former Cadets*. New York: West Point Association of Graduates, 2020.

"Egbert L. Viele, Class of 1847." In *The Register of Graduates and Former Cadets*. New York: West Point Association of Graduates, 2020.

George L. Gillespie obituary. In *45th Annual Reunion of the Association of Graduates of the United States Military Academy, June 12, 1914*. Saginaw, MI: Seeman & Peters, 1914.

"George L. Irwin, Class of 1889." In *The Register of Graduates and Former Cadets*. New York: West Point Association of Graduates, 2020.

George Le Roy Irwin obituary. In *62nd Annual Report of the Association of Graduates of the United States Military Academy, June 10th, 1941*. Crawfordsville, IN: Lakeside, 1941.

"Hall of Fame: Joseph Michael Pallone." GoArmyWestPoint website. https://goarmywestpoint.com/honors/hall-of-fame/joseph-michael-palone/20.

"Helen Hunt Jackson." Wikipedia. https://en.wikipedia.org/wiki/Helen_Hunt_Jackson.

Henry Metcalfe obituary. In *61st Annual Report of the Association of Graduates of the United States Military Academy, June 11th, 1930*. Newburgh, NY: Moore, 1930.

"James G. Benton." University of Chicago website. https://penelope.uchicago.edu/Thayer/E/Gazetteer/Places/America/United_States/Army/USMA/Cullums_Register/1121*.html.

James G. Benton obituary. In *13th Annual Reunion of the Association of Graduates of the United States Military Academy, June 12th, 1882*. Philadelphia: Times Printing House, 1882.

John Taliaferro Thompson obituary. In *72nd Annual Report of the Association of Graduates of the United States Military Academy, June 10th, 1941*. Newburgh, NY: Moore, 1941.

Maher, Martin. *Bringing Up the Brass: My 55 Years at West Point.* New York: David McKay, 1951.

"Mathematics at West Point: The First Hundred Years—Albert E. Church, Mathematics Professor, 1837–1878." Mathematical Association of America website. https://www.maa.org/press/periodicals/convergence/mathematics-education-at-west-point-the-first-hundred-years-albert-e-church-mathematics-professor.

"Men's Soccer: Palone Announced to United Soccer Coaches Hall of Fame Class." GoArmyWestPoint website. https://goarmywestpoint.com/news/2020/10/15/mens-soccer-palone-announced-to-united-soccer-coaches-hall-of-fame-class.aspx.

"Robert Walter Weir." Wikipedia. https://en.wikipedia.org/wiki/Robert_Walter_Weir.

"Stafford L. Irwin, Class of 1915." In *The Register of Graduates and Former Cadets.* New York: West Point Association of Graduates, 2020.

William H. Benyaurd obituary. In *31st Annual Reunion of the Association of Graduates of the United States Military Academy, June 12th, 1900.* Saginaw, MI: Seeman & Peters, 1900.

William Holmes Chambers Bartlett obituary. In *24th Annual Reunion of the Association of Graduates of the United States Military Academy, June 9th, 1893.* Saginaw, MI: Seeman & Peters, 1893.

Chapter 8

Albert Mills obituary. In *48th Annual Report of the Association of Graduates of the United States Military Academy, June 12th, 1917.* Saginaw, MI: Seeman & Peters, 1917.

"Alexander M. Patch 1913." West Point Association of Graduates website. https://www.westpointaog.org/memorial-article?id=b9faa296-cf65-4a08-84bc-c41f2c367326.

"California War Dead; Matthew C. Ferrara, 24." *Los Angeles Times,* November 9, 2007. https://projects.latimes.com/wardead/name/matthew-c-ferrara/.

"COL Dean Hudnutt." Family Search website. https://ancestors.familysearch.org/en/LB2Z-KMD/col-dean-hudnutt-1891-1943.

"Edward H. DeArmond, Class of 1901." In *The Register of Graduates and Former Cadets.* New York: West Point Association of Graduates, 2020.

"Edward L. King, Class of 1896." In *The Register of Graduates and Former Cadets.* New York: West Point Association of Graduates, 2020.

"Elliott C. Cutler, Class of 1942." In *The Register of Graduates and Former Cadets.* New York: West Point Association of Graduates, 2020.

"Frank D. Merrill 1929." West Point Association of Graduates website. https://www.westpointaog.org/memorial-article?id=56acf79b-f960-417c-bdd8-bc1806d6bb46.

"Fred W. Sladen 1890." West Point Association of Graduates website. https://www.westpointaog.org/memorial-article?id=2d6e87bc-f0c4-42ba-ac73-2e4d9cd5df00.

"Hall of Valor: Stuart MacDonald." Military Times website. https://valor.militarytimes.com/hero/109264.

"Hamilton H. Howze 1930." West Point Association of Graduates website. https://www.westpointaog.org/memorial-article?id=2a6971a5-7952-49e2-87a5-130e3b642184.

"Joseph W. Stilwell 1904." West Point Association of Graduates website. https://www.westpointaog.org/memorial-article?id=f1ba9ff3-1aac-40f5-8867-604fc8f01266.

"Lemuel Mathewson 13 Jun 1922." West Point Association of Graduates website. https://www.westpointaog.org/memorial-article?id=d16b8c69-233a-4686-bc35-d2d5380bfb6c.

"Matthew C. Ferrara 2005." West Point Association of Graduates website. https://www.westpointaog.org/memorial-article?id=0227e42f-7594-4c06-b54a-eb38083fa431.

"Medal of Honor: Sergeant Kyle J. White." US Army website. https://www.army.mil/medalofhonor/white/battle/index.html.

Robert Lee Howze obituary. In *58th Annual Report of the Association of Graduates of the United States Military Academy, June 13th, 1927.* Saginaw, MI: Seeman & Peters, 1927.

"Stuart C. MacDonald 1915." West Point Association of Graduates website. https://www.westpointaog.org/memorial-article?id=6541e0de-a127-4cb5-86c6-ca9cd3121861.

Thomas Henry Barry obituary. In *51st Annual Report of the Association of Graduates of the United States Military Academy, June 14th, 1920.* Saginaw, MI: Seeman & Peters, 1920.

"Vauthier, Louis." Museum of American Fencing website. http://museumofamericanfencing.com/wp/vauthier-louis/.

"The Yale Daily News 31 March 1943." Yale Daily News Historical Archive website. *ROTC Pistol Team Disbanded for War; Training Still Given* article; https://ydnhistorical.library.yale.edu/?a=d&d=YDN19430331-01.2.25&e=-------en-20--1--txt-txIN-------.

Chapter 9

"Battery Paul D. Bunker, BCN-127." Fort MacArthur Museum Association website. http://www.ftmac.org/batterybunker127.htm.

"BG George Smith Anderson." Find A Grave website. https://www.findagrave.com/memorial/122686657/george-smith-anderson.

"Brigadier General Douglas Kinnard." Legacy.com website. https://www.legacy.com/us/obituaries/pe/name/douglas-kinnard-obituary?id=19294233.

"Calvert P. Benedict." West Point Association of Graduates website. https://www.westpointaog.org/rog-search-details?id=f34e81ee-f0c1-4d96-923c-80d8d68933c9.

Capt. James Oscar Green Sr." Find A Grave website. https://www.findagrave.com/memorial/124052614/james-oscar-green.

"Charles C. Benedict Jan 1943." West Point Association of Graduates website. https://www.westpointaog.org/memorial-article?id=76507746-16c3-409f-b11b-7268dc6b60aa.

Clarence Page Townsley obituary. In *61st Annual Report of the Association of Graduates of the United States Military Academy, June 11th, 1930.* Newburgh, NY: Moore, 1930.

"David H. Barger Jan 1943." West Point Association of Graduates website. https://www.westpointaog.org/memorial-article?id=b28eaaef-a9aa-4d64-9790-bc18d2e19f34.

"David Marcus, Class of 1924." In *The Register of Graduates and Former Cadets.* New York: West Point Association of Graduates, 2020.

"Douglas Kinnard." West Point Association of Graduates website. https://www.westpointaog.org/rog-search-details?id=e06afa79-157e-438b-966b-3aef6f451ca2.

"Douglas Kinnard 1944." West Point Association of Graduates website. https://www.westpointaog.org/memorial-article?id=e06afa79-157e-438b-966b-3aef6f451ca2.

"Elbert E. Farman Jr." University of Chicago website. https://penelope.uchicago.edu/Thayer/E/Gazetteer/Places/America/United_States/Army/USMA/Cullums_Register/4780*.html.

"Elvin R. Heiberg II 1926." West Point Association of Graduates website. https://www.westpointaog.org/memorial-article?id=b9fadcb5-f495-4147-a7a2-13e4ef34c056.

Elvin R. Heiberg obituary. In *48th Annual Report of the Association of Graduates of the United States Military Academy, June 12th, 1917.* Saginaw, MI: Seeman & Peters, 1917.

"General Frank S. Besson Jr." US Army Transportation Museum website. https://transportation.army.mil/museum/about/GenBesson.html.

George S. Anderson obituary. In *46th Annual Reunion of the Association of Graduates of the United States Military Academy, June 11th, 1915.* Saginaw, MI: Seeman & Peters, 1915.

"George S. Pappas 1944." West Point Association of Graduates website. https://www.westpointaog.org/memorial-article?id=278eda84-564a-4653-9274-cd9b48445471.

Gioia, Joe. *The Czar of Yellowstone.* Medium website. https://medium.com/@joe.gioia/the-czar-of-yellowstone-c337e7a53a04.

"Hall of Valor: Calvert Potter Benedict." Military Times website. https://valor.militarytimes.com/hero/4796.

"Harrison H. Heiberg 1919." West Point Association of Graduates website. https://www.westpointaog.org/memorial-article?id=a46cb4a9-3ec6-4a87-9f55-31277862a7a5.

"Harrison Lobdell Jr. 1946." West Point Association of Graduates website. https://www.westpointaog.org/memorial-article?id=ed55324a-df3e-4044-97c8-1990cce5b053.

James O. Green Jr. obituary. In *69th Annual Report of the Association of Graduates of the United States Military Academy, June 13th, 1938.* Newburgh, NY: Moore, 1938.

"James Oscar Green III." Find A Grave website. https://www.findagrave.com/memorial/126625016/james-oscar-green.

"James O. Green." University of Chicago website. https://penelope.uchicago.edu/Thayer/E/Gazetteer/Places/America/United_States/Army/USMA/Cullums_Register/2966*.html.

"James O. Green III 1941." West Point Association of Graduates website. https://www.westpointaog.org/memorial-article?id=3a2a7113-22ae-4113-964d-6b371eb94bb1.

"John R. Jannarone 1938." West Point Association of Graduates website. https://www.westpointaog.org/memorial-article?id=fec3fed1-2f15-493d-997c-1e7f6c7ee891.

"In Memorium: George S. Pappas, 1919–2010." US Army War College Archives website. https://www.armywarcollege.edu/News/archives/12867.pdf.

"Louis A. Kunzig 1905." West Point Association of Graduates website. https://www.westpointaog.org/memorial-article?id=73ebfac7-ca27-4220-be26-c36be59f8d9e.

"Maj Charles Calvert Benedict Sr." Find A Grave website. https://www.findagrave.com/memorial/124122981/charles-calvert-benedict.

"Major General Thomas J. Hayes Jr." US Army Ordnance Corps website. https://goordnance.army.mil/hof/1970/1976/hayes.html.

"Maj James Oscar 'Jimmy' Green Jr." Find A Grave website. https://www.findagrave.com/memorial/124052661/james-oscar-green.

"MG James Leland Benedict." Find A Grave website. https://www.findagrave.com/memorial/35668866/jay-leland-benedict.

Miller, Jeremy King. USMA Cadet Album Write-Ups full page.docx, n.d. Personal correspondence with the author.

"Paul D. Bunker 1903." West Point Association of Graduates website. https://www.westpointaog.org/memorial-article?id=1e44d2a3-5943-46f9-85a6-ba561087e768.

Paul Delmont Bunker Jr. obituary. In *70th Annual Report of the Association of Graduates of the United States Military Academy, June 10th, 1939*. Newburgh, NY: Moore, 1939.

"Thomas J. Hayes III 1936." West Point Association of Graduates website. https://www.westpointaog.org/memorial-article?id=5e20f5ac-e2ba-4379-a428-b2e258df7c26.

"Thomas J. Hayes IV 1966." West Point Association of Graduates website. https://www.westpointaog.org/memorial-article?id=22a882c1-335b-4990-b54f-4a9b1ca5cd57.

"2003 Hall of Fame Inductee John R. Jannarone." Nutley Public Library Hall of Fame website. https://nutleyhalloffame.nutleypubliclibrary.org/2003-jannarone/.

"William B. Kunzig 1932." West Point Association of Graduates website. https://www.westpointaog.org/memorial-article?id=56215fb7-5562-43fb-87d8-b20a043e3d41.

"William L. Heiberg 1961." West Point Association of Graduates website. https://www.westpointaog.org/memorial-article?id=e4071a0f-c40c-43ae-a729-34cabd965ef3.

"William L. Heiberg 'Bill.'" USMA Class of 1961 website. http://www.usma1961.org/Heiberg.htm.

"William Rice King." Find A Grave website. https://www.findagrave.com/memorial/42697233/william-rice-king.

Chapter 10

"Andre C. Lucas 1954." West Point Association of Graduates website. https://www.westpointaog.org/memorial-article?id=004c6d01-4a0e-4fe3-8801-1d7f7bb13e47.

"Bryant E. Moore Aug 1917." West Point Association of Graduates website. https://www.westpointaog.org/memorial-article?id=b015d8e6-ac95-4470-855e-e3029489b4a0.

"Chancellor Martin." University of Chicago website. https://penelope.uchicago.edu/Thayer/E/Gazetteer/Places/America/United_States/Army/USMA/Cullums_Register/2258*.html.

Chancellor Martin obituary. In *48th Annual Report of the Association of Graduates of the United States Military Academy, June 12th, 1917*. Saginaw, MI: Seeman & Peters, 1917.

"*Chaplain H. Percy Silver and Lieutenant Charles Weeks Come Home from Manila*." Clipping from *Lincoln Journal Star*. Newspapers.com website. https://www.newspapers.com/clip/17618245/lincoln-journal-star/.

"Charles P. Echols." Century Association Archives Foundation website. https://centuryarchives.org/caba/bio.php?PersonID=903.

Charles Patton Echols obituary. In *72nd Annual Report of the Association of Graduates of the United States Military Academy, June 10th, 1941*. Newburgh, NY: Moore, 1941.

"Church of the Incarnation, Episcopal (Manhattan)." Wikipedia entry. https://en.wikipedia.org/wiki/Church_of_the_Incarnation,_Episcopal_(Manhattan).

"The Class of 1946: 15404 Nye, Roger Hurless." West Point.org website. https://www.west-point.org/users/usma1946/15405/.

"The Class of 1949: 17313 George William Tow." West Point.org website. https://www.west-point.org/users/usma1949/17313/.

"The Class of 2010: 1st Lt. Todd W. Lambka USA KIA." West Point.org website. https://www.west-point.org/users/usma2010/66560/.

"Courtlandt V. Schuyler 13 Jun 22." West Point Association of Graduates website. https://www.westpointaog.org/memorial-article?id=9bb21866-2d48-48eb-82a6-48695ae87cf0.

"Courtney C. Davis Jr. 1949." West Point Association of Graduates website. https://www.westpointaog.org/memorial-article?id=74155d04-1a7c-4935-b7b8-89d089669637.

"David Marcus 1924." West Point Association of Graduates website. https://www.westpointaog.org/memorial-article?id=1567a71a-244c-4eb6-aeef-25a07fd81a37.

"Dr. William Heaton Schempf." *New York Times* obituary website. https://www.legacy.com/us/obituaries/nytimes/name/william-schempf-obituary?pid=368247.

"Flags Lowered Wednesday for 1st Lt. Todd Lambka." Western Michigan University website. https://wmich.edu/news/2012/08/1245.

"George S. Eyster Jr. 1945." West Point Association of Graduates website. https://www.westpointaog.org/memorial-article?id=3810b00e-f19e-4ced-a6b1-fe56d32ead4b.

John Biddle obituary. In *67th Annual Report of the Association of Graduates of the United States Military Academy, June 11th, 1936*. Newburgh, NY: Moore, 1936.

"John L. Weaver 1950." West Point Association of Graduates website. https://www.westpointaog.org/memorial-article?id=8cd969dd-9d55-4f86-8dc7-b1ae1e805350.

John William Heard obituary. In *53rd Annual Report of the Association of Graduates of the United States Military Academy, June 12th, 1922*. Saginaw, MI: Seeman & Peters, 1922.

"Joseph E. McCarthy 1945." West Point Association of Graduates website. https://www.westpointaog.org/memorial-article?id=0bfccdb3-b545-4692-92c9-57d3848f2cf7.

"LTC Mortimer Lenane "Mort" O'Connor." Find A Grave website. https://www.findagrave.com/memorial/125024058/mortimer-lenane-o'connor.

"Mortimer L. O'Connor 1953." West Point Association of Graduates website. https://www.westpointaog.org/memorial-article?id=cc681cb3-8b9a-44eb-9572-55bcd8bc06b0.

"1997 Distinguished Graduate Award: GEN Michael S. Davison '39."
West Point Association of Graduates website. https://www
.westpointaog.org/page.aspx?pid=544.

"Ret Army Brig. Gen Joseph E. McCarty." Cumberlink website.
https://cumberlink.com/lifestyles/announcements/obituaries
/joseph-edward-mccarthy-brigadier-general-u-s-army-retired
/article_901d894b-c5aa-589d-b05f-acd000a5c522.html.

Robert M. Losey obituary. In *72nd Annual Report of the Association of
Graduates of the United States Military Academy, June 10th, 1941*.
Newburgh, NY: Moore, 1941.

"Samuel S. Coursen 1949." West Point Association of Graduates
website. https://www.westpointaog.org/memorial-article?id
=33157e48-79ed-4975-bf9d-eb8c19038081.

"Stars and Stripes over the Rhine. The American Occupation, 1918–
1923." Regionalgeschichte.net website. https://www
.regionalgeschichte.net/bibliothek/ausstellungen/stars-and-
stripes-over-the-rhine-the-american-occupation-1918-1923/
the-press-and-information-policies.html.

Walter Herman Schulze obituary. In *52nd Annual Report of the
Association of Graduates of the United States Military Academy,
June 11th, 1921*. Saginaw, MI: Seeman & Peters, 1921.

"William H. Wilbur 1912." West Point Association of Graduates website. https://www.westpointaog.org/memorial-article?id
=be64e43c-3cbe-4e20-b1ff-0f6127642c6c.

Chapter 11

"Army Nuclear Power Program." Wikipedia. https://en.wikipedia.org
/wiki/Army_Nuclear_Power_Program.

"Bruce I. Staser 1944." West Point Association of Graduates website.
https://www.westpointaog.org/memorial-article?id=7ba77ca6
-7806-4216-a4cf-8bc411e54645.

"Charles H. Schilling 1941." West Point Association of Graduates
website. https://www.westpointaog.org/memorial-article?id
=b1a18a61-4382-4e40-b3bb-3ac7016436ca.

"Donovan. Robert E. Donovan." *Hartford (CT) Courant*, April 10,
1996. https://www.courant.com/news/connecticut/hc-xpm-1996
-04-10-9604100707-story.html.

"East Stroudsburg University Lists Organizational Changes." *Morning
Call*, October 1, 1986. https://www.mcall.com/news/mc
-xpm-1986-10-01-2557301-story.html.

"Leader of WWII's 'Great Raid' Looks Back At Real-Life POW
Rescue." *Seattle Post Intelligencer*, August 24, 2005. https://www
.seattlepi.com/local/article/Leader-of-WWII-s-Great-Raid-looks
-back-at-1181340.php.

"Lieutenant Colonel Henry A. Mucci." Army Special Operations
Command website. https://arsof-history.org/icons/mucci.html.

"MSGT Pasquale 'Pat' Nappi." Find A Grave website. https://www
.findagrave.com/memorial/126544080/pasquale-nappi.

"Norman B. Edwards 1935." West Point Association of Graduates
website. https://www.westpointaog.org/memorial-article?id
=04469bf9-0f2b-4e85-9796-3b1eb9848569.

"Oh, Brothers—They Put Punch into It." Sports Illustrated website.
https://vault.si.com/vault/1976/08/09/oh-
brothersthey-put-punch-into-it.

"Robert E. Donovan." West Point Association of Graduates website.
https://www.westpointaog.org/rog-search-details?id=90733c9a
-d9a2-4d6d-a766-9eeeedd36cd6.

"Roger H. Nye 1946." West Point Association of Graduates website.
https://www.westpointaog.org/memorial-article?id=810dd2ad
-f17a-44df-bfeb-2c2a5b3bddd3.

"Section 10. The Library." In *Annual Report of the Superintendent of
the United States Military Academy 1944*. West Point, NY: United
States Military Academy Printing Office, 1944.

"Section 12. Library," In *Annual Report of the Superintendent of the
United States Military Academy 1948*. West Point, NY: United
States Military Academy Printing Office, 1948.

"Timothy E. Krebs." Legacy.com website. https://www.legacy.com
/us/obituaries/centredaily/name/timothy-krebs-obituary?id
=12839985.

"Timothy E. Krebs." West Point Association of Graduates website.
https://www.westpointaog.org/rog-search-details?id=a7ef1e41
-cb68-486c-9442-86463b04d8f1.

Chapter 12

"Benjamin Gilman." Wikipedia. https://en.wikipedia.org/wiki
/Benjamin_Gilman.

"Charles R. Meyer, Class of 1937." In *The Register of Graduates and
Former Cadets*. New York: West Point Association of Graduates,
2020.

"Chinese-American General Ying Hsing Wen, Who Pioneered Warm
Relations 100 Years Ago, Offers Lesson for Today, Honour Says."
South China Morning Post, November 17, 2018. https:
//www.scmp.com/news/china/diplomacy/article/2173686/
chinese-american-who-pioneered-warm-relations-100-years-ago.

"COL Seth Foster Hudgins Jr. USA (Retired)." West Point.org website. https://www.west-point.org/users/usma1964/25293/.

"Command Sergeant Major Mary E. Sutherland." Tribute Archive
website. https://www.tributearchive.com/obituaries/2564166
/Command-Sergeant-Major-Mary-E-Sutherland.

"Emily J. Perez 2005." West Point Association of Graduates website. https://www.westpointaog.org/memorial-article?id=29c9a61c-6eff-46d3-b65b-b99d5d177058.

"1LT Laura Margaret Walker USA." West Point.org website. https://www.west-point.org/users/usma2003/60262/.

"Henry R. McKenzie 1929." West Point Association of Graduates website. https://www.westpointaog.org/memorial-article?id=b5910695-7146-4845-9ea1-07e603548052.

"Hottell, John A." West Point.org website. https://www.west-point.org/users/usma1964/24930/.

"Jaimie E. Leonard." West Point Association of Graduates website. https://www.westpointaog.org/rog-search-details?id=c980aabb-da08-4082-873b-1083b6cd7358.

"John A. Heintges, Class of 1936." In *The Register of Graduates and Former Cadets*. New York: West Point Association of Graduates, 2020.

"Laura Margaret Walker." *Washington Post*, September 11, 2005. https://www.legacy.com/us/obituaries/washingtonpost/name/laura-walker-obituary?id=5540450.

"Lawrence K. White, Class of 1933." In *The Register of Graduates and Former Cadets*. New York: West Point Association of Graduates, 2020.

"McKenzie, Henry, BG." Together We Served website. https://army.togetherweserved.com/army/servlet/tws.webapp.WebApp?cmd=ShadowBoxProfile&type=AssignmentExt&ID=719735.

"MAJ John Alexander 'Alex' Hottell III." Find A Grave website. https://www.findagrave.com/memorial/8642077/john-alexander-hottell.

"Rene Edward DeRussy." Find A Grave website. https://www.findagrave.com/memorial/5949428/rene-edward-derussy.

"Theodore W. Parker 1931." West Point Association of Graduates website. https://www.westpointaog.org/memorial-article?id=73b3e686-49b0-4946-a8ae-38c080f521bb.

"Thomas E. Selfridge, Class of 1903." In *The Register of Graduates and Former Cadets*. New York: West Point Association of Graduates, 2020.

"Wang Zhi." World War II Database website. https://ww2db.com/person_bio.php?person_id=931.

"West Point Honors Command Sgt. Maj. Mary Sutherland." Army.mil website. https://www.army.mil/article/154416/west_point_honors_command_sgt_maj_mary_sutherland.

"Ying H. Wen 1909." West Point Association of Graduates website. https://www.westpointaog.org/memorial-article?id=4cc49e91-4b35-4324-8ebe-63e73b139dbd.

Photo Credits

This section credits the photographs used in this book. The vast majority of the photographs in the book were able to be used through the kind permission of the West Point Association of Graduates and the USMA Library, including all the photos that were taken from the *Howitzer*, the annual yearbook of the Corps of Cadets. All the *Howitzer* photos were taken from the US Military Academy Library Digital Collections. Many photographs of officers in their more senior years were found at the extensive archives of the US Army Historical and Education Center in Carlisle, Pennsylvania. Any photograph in the book not explicitly attributed below was taken by the author.

Page	Description	Attribution	Page	Description	Attribution
1	Buford Monument, no leaves on trees	Author	19	Organ view from floor	Author
2	Cadet Monument, close-up	Author	20	Right side of chapel, sunlit through windows	Author
3	Cadet Chapel in sunlight, tree in foreground	Author	20	Detail of "GR" on cannon on right wall	Author
4	LOVE headstone in black	Author	21	General George Washington plaque	Author
10	Thayer headstone, very transparent	Author	21	Major General Nathaniel Greene plaque	Author
12	Entrance gate	Author	21	Major General von Steuben plaque	Author
12	Entrance Gate detail	Author	22	Brigadier Generals plaque	Author
13	Cadet Chapel from entrance gates	Author	22	Major General effaced plaque	Author
14	Old photo of Cadet Chapel from columbarium	Author	23	Officers, soldiers, and sailors plaque, Revolution	Author
14	Egret fountain in front of Chapel	Author	23	Officers and enlisted men, Spanish-American War	Author
15	View of back of Cadet Chapel	Author	24	Altar and pulpit in chapel	Author
16	Interior of Cadet Chapel	Author	25	Plaques and cannons from Mexican War	Author
17	Close-up of vase on altarpiece	Author	25	Minor Actions plaque, Indian Wars	Author
17	Close-up of flag on altarpiece	Author	26	Detail of Mexican cannon-lifting shackles	Author
18	Winfield Scott's silver nameplate	Author	26	Detail of Mexican cannon	Author
18	Full altarpiece from back of chapel	Author	27	Map detail of Sections IX and X	Author
18	Proverbs quote on altarpiece	Author	28	Blaik headstone	Author
18	Close-up of eagle and fasces	Author			
18	Light sconce on pillar	Author			

Page	Description	Attribution
28	Blaik B&W coach picture	Photo courtesy of Army Football, from website https://footballfoundation.org//news 2021 /12/21/football-blaik-family-proudly-recalls-hall-of-fame-patriarchs-epic-career.aspx
28	Blaik *Howitzer* picture	Photo courtesy of the USMA Library, taken from the Library Digital Collection, 1920 *Howitzer*
29	Glenn Davis *Howitzer* picture	Photo courtesy of the USMA Library, taken from the Library Digital Collection, 1947 *Howitzer*
29	Glenn Davis headstone	Author
29	Glenn Davis receiving Heisman	Photo courtesy of the Heisman Trophy, from website https://www.heisman.com/heisman -winners/glenn-davis/
30	Maggie Dixon headstone	Author
30	Maggie Dixon color portrait	Photo courtesy of Army Athletics, from website https://web.archive.org/web /20060618122358/http://goarmysports.cstv.com/sports/w-baskbl/mtt/dixon_maggie00.html
30	Maggie Dixon with championship basketball team	Photo courtesy of USMA, from website https://www.swishappeal.com/2010/12/18 /1882691/ maggie-dixon-classic-a-great-event-missing-an-important-element
31	Class Crest 1943	Photo courtesy of the USMA Library, taken from the Library Digital Collection, 1943 Howitzer
31	Ronan Grady *Howitzer*	Photo courtesy of the USMA Library, portraittaken from the Library Digital Collection, 1943 Howitzer
31	Ducrot Pepys cartoon 1	Image courtesy of the University of Chicago, from University of Chicago website; "The Collected Works of Ducrot Pepys" entry; https://penelope.uchicago.edu/ Thayer/E /Gazetteer/Places/America/United_States/Army/USMA/Collected_Works_of_Ducrot _Pepys/home.html
31	Ducrot Pepys cartoon 2	Image courtesy of the University of Chicago, from University of Chicago website; "The Collected Works of Ducrot Pepys" entry; https://penelope.uchicago.edu/Thayer/E /Gazetteer/Places/America/United_States/Army/USMA/Collected_Works_of_Ducrot _Pepys/home.html
31	Ronan Grady headstone	Author
32	Cadet Chapel from Section X	Author
33	Larry Jones *Howitzer* photo	Photo courtesy of the USMA Library, taken from the Library Digital Collection, 1945 *Howitzer*
33	Larry Jones command photo	Photo courtesy of the US Army Heritage and Education Center photo archives, Carlisle, PA
33	Larry Jones headstones	Author
34	Jack Norton *Howitzer* photo	Photo courtesy of the USMA Library, taken from the Library Digital Collection, 1941 *Howitzer*
34	Jack Norton headstone	Author
34	Jack Norton B&W official photo	Photo courtesy of US Army, from website http://www.arlingtoncemetery.net/john-norton .htm
35	Red Reeder *Howitzer* photo	Photo courtesy of the USMA Library, taken from the Library Digital Collection, 1926 *Howitzer*
35	Red Reeder B&W with General Marshall	Photo courtesy of US Army Heritage and Education Center photo archives, Carlisle, PA
35	Red Reeder baseball uniform	Photo courtesy of US Army, from website https://forwhattheygave.com/2009/12/28 /red-reeder/
35	Red Reeder headstone	Author
36	Two fawns in cemetery	Author

296 *Stone Tapestry*

Page	Description	Attribution
37	H. Norman Schwarzkopf Sr. headstone	Author
37	H. Norman Schwarzkopf Sr. B&W in uniform	Photo courtesy of the USMA Library, taken from the Library Digital Collection, 1917 *Howitzer*
37	H. Norman Schwarzkopf Sr. in suit photo	Photo courtesy of Walter Albertin, World Telegram staff photographer, from website http://hdl.loc.gov/loc.pnp/cph.3c15940
38	Biff Jones B&W uniform portrait	Photo courtesy of the USMA Library, taken from the Library Digital Collection, 1945 Howitzer
38	Biff Jones football uniform photo	Photo courtesy of the USMA Library, taken from the Library Digital Collection, 1917 Howitzer
38	Biff Jones headstone	Author
39	General Schwarzkopf *Howitzer* photo	Photo courtesy of the USMA Library, taken from the Library Digital Collection, 1956 *Howitzer*
39	General Schwarzkopf command photo	Photo courtesy of US Army Heritage and Education Center photo archives, Carlisle, PA
39	General Schwarzkopf at Pentagon	Photo courtesy of US Army Heritage and Education Center photo archives, Carlisle, PA
39	General Schwarzkopf headstone	Author
40	Sunlit with red berry tree in foreground	Author
41	Jim Gavin headstone	Author
41	Jim Gavin *Howitzer* photo	Photo courtesy of the USMA Library, taken from the Library Digital Collection, 1929 *Howitzer*
41	Jim Gavin B&W CG of 82nd photo	Photo courtesy of Pennsylvania State Archives, taken from website https://explorepahistory.com/displayimage.php?imgId=1-2-ECF
42	Dutch Cota *Howitzer* photo	Photo courtesy of the USMA Library, taken from the Library Digital Collection, April 1917 *Howitzer*
42	B&W D-day photo	Photo courtesy of US Army Heritage and Education Center photo archives, Carlisle, PA
42	Dutch Cota with Ike B&W combat photo	Photo by unknown War Department photographer, taken from website http://liberationtrilogy.com/books/guns-at-last-light/historical-photos/slideshow/
42	Dutch Cota headstone	Author
43	Snow-covered view of Caretaker's Cottage	Author
44	B&W photo of Pat Buyers from *Howitzer*	Photo courtesy of the USMA Library, taken from the Library Digital Collection, 1973 *Howitzer*
44	Buyers headstone	Author
44	Gingerbread cottage	Author
45	Class Crest 1943	Photo courtesy of the USMA Library, taken from the Library Digital Collection, 1943 *Howitzer*
45	B&W portrait of Pinkerton	Photo courtesy of Pinkerton family, taken from West Point Association of Graduates website; "Charles C. Pinkerton Jr. Jan 1943" entry; https://www.westpointaog.org/memorial-article?id=1592d745-0403-4058-9ca8-ad12c4dcf208.
45	Pinkerton's headstones	Author
45	B&W photo of Mustang in flight	Photo by unknown War Department photographer, taken from website https://www.mustangsmustangs.com/p-51/image_viewer/sepia/Home/27382435/114590917/1
46	Cadet Monument looking south	Author
47	B&W Frederick Terry in uniform	Photo courtesy of the USMA Library, taken from the Library Digital Collection, 1960 *Howitzer*
47	Frederick Terry Jr. *Howitzer* photo	Photo courtesy of the USMA Library, taken from the Library Digital Collection, 1930 *Howitzer*
47	Terry headstones	Author
48	General Harkins headstone	Author
48	General Harkins *Howitzer* photo	Photo courtesy of the USMA Library, taken from the Library Digital Collection, 1929 *Howitzer*
48	General Harkins command photo	Photo courtesy of US Army Heritage and Education Center photo archive, Carlisle, PA
49	Caretaker's Cottage in winter	Author
50	Caretaker's Cottage in antiquity	Photo courtesy of the USMA Library, taken from the Library Stockbridge Collection
50	Caretaker's Cottage contemporary	Author

Photo Credits **297**

Page	Description	Attribution
50	Anderson fountain and cottage	Author
51	Anderson fountain with gates and light on cottage	Author
52	Light snow, brown-leaved tree in foreground	Author
53	Map detail of Sections XVIII and XXVI	Author
54	Philip Feir *Howitzer* photo	Photo courtesy of the USMA Library, taken from the Library Digital Collection, 1949 *Howitzer*
54	Philip Feir headstone	Author
54	Philip Feir B&W portrait photo	Photo courtesy of the USMA Library, taken from the Library Digital Collection, 1973 *Howitzer*
55	Howard Graves headstone	Author
55	Howard Graves color portrait	Photo courtesy of US Army Heritage and Education Center photo archive, Carlisle, PA
55	Howard Graves standing	Photo courtesy of the USMA Library, taken from the Library Digital Collection
56	Richard Tallman *Howitzer* photo	Photo courtesy of the USMA Library, taken from the Library Digital Collection, 1949 *Howitzer*
56	Tallman headstone	Author
56	Tallman cutting cake	Photo courtesy of the USMA Library, taken from the Library Digital Collection
57	Turkey among headstones	Photo credit: David R. Rose, release from photographer on hand
58	Blackshear Bryan *Howitzer* photo	Photo courtesy of the USMA Library, taken from the Library Digital Collection, 1918 *Howitzer*
58	Blackshear Bryan headstone	Author
58	Blackshear Bryan B&W official portrait	Photo courtesy of US Army Heritage and Education Center photo archives, Carlisle, PA
59	Gar Davidson headstone	Author
59	Gar Davidson B&W coach photo	Photo courtesy of the USMA Library, taken from the Library Digital Collection, 1934 *Howitzer*
59	Gar Davidson as Supe	US Army photograph, taken from http://www.usma.edu/bicentennial/history/images/GDavidson_l.jpg via http://www.usma.edu/bicentennial/history/1950.asp
60	Willard Scott color portrait	US Army photo, taken from http://www.e-yearbook.com/books/61/1984/jpg180/36.jpg
60	Willard Scott B&W on mule at football game	Photo courtesy of the USMA Library, taken from the Library Digital Collection, 1985 *Howitzer*
60	Willard Scott headstone	Author
61	Wayne Downing color saluting	US Army photo, taken from http://defender.west-point.org/service/display.mhtml?u=24096&i=39615
61	USSOCOM patch line drawing	Line drawing of USSOCOM insignia, taken from https://www.etsy.com/fi-en/listing/666067941/us-special-operations-command-patch
61	Wayne Downing headstone	Author
62	Fall Sunset of old section	Photo credit: Scott R. Gourley, release from photographer on hand
63	Bernard Rogers B&W portrait	Photo courtesy of US Army Heritage and Education Center photo archives, Carlisle, PA
63	Bernard Rogers, color portrait as CSA	Photo courtesy of US Army Heritage and Education Center photo archives, Carlisle, PA
63	Bernard Rogers headstone	Author
64	Red Newman headstone	Author
64	Red Newman B&W portrait	Photo courtesy of US Army Heritage and Education Center photo archives, Carlisle, PA
64	Red Newman, color painting of *Follow Me*	US Army painting, taken from https://www.wikiwand.com/en/Aubrey_Newman#Media/File:%22Follow_Me!%22_DA_Poster_21-43.png
65	Vincent Esposito *Howitzer* photo	Photo courtesy of the USMA Library, taken from the Library Digital Collection, 1925 *Howitzer*
65	Vincent Esposito headstone	Author
65	Vincent Esposito Army map books	Author
66	Gnarled tree in winter	Author

Page	Description	Attribution
67	Sam Walker headstone	Author
67	Sam Walker command photo	Photo courtesy of US Army Heritage and Education Center photo archives, Carlisle, PA
67	Sam Walker, with Bernie Rogers	Photo courtesy of US Army Heritage and Education Center photo archives, Carlisle, PA
68	William Westmoreland *Howitzer* photo	Photo courtesy of the USMA Library, taken from the Library Digital Collection, 1939 *Howitzer*
68	William Westmoreland headstone	Author
68	William Westmoreland with troops in Vietnam	Courtesy of *Life* magazine, taken from https://www.flickr.com/photos/97930879@N02/10501504655
69	Ed White Sr. *Howitzer* photo	Photo courtesy of the USMA Library, taken from the Library Digital Collection, 1924 *Howitzer*
69	Class Crest 1924	Photo courtesy of the USMA Library, taken from the Library Digital Collection, 1924 *Howitzer*
69	Ed White, Sr. headstone	Author
69	Ed White Sr. B&W portrait as a major general	US Air Force photograph, taken from http://digital-library.usma.edu/digital/collection/assembly/id/19219/rec/1
70	Snow covered tombstones	Author
71	Lucius Clay color portrait as LTG	US Army photograph, taken from https://catalog.archives.gov/id/74864256?objectPage=825
71	Lucius Clay headstone	Author
71	Lucius Clay Berlin marker	Author
71	Lucius Clay, *Time* magazine	Photo courtesy of *Time* magazine
72	Ed White Jr. headstone	Author
72	Ed White Jr. *Howitzer* photo	Photo courtesy of the USMA Library, taken from the Library Digital Collection, 1952 *Howitzer*
72	Ed White Jr. color portrait as LTC	Photo courtesy of NASA, taken from http://spaceflight.nasa.gov/gallery/images/apollo/apollo1/html/s66-35219.html (direct link) (JSC reference/uncropped version of original upload)
72	Ed White Jr. EVA in Gemini program	Photo courtesy of NASA, taken from https://www.nasa.gov/audience/foreducators/k-4/features/F_Going_Out.html
73	George Goethals headstone	Author
73	George Goethals B&W seated	Photo courtesy of USMA Library Digital Collection
74	Yellow flowers on gravesite	Photo credit: David R. Rose, release from photographer on hand
75	Donald V. Bennett *Howitzer* photo	Photo courtesy of the USMA Library, taken from the Library Digital Collection, 1940 *Howitzer*
75	Class Crest 1940	Photo courtesy of the USMA Library, taken from the Library Digital Collection, 1940 *Howitzer*
75	Donald V. Bennett B&W command photo	Photo courtesy of US Army Heritage and Education Center photo archives, Carlisle, PA
75	Donald V. Bennett headstone	Author
76	Sam Koster *Howitzer* photo	Photo courtesy of the USMA Library, taken from the Library Digital Collection, 1942 *Howitzer*
76	Sam Koster command photo	Photo courtesy of US Army Heritage and Education Center photo archives, Carlisle, PA
76	Sam Koster headstone	Author
77	John Buford B&W official photo	Photo courtesy of Brady National Photographic Art Gallery, taken from http://loc.gov/pictures/resource/cwpb.06372/
77	John Buford Monument, looking upward	Author
77	John Buford Monument, base	Author
77	John Buford in Gettysburg, sketch	Author scan of sketch in *Thirty Years After: An Artist's Memoir of the Civil War*, by Edward Forbes
78	Section XVIII signpost	Author
79	Old-style Medal of Honor line drawing	Drawing courtesy of US Army Institute of Heraldry, taken from https://commons.wikimedia.org/wiki/File:US-MOH-1896.png
79	Alonzo Cushing headstone	Author
79	Alonzo Cushing *Howitzer* photo	Photo courtesy of the USMA Library, taken from the Library Digital Collection, 1861 *Howitzer*

Photo Credits **299**

Page	Description	Attribution
79	Gettysburg battlefield	Photo courtesy of Clay Gilliland, taken from https://commons.wikimedia.org/wiki/File: Gilliland_(8819808704).jpg
80	Judson Kilpatrick B&W	Photo courtesy of Mathew B. Brady, US National Archives and Record Administration, taken from https://commons.wikimedia.org/wiki/File:Gen._Judson_Kilpatrick_-_NARA_-_528309 -crop.jpg
80	Judson Kilpatrick *Howitzer* photo	Photo courtesy of the USMA Library, taken from the Library Digital Collection, 1861 *Howitzer*
80	Judson Kilpatrick Monument in snow	Author
81	Fred Grant *Howitzer* photo	Photo courtesy of the USMA Library, taken from the Library Digital Collection, 1871 *Howitzer*
81	Fred Grant B&W official photo as MG	Photo courtesy of Library of Congress, taken from https://lccn.loc.gov/99406215
81	Fred Grant Monument	Author
81	Fred Grant Monument base	Author
82	Monuments with Buford, Foster in view	Author
83	Section XXX signpost	Author
83	Map detail of Section XXX	Author
84	B&W engraving of Wood Monument	Engraving by unknown author, taken from https://www.123rf.com/photo_133362165_wood -s-monument-in-honor-of-colonel-eleazer-derby-wood-who-died-during-the-american-civil-war -1812-v.html?vti=o75lha57o82rduz8bq-1-31
84	Wood Monument	Author
84	Wood Monument with cottage in background	Author
85	Edward Holden B&W portrait	Photo courtesy of the Library of Congress, taken from http://hdl.loc.gov/loc.pnp/cwpbh.03688
85	Cover of Holden's book on Herschel	Photo courtesy of Barnes and Noble, taken from https://www.barnesandnoble.com/w/sir -william-herschel-his-life-and-works-edward-singleton-holden/1129210199
85	Edward Holden Monument	Author
86	John Lillie Monument	Author
86	John Lillie B&W engraving with signature	Engraving by unknown author, taken from https://www.wikitree.com/photo/png/Lillie-548
86	John Lillie Monument detail	Author
87	Sunlit view of JFH gravesite	Author
88	Trant family crest line drawing	Line drawing courtesy of Heraldry, taken from https://fineartamerica.com/featured/trant-coat -of-arms-irish-heraldry.html
88	Revolutionary War soldier color painting	Painting taken from https://www.facebook.com/photo/?fbid=177968541463184&set= pb.100077501172759.-2207520000.
88	Dominick Trant tombstone	Author
89a	Susan Warner	Photo by unknown author, taken from https://www.military.com/history/susan-and-anna -warner.html
89b	Anna Warner	Photo by unknown author, taken from https://www.military.com/history/susan-and-anna -warner.html
89	Warner house color photograph	Photo courtesy of A. Hodges, taken from https://www.hhhistory.com/2014/01/miss-warners -boys-west-point-cadets_22.html
89	Warner sisters tombstones	Author
90	Cadet Monument	Author
90	Cadet Monument, detail 1	Author
90	Cadet Monument, detail 2	Author

Page	Description	Attribution
91	Page from *1876 Surgeon Report*	Author
91	Cadet Monument, detail of shaft	Author
91	Cadet Monument in winter	Author
92	Cemetery in snow at dawn	Author
93	Unknown Infant headstones in sunlight	Author
93	Unknown headstone	Author
93	Unknown Infant headstone close-up	Author
94	Louis Bentz headstone	Author
94	Louis Bents B&W portrait	Photo courtesy of the USMA Library, taken from the Library Digital Collection, 1871 Howitzer
94	Louis Bentz headstone detail	Author
94	B&W photo of Bentz in sallyport	Photo courtesy of the USMA Library Digital Collection, Stockdale Collection
95	Map detail of Sections XXIX, etc.	Author
96	Paul Kendall *Howitzer* photo	Photo courtesy of the USMA Library, taken from the Library Digital Collection, 1918 *Howitzer*
96	Paul Kendall B&W portrait as a MG	Photo courtesy of US Army Heritage and Education Center photo archives, Carlisle, PA
96	Paul Kendall headstone	Author
97	William M. Black headstone	Author
97	William M. Black sepia portrait as an MG	Photo courtesy of US Army Heritage and Education Center photo archives, Carlisle, PA
97	USS *William M. Black* ship photo	US Navy Yard Mare Island photo, taken from http://www.navsource.org/archives/09/22/22135.htm
98	Old-style Medal of Honor line drawing in color	Drawing courtesy of US Army Institute of Heraldry, taken from https://commons.wikimedia.org/wiki/File:US-MOH-1896.png
98	Mary Godfrey Monument	Author
98	B&W portrait of Edward Godfrey standing	US Army photograph, taken from https://www.arlingtoncemetery.net/egodfrey.htm
99	B&W portrait of George Derby seated	US Army photograph, taken from http://content.cdlib.org/ark:/13030/tf5d5nb3vb/?layout=metadata&brand=calisphere
99	George Derby headstone	Author
99	George M. Derby headstone	Author
99	Derby family plot 1	Author
99	George K. Derby headstone	Author
99	Derby family plot 2	Author
100	Section XXVII signpost	Author
101	George Custer B&W portrait, arms folded	Photographer unknown, taken from https://www.wchsmuseum.org/blog/on-this-day-in-history-custers-last-stand
101	Custer Monument, entire	Author
101	Custer Monument, detail with red flower	Author
102	Robert Anderson B&W portrait, standing	Photo by Mathew Brady, taken from https://en.wikipedia.org/wiki/Robert_Anderson_(Civil_War)#/media/File:Major_Robert_Anderson_by_Mathew_Brady.jpg
102	Robert Anderson Monument, front	Author
102	Robert Anderson Monument, rear	Author
103	Ethan Allen Hitchcock, B&W portrait, seated	Photo courtesy of the Library of Congress, taken from https://commons.wikimedia.org/wiki/File:Gen_Ethan_Allen_Hitchcock.jpg
103	Ethan Allen Hitchcock headstone	Author
104	Butterfield in distance, sunlit	Author

Photo Credits **301**

Page	Description	Attribution
105	Winfield Scott, B&W painting	Photo courtesy of USMA Library, Digital Collections
105	Winfield Scott Monument	Author
105	Winfield Scott B&W photo, seated as CSA	Photo courtesy of the Gilder Lehrman Collection of New York, taken from http://www.mrlincolnandnewyork.org/mr-lincolns-visits/general-winfield-scott/
106	John Eisenhower, *Howitzer* photo	Photo courtesy of the USMA Library, taken from the Library Digital Collection, 1944 *Howitzer*
106	John Eisenhower headstone	Author
106	John Eisenhower B&W portrait	Photo courtesy of US Army Heritage and Education Center photo archives, Carlisle, PA
107	Class Crest 1905	Photo courtesy of the USMA Library, taken from the Library Digital Collection, 1905 *Howitzer*
107	Clarence Ridley headstone	Author
107	Clarence Ridley *Howitzer* photo	Photo courtesy of the USMA Library, taken from the Library Digital Collection, 1905 *Howitzer*
107	Clarence Ridley B&W portrait, head	Photo courtesy of US Army Heritage and Education Center photo archives, Carlisle, PA
108	Ora Hunt Monument	Author
108	Ora Hunt *Howitzer* photo	Photo courtesy of the USMA Library, taken from the Library Digital Collection, 1894 *Howitzer*
108	Class Crest 1894	Photo courtesy of the USMA Library, taken from the Library Digital Collection, 1894 *Howitzer*
108	Ora Hunt B&W photo standing	Photo courtesy of US Army Heritage and Education Center photo archives, Carlisle, PA
109	Viele Monument in background, sunlit	Author
110	Painting of Sylvanus Thayer, seated	Painting by Robert W. Weir, taken from USMA Library Digital Collections
110	Sylvanus Thayer Monument	Author
110	Sylvanus Thayer statue on the Plain	Photo courtesy of the USMA Library Digital Collection
111	John Tidball Monument	Author
111	John Tidball face close-up	US Army photograph, taken from https://www.santafenewmexican.com/news/trail_dust/trail-dust-some-cannons-gained-fame-in-new-mexico/article_ee84fdc6-b425-11e2-a92e-001a4bcf6878.html
111	John Tidball with staff on cannon	US Army photograph, taken from https://www.santafenewmexican.com/news/trail_dust/trail-dust-some-cannons-gained-fame-in-new-mexico/article_ee84fdc6-b425-11e2-a92e-001a4bcf6878.html
112	Herman Koehler B&W portrait	Photo courtesy of the USMA Library Digital Collections
112	Herman Koehler B&W portrait	Photo courtesy of the USMA Library Digital Collections
112	Herman Koehler Monument	Author
113	Muro/Finkenaur headstones in shade of tree	Author
114	Old-style Medal of Honor line drawing in color	Drawing courtesy of US Army Institute of Heraldry, taken from https://commons.wikimedia.org/wiki/File:US-MOH-1896.png
114	Alexander Webb B&W portrait, seat, as BG	Photo courtesy of the Library of Congress
114	Alexander Webb headstone	Author
114	Alexander Webb Medal of Honor plaque	Author
115	Peter Michie B&W portrait, seated	Photo courtesy of the USMA Library Digital Collections, Stockbridge Collection
115	Peter Michie B&W painting	Photo courtesy of the USMA Library Digital Collections, Stockbridge Collection
115	Peter Michie headstone	Author
116	Dennis Michie *Howitzer* photo	Photo courtesy of the USMA Library, taken from the Library Digital Collection, 1882 *Howitzer*
116	Dennis Michie officer uniform portrait	US Army photo, unknown photographer, taken from https://www.findagrave.com/memorial/41645751/dennis-mahan-michie
116	Dennis Michie headstone	Author
116	Michie Stadium color photograph	Photo courtesy of USMA Public Affairs Office

302 *Stone Tapestry*

Page	Description	Attribution
117	Viele Monument in background, winter	Author
118	Old-style Medal of Honor line drawing in color	Drawing courtesy of US Army Institute of Heraldry, taken from https://commons.wikimedia .org/wiki/File:US-MOH-1896.png
118	William Beebe B&W portrait	US Army photograph, taken from https://goordnance.army.mil/hof/1969/beebe.html
118	William Beebe Howitzer portrait	Photo courtesy of the USMA Library, taken from the Library Digital Collection, 1863 *Howitzer*
118	William Beebe Medal of Honor plaque	Author
118	William Beebe headstone	Author
119	Thomas Devin headstone	Author
119	B&W sketch of cavalry	Author scan of sketch in *Thirty Years After: An Artists Memoir of the Civil War*, by Edward Forbes
119	Thomas Devin B&W photo seated	Photograph courtesy of the Library of Congress
120	Frank Kobes headstone	Author
120	Frank Kobes *Howitzer* photo	Photo courtesy of the USMA Library, taken from the Library Digital Collection, 1939 *Howitzer*
120	Frank Kobes B&W official portrait	Photo courtesy of the USMA Library, taken from the Library Digital Collection, 1955 *Howitzer*
121	Snow covered, with Cottage	Author
122	Map detail of Sections XXVIII, etc.	Author
123	Charles Raymond sepia photo portrait	US Army photo, unknown photographer, taken from https://www.findagrave.com/memorial /34195960/charles-walker-raymond
123	Charles Raymond family plot #1	Author
123	Charles Raymond B&W photo standing	Photo courtesy of USMA Library Digital Collections
123	Charles Raymond family plot #2	Author
124	Cyrus Comstock headstone	Author
124	Cyrus Comstock B&W	Photo courtesy of USMA Library Digital Collections
124	Cyrus Comstock B&W	Photo courtesy of USMA Library Digital Collections
125	Old-style Medal of Honor line drawing in color	Drawing courtesy of US Army Institute of Heraldry, taken from https://commons .wikimedia.org/wiki/File:US-MOH-1896.png
125	Bernard J. D. Irwin portrait	US Army photograph, unknown photographer, taken from https://www.findagrave.com /memorial/6412481/bernard-john_dowling-irwin
125	Bernard J. D. Irwin headstone	Author
125	George LeRoy Irwin B&W standing	Photo courtesy of US Army Heritage and Education Center photo archives, Carlisle, PA
125	Color photo of Main Gate, Fort Irwin, CA	Author
126	Water spraying over sunlit headstones	Author
127	B&W photo of Albert Church	Photo courtesy of USMA Library Digital Collections
127	Albert Church headstone	Author
127	Color photo of Descriptive Geometry textbook	Unknown photographer, taken from https://www.biblio.com/book/plates-descriptive -geometry-shades-shadows-linear/d/305611124
128	B&W photo of William Barlett	Photo courtesy of USMA Library Digital Collections
128	Color photo of front of Bartlett Hall	Unknown photographer, taken from https://www.walshgroup.com/ourexperience/building /education/westpointmilitaryacademybartletthallsciencecenter.html
128	Bartlett headstone	Author
128	Bartlett family plot	Author
129	Edward B. Hunt headstone	Author
129	B&W photo of Edward Hunt, standing	Photographer unknown, taken from https://www.findagrave.com/memorial/14244842 /edward-bissell-hunt

Page	Description	Attribution
129	Detail of Murray Hunt's headstone with his father	Author
129	B&W photo of Helen Jackson Hunt	Photo courtesy of USMA Library Digital Collections
130	Sylvanus Thayer grave, covered by tree	Author
131	Robert W. Weir B&W photo seated	Photo courtesy of USMA Library Digital Collections
131	Robert Weir headstone	Author
131	Color painting of *Embarkation of the Pilgrims*	Photo courtesy of the architect of the Capitol, original painting by Robert W. Weir, taken from https://en.wikipedia.org/wiki/United_States_Capitol_rotunda#/media/File: Embarkation_of_the_Pilgrims.jpg
131	Color painting of Winfield Scott	Photo courtesy of the USMA Library Digital Collections
132	James G. Benton headstone	Author
132	B&W photo of James Benton	Photo courtesy of USMA Library Digital Collections
132	Color photo of Ordnance Manual	Unknown photographer, taken from https://www.walmart.com/ip/A-Course-of-Instruction-in -Ordnance-and-Gunnery-Compiled-for-the-Use-of-the-Cadets-of-the-United-States-Military -Academy-9781361617786/736123029?wmlspartner=wlpa&selectedSellerId=1719
133	Sepia photo of Henry Metcalfe with signature	Photo courtesy of USMA Library Digital Collections, 1868 Howitzer
133	B&W photo of Henry Metcalfe	Photo courtesy of USMA Library Digital Collections
133	Henry Metcalfe headstone	Author
134	Detail, eagle on top of Buford Monument	Author
135	Old-style Medal of Honor line drawing in color	Drawing courtesy of US Army Institute of Heraldry, taken from https://commons.wikimedia .org/wiki/File:US-MOH-1896.png
135	Colorized photo of Butterfield	Courtesy of Daniel Hass, taken from https://commons.wikimedia.org/wiki/File: Colorbutterfield1.jpg
135	Butterfield Monument	Author
135	Color photo of two bandsmen playing "Taps"	Unknown photographer, courtesy of the USMA Band, taken from https://westpointband .wordpress.com/category/funeral/
135	Detail, top of Butterfield Monument	Author
136	Egbert Viele Monument	Author
136	B&W photo of Egbert Viele	Photo courtesy of USMA Library Digital Collections
136	Detail of topographical map of Manhattan	Photo of detail of the Veile map (1865) of New York City, taken from https://en.wikipedia.org /wiki/File:Viele_Map_1865-Topographical_New_York_City.jpg
136	Interior of Viele Monument	Author
137	B&W photo of Dennis Hart Mahan	Photo courtesy of USMA Library Digital Collections
137	Mahan headstone	Author
137	Photo of Mahan Hall	Photo courtesy of USMA Library Digital Collections
137	Sepia photo of Mahan with signature	Photo courtesy of USMA Library Digital Collections, 1871 *Howitzer*
138	Interior of Cadet Chapel	Author
139	Marty Maher headstone	Author
139	B&W painting of Marty Maher	Photo courtesy of USMA Library Digital Collections
139	B&W photo of Marty Maher	Author scanned from *Bringing Up The Brass*, by Marty Maher
139	Marty Maher with Red Reeder	Author scanned from *Bringing Up The Brass* by Marty Maher
140	Coach Palone headstone	Author
140	B&W photo of Palone	Photo courtesy of USMA Library Digital Collections, 1973 *Howitzer*

Page	Description	Attribution
140	B&W photo of Joe Palone	Photo courtesy of USMA Library Digital Collections, 1973 *Howitzer*
140	B&W photo of Coach Palone with players	Photo courtesy of USMA Library Digital Collections, 1971 *Howitzer*
141	B&W photo of John Thompson in uniform	Photo courtesy of USMA Library Digital Collections
141	John Thompson headstone	Author
141	B&W photo of Churchill with Tommy Gun	Author scanned from *Churchill at War: The Finest Hour in Photographs, 1940–1945*, by Martin Gilbert
142	Viele and Butterfield Monuments in light snow	Author
143	Old-style Medal of Honor line drawing in color	Drawing courtesy of US Army Institute of Heraldry, taken from https://commons.wikimedia .org/wiki/File:US-MOH-1896.png
143	New-style Medal of Honor line drawing in color	Drawing courtesy of US Army Institute of Heraldry, taken from https://commons .wikimedia.org/wiki/File:US-MOH-1904.png
143	George Gillespie *Howitzer* photo	Photo courtesy of the USMA Library, taken from the Library Digital Collection, 1862 *Howitzer*
143	George Gillespie headstone	Author
143	B&W photo portrait of George Gillespie	Photo courtesy of USMA Library Collections
143	Gillespie Medal of Honor plaque	Author
144	Old-style Medal of Honor line drawing in color	Drawing courtesy of US Army Institute of Heraldry, taken from https://commons.wikimedia .org/wiki/File:US-MOH-1896.png
144	B&W portrait photo of Benyaurd, standing	US Army photograph, taken from https://www.cmohs.org/recipients/william-h-benyaurd
144	B&W photo portrait of Benyaurd, seated	Photo courtesy of USMA Library Digital Collections, 1862 *Howitzer*
144	Benyaurd Medal of Honor plaque	Author
144	Benyaurd headstone	Author
145	Child statue on headstone	Author
146	Map detail of Sections I, II, III, and IV	Author
147	Hamilton Howze, *Howitzer* photo	Photo courtesy of the USMA Library, taken from the Library Digital Collection, 1930 *Howitzer*
147	Hamilton Howze headstone	Author
147	B&W photo of Hamilton Howze	US Army photograph, taken from http://ahecwebdds.carlisle.army.mil/awweb/main.jsp?flag= browse&smd=2&awdid=11
148	Old-style Medal of Honor line drawing in color	Drawing courtesy of US Army Institute of Heraldry, taken from https://commons.wikimedia .org/wiki/File:US-MOH-1896.png
148	Robert L. Howze, *Howitzer* photo	Photo courtesy of the USMA Library Digital Collection, taken from the 1880 *Howitzer*
148	B&W portrait of MG Robert Howze	Photo courtesy of USMA Library Digital Collections
148	Robert Howze headstone	Author
149	Alexander Patch headstone	Author
149	Alexander Patch *Howitzer* photo	Photo courtesy of the USMA Library, taken from the Library Digital Collection, 1913 *Howitzer*
149	Alexander Patch B&W command photo	Photo courtesy of US Army Heritage and Education Center photo archives, Carlisle, PA
150	Thomas Barry, B&W photo, standing portrait	Photo courtesy of USMA Library, taken from the Library Digital Collections
150	Thomas Barry, B&W photo, seated portrait	Photograph taken from *51st Annual Report of the Association of Graduates of the United States Military Academy, June 14th, 1920*
150	B&W photo of USS *Thomas H. Barry*	US Navy photograph, taken by USS *Tangier*, taken from https://www.shipscribe.com/usnaux /AP/AP45-p.html
150	Thomas Barry headstone	Author

Photo Credits **305**

Page	Description	Attribution
151	headstones framed by fall foliage	Photo credit: Scott R. Gourley, release from photographer on hand
152	Joseph Stilwell *Howitzer* photo	Photo courtesy of the USMA Library, taken from the Library Digital Collection, 1904 *Howitzer*
152	B&W Joseph Stilwell command photo	Photo courtesy of US Army Heritage and Education Center photo archives, Carlisle, PA
152	Stilwell headstone	Author
152	B&W photo of Stilwell walking out of Burma	US Army photograph, taken from https://forwhattheygave.com/2009/08/24/joe-stilwell/
153	Frank Merrill *Howitzer* photo	Photo courtesy of the USMA Library, taken from the Library Digital Collection, 1929 *Howitzer*
153	Frank Merrill headstone	Author
153	Frank Merrill B&W informal portrait in the field	US Army photo, taken from https://arsof-history.org/icons/merrill.html
153	Frank Merrill and Joe Stilwell B&W in the field	Photo courtesy of US Army Heritage and Education Center photo archives, Carlisle, PA
154	Color photo of a painting of Edward L. King	Painting by Joseph Cummings Chase, taken from https://americanhistory.si.edu/collections/search/object/nmah_447689
154	B&W informal portrait of Edward King in WWI	Photo courtesy of US Army Heritage and Education Center photo archives, Carlisle, PA
154	Edward L. King headstone	Author
155	Single deer fawn among headstones	Author
156	Edward DeArmond *Howitzer* photo	Photo courtesy of the USMA Library, taken from the Library Digital Collection, 1901 *Howitzer*
156	Edward DeArmond headstone	Author
156	Sepia tone BG DeArmond head portrait	US Army photograph, taken from https://www.findagrave.com/memorial/122685748/edward-harrison-dearmond
156	B&W photo of 32nd Infantry division staff WWI	Photograph taken by Fred Gildersleeve, taken from the Texas Collection at Baylor University, https://wacotexashistoryinpictures.com/2022/08/24/gildersleeves-views-of-camp-macarthur/
157	B&W informal head portrait of Fred Sladen	Photo courtesy of the USMA Library, from the Library Digital Collection
157	Fred Sladen headstone	Author
157	B&W photo of Fred Sladen	US Army photograph, taken from https://www.findagrave.com/memorial/122959687/fred-winchester-sladen
158	B&W portrait of Professor Louis Vauthier	US Army photograph, taken from https://museumofamericanfencing.com/wp/vauthier-louis/
158	Louis Vauthier headstone	Author
158	B&W photo of fencing team	Photo courtesy of the USMA Library, taken from the Library Digital Collection, 1904 *Howitzer*
158	B&W photo of Vauthier in fencing attire	Photo courtesy of the USMA Library, taken from the Library Digital Collection, 1923 *Howitzer*
159	Rock saying, "I Love You"	Author
160	Elliott Cutler headstone	Author
160	Elliott Cutler *Howitzer* photo	Photo courtesy of the USMA Library, taken from the Library Digital Collection, 1942 *Howitzer*
160	Elliot Cutler formal portrait B&W	Photo courtesy of the USMA Library, taken from the Library Digital Collections
161	Dean Hudnutt *Howitzer* photo	Photo courtesy of the USMA Library, taken from the Library Digital Collection, 1916 *Howitzer*
161	Class Crest 1916	Photo courtesy of the USMA Library, taken from the Library Digital Collection, 1916 *Howitzer*
161	B&W photo of 1936 Olympic Program	Photo taken from https://www.flickr.com/photos/57440551@N03/16252650030
161	Dean Hudnutt headstone	Author
162	Old-style Medal of Honor line drawing in color	Drawing courtesy of US Army Institute of Heraldry, taken from https://commons.wikimedia.org/wiki/File:US-MOH-1896.png
162	Albert Mills Monument	Author
162	B&W photo of Albert Mills, seated portrait	Photo courtesy of USMA Library, taken from the Library Digital Collection

Page	Description	Attribution
162	Albert Mills Medal of Honor plaque	Author
162	Albert Mills B&W portrait, seated	US Army photograph, taken from https://mohmuseum.org/medal_of_honor/albert-mills/
163	Penny headstone framed in red berry tree	Author
164	Matthew Ferrara color portrait from 2-503 PIR	US Army photograph, taken from https://www.findagrave.com/memorial/23018311/matthew-charles-ferrara
164	Class Crest 2005	Photo courtesy of the USMA Library, taken from the Library Digital Collection, 2005 *Howitzer*
164	Matthew Ferrara headstone	Author
164	Color photo of Ferrara briefing senior officer	Photo courtesy of Greg Zoroya, taken from the Chosen Few, https://m.facebook.com/media/set/?vanity=chosenfewbook&set=a.780908872087156
165	Stuart MacDonald *Howitzer* photo	Photo courtesy of the USMA Library, taken from the Library Digital Collection, 1915 *Howitzer*
165	B&W photo, Stuart MacDonald obituary	US Army photograph, taken from West Point Association of Graduates website, "Stuart C. MacDonald 1915" entry; https://www.westpointaog.org/memorial-article?id=6541e0de-a127-4cb5-86c6-ca9cd3121861.
165	B&W photo of Bataan Death March	US Army photograph by unknown Japanese soldier, taken from https://www.businessinsider.com/bataan-death-march-photos-from-world-war-ii-2017-4
165	Stuart MacDonald headstone	Author
166	Lemuel Mathewson *Howitzer* photo	Photo courtesy of the USMA Library, taken from the Library Digital Collection, 1922 *Howitzer*
166	Lemuel Mathewson headstone	Author
166	B&W photo of Lemuel Mathewson	Photo courtesy of US Army Heritage and Education Center photo archives, Carlisle, PA
166	Color photo of White House Military Office patch	US Army photograph, taken from https://army.togetherweserved.com/army/servlet/tws.webapp.WebApp?cmd=ShadowBoxProfile&type=AssignmentExt&ID=311069
167	Anderson Fountain	Author
168	"Died at West Point" headstone	Author
169	Map detail of Sections V and VI	Author
170	George Anderson headstone	Author
170	B&W photo of George Anderson, formal portrait	US Army photograph, taken from 46th Annual Reunion of the Association of Graduates of the United States Military Academy, June 11, 1915 (George S. Anderson obituary); Saginaw, MI: Seeman & Peters
170	B&W photo of Anderson at Yellowstone	Photo courtesy of Montana Historical Society, taken from https://medium.com/@joe.gioia/the-czar-of-yellowstone-c337e7a53a04
171	Color photo of Frank Besson, official portrait	Photo courtesy of US Army Heritage and Education Center photo archives, Carlisle, PA
171	Frank Besson *Howitzer* photo	Photo courtesy of the USMA Library, taken from the Library Digital Collection, 1932 *Howitzer*
171	Frank Besson headstone	Author
172	David Barger *Howitzer* photo	Photo courtesy of the USMA Library, taken from the Library Digital Collection, January 1943 *Howitzer*
172	David Barger headstone	Author
172	David Barger B&W official portrait	US Air Force photograph, taken from https://www.westpointaog.org/memorial-article?id=b28eaaef-a9aa-4d64-9790-bc18d2e19f34.
172	Color photo of Gemini two-ship mission	Photograph courtesy of NASA
173	Outside Columbarium in fall	Author
174	John Jannarone headstone	Author
174	B&W *Howitzer* photo of Dean Jannarone	Photo courtesy of the USMA Library, taken from the Library Digital Collection, 1938 *Howitzer*

Page	Description	Attribution
174	B&W photo of Jannarone with Leslie Groves	Photo courtesy of Atomic Heritage Foundation, taken from https://commons.wikimedia.org/wiki/File:Edgar_Sengier_receiving_the_Medal_of_Merit.jpg
175	Sepia *Howitzer* photo of Clarence Townsley	Photo courtesy of the USMA Library, taken from the Library Digital Collection, 1944 *Howitzer*
175	B&W formal portrait of Clarence Townsley	Photo courtesy of US Army Heritage and Education Center photo archives, Carlisle, PA
175	B&W photo of Townsley as superintendent	Photo courtesy of USMA Library, taken from Library Digital Collections
175	Townsley headstone	Author
176	James O. Green West Point ring, top	Photograph courtesy of Green family, taken from https://www.findagrave.com/memorial/124052614/james-oscar-green/photo
176	James O. Green West Point ring, side	Photograph courtesy of Green family, taken from https://www.findagrave.com/memorial/124052614/james-oscar-green/photo
176	B&W photo portrait of James O. Green Jr.	Photo courtesy of the USMA Library, taken from the Library Digital Collection, 1917 *Howitzer*
176	Class Crest 1917	Photo courtesy of the USMA Library, taken from the Library Digital Collection, 1917 *Howitzer*
177	James O. Green *Howitzer* photo	Photo courtesy of the USMA Library, taken from the Library Digital Collection, 1941 *Howitzer*
177	Class Crest 1941	Photo courtesy of the USMA Library, taken from the Library Digital Collection, 1941 *Howitzer*
177	B&W informal portrait of James O. Green	Photograph courtesy of the Green family, taken from https://www.westpointaog.org/memorial-article?id=3a2a7113-22ae-4113-964d-6b371eb94bb1.
177	Green family headstones	Author
178	Walking path by Lorentz	Author
179	B&W photo of Elvin Heiberg, official portrait	Photo courtesy of US Army Heritage and Education Center photo archives, Carlisle, PA
179	Elvin R. Heiberg Monument	Author
179	Elvin R. Heiberg Monument, detail of base	Author
179	B&W photo of Harrison Heiberg, official portrait	US Army photograph, taken from https://www.westpointaog.org/memorial-article?id=a46cb4a9-3ec6-4a87-9f55-31277862a7a5
180	Harrison Heiberg Monument	Author
180	Class Crest 1919	Photo courtesy of the USMA Library, taken from the Library Digital Collection, 1919 *Howitzer*
180	B&W photo of Elvin R. Heiberg II	US Army photograph, taken from https://www.westpointaog.org/memorial-article?id=b9fadcb5-f495-4147-a7a2-13e4ef34c056.
180	Elvin R. Heiberg II Monument	Author
180	Class Crest 1926	Photo courtesy of the USMA Library, taken from the Library Digital Collection, 1926 *Howitzer*
181	Class Crest 1961	Photo courtesy of the USMA Library, taken from the Library Digital Collection, 1961 *Howitzer*
181	William Heiberg *Howitzer* photo	Photo courtesy of the USMA Library, taken from the Library Digital Collection, 1961 *Howitzer*
181	William Heiberg B&W official photo	US Army photograph, taken from https://www.westpointaog.org/memorial-article?id=e4071a0f-c40c-43ae-a729-34cabd965ef3
181	William Heiberg Monument	Author
182	Elbert Farman Jr. headstone	Author
182	Class Crest 1909	Photo courtesy of the USMA Library, taken from the Library Digital Collection, 1909 *Howitzer*
182	Elbert Farman *Howitzer* photo	Photo courtesy of the USMA Library, taken from the Library Digital Collection, 1909 *Howitzer*
183	Back of Chapel with rifle/helmet monument	Author
184	Charles C. Benedict *Howitzer* photo	Photo courtesy of the USMA Library, taken from the Library Digital Collection, 1915 *Howitzer*
184	Benedict Family headstone	Author
184	B&W official photo, Charles C. Benedict	US Army photograph, taken from https://www.findagrave.com/memorial/124122981/charles-calvert-benedict

Page	Description	Attribution
184	Charles C. Benedict Jr. *Howitzer* photo	Photo courtesy of the USMA Library, taken from the Library Digital Collection, January 1943 *Howitzer*
185	Calvert P. Benedict *Howitzer* photo	Photo courtesy of the USMA Library, taken from the Library Digital Collection, 1946 *Howitzer*
185	Class Crest 1946	Photo courtesy of the USMA Library, taken from the Library Digital Collection, 1946 *Howitzer*
185	Color photo of Calvert Benedict	US Army photograph, taken from https://www.findagrave.com/memorial/66438746/calvert-potter-benedict
186	Class Crest 1946	Photo courtesy of the USMA Library, taken from the Library Digital Collection, 1946 *Howitzer*
186	Harrison Lobdell *Howitzer* photo	Photo courtesy of the USMA Library, taken from the Library Digital Collection, 1946 *Howitzer*
186	Color portrait, MG Lobdell seated	Photo courtesy of the US Air Force
187	Paul Bunker *Howitzer* photo	Photo courtesy of the USMA Library, taken from the Library Digital Collection, 1903 *Howitzer*
187	Paul Bunker Jr. *Howitzer* photo	Photo courtesy of the USMA Library, taken from the Library Digital Collection, 1932 *Howitzer*
187	Paul Bunker headstone	Author
187	Paul Bunker Jr. headstone	Author
188	William Kunzig *Howitzer* photo	Photo courtesy of the USMA Library, taken from the Library Digital Collection, 1932 *Howitzer*
188	William Kunzig headstone	Author
188	B&W photo of William Kunzig by jeep, WWII	Photograph courtesy of William Kunzig, taken from https://www.sfgate.com/bayarea/article/Gen-William-Kunzig-dies-Presidio-last-post-3285453.php
189	Hanna headstone in water	Author
190	Mickey Marcus headstone	Author
190	Marcus Howitzer photo	Photo courtesy of the USMA Library, taken from the Library Digital Collection, 1924 *Howitzer*
190	B&W photo of Mickey Marcus, official portrait	US Army photograph, taken from https://www.geni.com/people/David-Mickey-Marcus/6000000000631622551
191	Hayes family headstones	Author
191	Thomas J. Hayes Jr. *Howitzer* photo	Photo courtesy of the USMA Library, taken from the Library Digital Collection, 1912 *Howitzer*
191	Thomas J. Hayes Jr. B&W photo, official portrait	US Army photograph, taken from https://goordnance.army.mil/hof/1970/1976/hayes.html
191	Thomas J. Hayes III *Howitzer* photo	Photo courtesy of the USMA Library, taken from the Library Digital Collection, 1936 *Howitzer*
192	Class Crest 1936	Photo courtesy of the USMA Library taken from the Library Digital Collections, 1936 *Howitzer*
192	Thomas J. Hayes III headstone	Author
192	Class Crest 1966	Photo courtesy of the USMA Library, taken from the Library Digital Collection, 1966 *Howitzer*
192	Thomas J. Hayes IV *Howitzer* photo	Photo courtesy of the USMA Library, taken from the Library Digital Collection, 1966 *Howitzer*
192	Thomas J. Hayes IV headstone	Author
193	Field of headstones	Author
194	Douglas Kinnard headstone	Author
194	Douglas Kinnard *Howitzer* photo	Photo courtesy of the USMA Library, taken from the Library Digital Collection, 1944 *Howitzer*
194	Color photo of cover of The War Managers	Image taken from https://www.amazon.com/War-Managers-Thirtieth-Anniversary/dp/159114437X
194	B&W photo of Douglas Kinnard, portrait	Photo courtesy of Kinnard family, taken from https://www.westpointaog.org/memorial-article?id=e06afa79-157e-438b-966b-3aef6f451ca2.
194	Color photo from *Adventures in Two Worlds*	US Army photograph, taken from https://www.amazon.com/Adventures-Two-Worlds-Vietnam-Professor-ebook/dp/B079K23WGS
195	Ike Pappas *Howitzer* photo	Photo courtesy of the USMA Library, taken from the Library Digital Collection, 1944 *Howitzer*
195	Ike Pappas headstone	Author

Page	Description	Attribution
195	B&W photo of Ike Pappas in library at Carlisle	US Army photograph, taken from https://www.westpointaog.org/rog-search-details?id=278eda84-564a-4653-9274-cd9b48445471.
196	William Rice King headstone	Author
197	Viele and Butterfield Monuments	Author
198	Map detail of Sections VII and VIII	Author
199	New-style Medal of Honor line drawing	Drawing courtesy of US Army Institute of Heraldry, taken from https://commons.wikimedia.org/wiki/File:US-MOH-1904.png
199	William Wilbur *Howitzer* photo	Photo courtesy of the USMA Library, taken from the Library Digital Collection, 1912 *Howitzer*
199	William Wilbur headstone	Author
199	B&W of William Wilbur wearing Medal of Honor	Photo courtesy of US Army Heritage and Education Center photo archives, Carlisle, PA
199	B&W of William Wilbur at Casablanca	Photo courtesy of US Army Heritage and Education Center photo archives, Carlisle, PA
200	Michael Davison *Howitzer* photo	Photo courtesy of the USMA Library, taken from the Library Digital Collection, 1944 *Howitzer*
200	Michael Davison headstone	Author
200	Color portrait of Michael Davison, official portrait	Photo courtesy of US Army Heritage and Education Center photo archives, Carlisle, PA
201	New-style Medal of Honor line drawing in color	Drawing courtesy of US Army Institute of Heraldry, taken from https://commons.wikimedia.org/wiki/File:US-MOH-1904.png
201	Andre Lucas *Howitzer* photo	Photo courtesy of the USMA Library, taken from the Library Digital Collection, 1954 *Howitzer*
201	Andre Lucas headstone	Author
201	B&W photo, LTC Andre Lucas at Ripcord	US Army photograph, taken from https://commons.wikimedia.org/wiki/File:Andre_C._Lucas.jpg
202	Close-up of bronze USMA crest on a headstone	Author
203	Mort O'Connor headstone	Author
203	Mort O'Connor *Howitzer* photo	Photo courtesy of the USMA Library, taken from the Library Digital Collection, 1953 *Howitzer*
203	B&W Mort O'Connor official photo	US Army photograph, taken from https://www.vvmf.org/Wall-of-Faces/38351/MORTIMER-L-OCONNOR/
204	John Weaver *Howitzer* photo	Photo courtesy of the USMA Library, taken from the Library Digital Collection, 1950 *Howitzer*
204	B&W photo of LT John Weaver in uniform	US Army photograph, taken from https://www.westpointaog.org/memorial-article?id=8cd969dd-9d55-4f86-8dc7-b1ae1e805350.
204	John Weaver headstone	Author
205	New-style Medal of Honor line drawing in color	Drawing courtesy of US Army Institute of Heraldry, taken from https://commons.wikimedia.org/wiki/File:US-MOH-1904.png
205	Sam Coursen headstone	Author
205	Sam Coursen *Howitzer* photo	Photo courtesy of the USMA Library, taken from the Library Digital Collection, 1949 *Howitzer*
205	Ferry boat the Lt Samuel S. Coursen	Photo courtesy of Luis Zunino, taken from https://www.shipspotting.com/photos/2703756
206	Courtenay Davis *Howitzer* photo	Photo courtesy of the USMA Library, taken from the Library Digital Collection, 1949 *Howitzer*
206	Color drawing odDistinguished Service Cross	Line drawing taken from https://en.wikipedia.org/wiki/Distinguished_Service_Cross_%28United_States%29
206	Courtenay Davis headstone	Author
207	Shaded view of tree with Buford in background	Author

310 *Stone Tapestry*

Page	Description	Attribution
208	George Tow *Howitzer* photo	Photo courtesy of the USMA Library, taken from the Library Digital Collection, 1949 *Howitzer*
208	George Tow in bathrobe, B&W portrait	Photo courtesy of USMA Library, taken from the Library Digital Collection, 1949 *Howitzer*
208	George Tow headstone	Author
208	Class Crest 1949	Photo courtesy of the USMA Library, taken from the Library Digital Collection, 1949 *Howitzer*
209	Bryant Moore headstone	Author
209	Bryant Moore, B&W formal portrait as a MG	US Army photograph, taken from https://www.usmilitariaforum.com/forums/index.php?/topic/330569-major-general-bryant-e-moore-wwii-identify-foreign-awards/
209	Bryant Moore, B&W informal portrait	Photo courtesy of US Army Heritage and Education Center photo archives, Carlisle, PA
210	William Schempf, formal B&W portrait	US Army photograph, taken from https://www.discogs.com/artist/3593332-William-H-Schempf
210	William Schempf headstone	Author
210	B&W photo of band Trophy Point	Photo courtesy of USMA Library, taken from Library Digital Collections
211	Chancellor Martin headstone	Author
211	B&W photo in Egyptian uniform dress	Unknown photographer, taken from the 48th Annual Report of the Association of Graduates of the United States Military Academy, June 12th, 1917
212	White dogwood tree in bloom near Section II	Author
213	John Biddle, B&W photo, standing	Photo courtesy of USMA Library, taken from Library Digital Collections
213	John Biddle headstone	Author
213	John Biddle, B&W photo	Photo courtesy of USMA Library, taken from the Library Digital Collections
214	Percy Silver, B&W photo in clerical garb	Photo courtesy of the USMA Library, taken from the Library Digital Collection, 1917 *Howitzer*
214	Line drawing of Episcopal Church logo	Line drawing taken from https://en.wikipedia.org/wiki/Episcopal_Church_(United_States)
214	Church of the Incarnation	Photograph courtesy of the New York Architecture website, taken from https://www.newyorkitecture.com/church-of-the-incarnation/
214	Percy Silver headstone	Author
215	Todd Lambka headstone	Author
215	Lambka command photo	US Army photograph
215	Todd Lambka *Howitzer* photo	Photo courtesy of the USMA Library, taken from the Library Digital Collection, 2010 *Howitzer*
216	New-style Medal of Honor line drawing in color	Drawing courtesy of US Army Institute of Heraldry, taken from https://commons.wikimedia.org/wiki/File:US-MOH-1904.png
216	William Heard headstone	Author
216	William Heard *Howitzer* photo	Photo courtesy of the USMA Library, taken from the Library Digital Collection, 1883 *Howitzer*
216	William Heard, B&W photo official portrait	Photo courtesy of the USMA Library, taken from the Library Digital Collections
217	Watkins headstone in foreground	Author
218	Courtland Schuyler *Howitzer* photo	Photo courtesy of the USMA Library, taken from the Library Digital Collection, 1922 *Howitzer*
218	Courtlandt Schuyler headstone	Author
218	Courtland Schuyler portrait	Photo courtesy of US Army Heritage and Education Center photo archives, Carlisle, PA
219	Joseph McCarthy *Howitzer* photo	Photo courtesy of the USMA Library, taken from the Library Digital Collection, 1945 *Howitzer*
219	Class Crest 1945	Photo courtesy of the USMA Library, taken from the Library Digital Collection, 1945 *Howitzer*
219	Joseph McCarthy headstone	Author
219	BG Joseph McCarthy, B&W official photo	Photo courtesy of US Army Heritage and Education Center photo archives, Carlisle, PA
220	George Eyster *Howitzer* photo	Photo courtesy of the USMA Library, taken from the Library Digital Collection, 1945 *Howitzer*
220	Class Crest 1945	Photo courtesy of the USMA Library, taken from the Library Digital Collection, 1945 *Howitzer*
220	George Eyster headstone	Author

Photo Credits **311**

Page	Description	Attribution
220	George Eyster, B&W seated portrait head shot	Photo courtesy of the Eyster family
221	Snow-covered headstone with wreaths	Author
222	Robert Losey headstone	Author
222	Robert Losey *Howitzer* photo	Photo courtesy of the USMA Library, taken from the Library Digital Collection, 1929 *Howitzer*
222	Robert Losey, B&W head shot seated in airplane	Unknown photographer, taken from https://www.findagrave.com/memorial/7411175/robert-moffat-losey
223	Walter Schulze headstone	Author
223	B&W photo of Schultze monument in France	Unknown photographer, taken from https://www.findagrave.com/memorial/5290859/walter-herman-schulze/photo
223	B&W photo of Schultze, standing in uniform	Unknown photographer, taken from https://www.findagrave.com/memorial/5290859/walter-herman-schulze/photo
224	B&W photo of Charles P. Echols	Photo courtesy of the USMA Library, taken from the Library Digital Collection, photographs of West Point Collection
224	Echols headstone	Author
225	George Tow's CIB on headstone	Author
226	Map of Sections XII, XXXI, XXXII, and XXXIII	Author
227	Pat Nappi headstone	Author
227	Nappi at ringside	Photo courtesy of USMA Library Digital Collections
227	Color photo of Nappi ringside	Unknown US Army photographer, taken from https://nara.getarchive.net/media/retired-master-sergeant-pat-nappi-us-army-left-head-coach-of-the-boxing-team-a0f3fd
228	Row of Infants headstones	Author
228	Ruth Bryan headstone	Author
228	Unknown Infant headstone	Author
228	Bertha Johnson infant headstone	Author
229	Constantine Child headstone	Author
229	Lapp Child headstone	Author
229	Tina Mae infant headstone	Author
229	Karen Marie infant headstone	Author
229	Irene and George Kulebokeon headstones	Author
230	Norman Edwards headstone	Author
230	Norman Edwards *Howitzer* photo	Photo courtesy of the USMA Library, taken from the Library Digital Collection, 1935 *Howitzer*
230	Class Crest 1935	Photo courtesy of the USMA Library, taken from the Library Digital Collection, 1935 *Howitzer*
231	View through cemetery framed by fall foliage	Photo credit: Scott R. Gourley, release from photographer on hand
232	Overhead view of library interior	Photo courtesy of the USMA Library, taken from the Library Digital Collection, Stockbridge Collection
232	William and Frances Lewis headstone	Author
232	Exterior of Library	Photo courtesy of the USMA Library, taken from the Library Digital Collection, 1929 *Howitzer*
233	Robert Donovan *Howitzer* photo	Photo courtesy of the USMA Library, taken from the Library Digital Collection, 1963 *Howitzer*
233	Class Crest 1963	Photo courtesy of the USMA Library, taken from the Library Digital Collection, 1963 *Howitzer*
233	Robert Donovan headstone	Author
234	Charles Schilling headstone	Author

Page	Description	Attribution
234	B&W photo, COL Schilling at his desk	Photo courtesy of the USMA Library, taken from the Library Digital Collection, 1973 *Howitzer*
234	Charles Schilling *Howitzer* photo	Photo courtesy of the USMA Library, taken from the Library Digital Collection, 1941 *Howitzer*
235	Cemetery view framed by dogwoods	Author
236	Color photo of interior of gym	Photo courtesy of USMA Library Digital Collections
236	William Penny headstone	Author
236	Color photo of exterior of gym	Photo courtesy of USMA Library Digital Collections
237	Bruce Staser *Howitzer* photo	Photo courtesy of the USMA Library, taken from the Library Digital Collection, 1944 *Howitzer*
237	Full-size photo of Betty Staser poem	Author
237	Detail of Bruce and Betty Staser headstone	Author
238	James Mahan headstone	Author
238	B&W detail of photo of Mahan, seated	Photo courtesy of the USMA Library, taken from the Library Digital Collection, 1945 *Howitzer*
238	Color photo of USMA Band in parade	Photo courtesy of SSG Torin Olsen, taken from https://en.wikipedia.org/wiki/West_Point_Band#/media/File:West_Point_Band_Army_vs_N_Illinois_Review.jpg
238	B&W photo of old USMA Band in formation	Photo courtesy of the USMA Library, taken from the Library Digital Collection
239	Photo of back gates to cemetery in shade	Author
240	Henry Mucci *Howitzer* photo	Photo courtesy of the USMA Library, taken from the Library Digital Collection, 1936 *Howitzer*
240	B&W photo of Henry Mucci with pipe in jungle	Photo courtesy of US Army Heritage and Education Center photo archives, Carlisle, PA
240	Henry Mucci headstone	Author
241	Tim Krebs headstone	Author
241	Tim Krebs *Howitzer* photo	Photo courtesy of the USMA Library, taken from the Library Digital Collection, 1971 *Howitzer*
241	Line drawing of Legion of Merit	Photo taken from https://en.wikipedia.org/wiki/Legion_of_Merit
242	Roger Nye *Howitzer* photo	Photo courtesy of the USMA Library, taken from the Library Digital Collection, 1946 *Howitzer*
242	Roger Nye headstone	Author
242	Color photo of cover of *The Patton Mind*	Photograph taken from https://www.amazon.com/Patton-Mind-Point-Military-History/dp/0895294281
242	*The Challenge of Command*	Photograph taken from https://www.amazon.com/Challenge-Command-Reading-Military-Excellence/dp/0399528040
242	B&W official portrait of COL Nye	US Army photograph, taken from https://www.westpointaog.org/memorial-article?id=810dd2ad-f17a-44df-bfeb-2c2a5b3bddd3
243	View of cemetery on summer day framed by trees 244	Author
	Map detail of Sections XXXVI and XXXIV	Author
245	Red White headstone	Author
245	Red White *Howitzer* photo	Photo courtesy of the USMA Library, taken from the Library Digital Collection, 1933 *Howitzer*
245	Class Crest 1933	Photo courtesy of USMA Library, taken from the Library Digital Collection, 1933 *Howitzer*
245	Line drawing of CIA seal	Drawing of CIA seal, taken from https://en.wikipedia.org/wiki/Central_Intelligence_Agency
246	Ted Parker *Howitzer* photo	Photo courtesy of the USMA Library, taken from the Library Digital Collection, 1931 *Howitzer*
246	Ted Parker headstone	Author
246	B&W official portrait of General Parker	Photo courtesy of US Army Heritage and Education Center photo archives, Carlisle, PA
247	Henry McKenzie *Howitzer* photo	Photo courtesy of the USMA Library, taken from the Library Digital Collection, 1929 *Howitzer*
247	Henry McKenzie headstone	Author
247	Line drawing of Quartermaster Corps insignia	Line drawing, taken from https://en.wikipedia.org/wiki/File:USA_-_Quartermaster_Corps_Branch_Insignia.png

Page	Description	Attribution
248	Cemetery view in fall	Photo credit: Scott R. Gourley, release from photographer on hand
249	Laura Walker headstone	Author
249	Laura Walker *Howitzer* photo	Photo courtesy of the USMA Library, taken from the Library Digital Collection, 2003 *Howitzer*
249	Laura Walker in Afghanistan	Photo courtesy of the Walker family
250	Emily Perez *Howitzer* photo	Photo courtesy of the USMA Library, taken from the Library Digital Collection, 2005 *Howitzer*
250	Emily Perez headstone	Author
250	Color informal photo of Emily Perez	Photograph courtesy of the Perez family, taken from http://www.salem-news.com/articles /may052010/perez-honors.php
251	CSM Mary Sutherland Monument	Author
251	Line drawing of CSM insignia	Line drawing, taken from https://en.wikipedia.org/wiki/Command_sergeant_major#:~:text =A%20command%20sergeant%20major%20(CSM,unit%20(battalion%20or%20higher).
251	Plaque for MES Community Center	US Army photograph, taken from https://www.army.mil/article/154416/west_point_honors _command_sgt_maj_mary_sutherland
251	Color informal portrait of CSM Sutherland	Unknown photographer, taken from https://www.tributearchive.com/obituaries/2564166 /Command-Sergeant-Major-Mary-E-Sutherland
252	Snow-covered wreath on front gates	Author
253	B&W informal photo of Chaplain Ford, seated	Photo courtesy of the USMA Library, taken from the Library Digital Collection, 1973 *Howitzer*
253	B&W photo of Cadet Chapel	Photo credit: Michael Lyons, release from photographer on hand
253	Line drawing of House of Representatives seal	Line drawing, taken from https://en.wikipedia.org/wiki/United_States_House_of _Representatives
253	Chaplain Ford headstone	Author
254	John Heintges headstone	Author
254	John Heintges *Howitzer* photo	Photo courtesy of the USMA Library, taken from the Library Digital Collection, 1936 *Howitzer*
254	B&W informal photo of Heintges in combat	US Army photograph
255	Chih Wang headstone	Author
255	Chih Wang *Howitzer* photo	Photo courtesy of the USMA Library, taken from the Library Digital Collection, 1932 *Howitzer*
255	B&W informal portrait of Chih Wang in uniform	Photo courtesy of the USMA Library, taken from the Library Digital Collection, 1932 *Howitzer*
256	Monk Meyers headstone	Author
256	Monk Meyers *Howitzer* photo	Photo courtesy of the USMA Library, taken from the Library Digital Collection, 1937 *Howitzer*
256	B&W face shot of Monk Meyers in old age	Unknown photographer, taken from https://footballfoundation.org/sports/general/roster /charles-r---monk--meyer/31
257	Sandstone triptych monument	Author
258	Ben Gilman headstone	Author
258	Line drawing of House of Representatives seal	Line drawing, taken from https://en.wikipedia.org/wiki/United_States_House_of _Representatives
258	Color portrait of Ben Gilman in Congress	Photo courtesy of the US House of Representatives, taken from https://www.wamc.org/wamc -news/2016-12-17/former-ny-congressman-ben-gilman-dies
259	Seth Hudgins *Howitzer* photo	Photo courtesy of the USMA Library, taken from the Library Digital Collection, 1964 *Howitzer*
259	Seth Hudgins headstone	Author
259	Color photo of AOG Seal	Photo courtesy of the USMA Association of Graduates
259	photo of Seth Hudgins seated at his desk	Photo courtesy of the USMA Association of Graduates

Page	Description	Attribution
260	Jaimie Leonard *Howitzer* photo	Photo courtesy of the USMA Library, taken from the Library Digital Collection, 1997 *Howitzer*
260	Jaimie Leonard headstone	Author
260	Color photo of Jaimie Leonard in Afghanistan	Photograph courtesy of Leonard family, taken from https://warriorsatease.org/the-meaning-of-memorial-day/
261	Garry Owen insignia on headstone	Author
262	John Hottell *Howitzer* Photo	Photo courtesy of the USMA Library, taken from the Library Digital Collection, 1964 *Howitzer*
262	B&W photo, John Hottell	US Army photograph, taken from https://www.west-point.org/users/usma1964/24930/.
262	John Hottell headstone	Author
263	Ying-Hsing Wen headstone	Author
263	Class Crest 1909	Photo courtesy of the USMA Library, taken from the Library Digital Collection, 1909 *Howitzer*
263	Ying-Hsing Wen, B&W portrait	Unknown photographer, taken from https://commons.wikimedia.org/wiki/File:Wen_Yingxing.jpg
263	Ying-Hsing Wen *Howitzer* photo	Photo courtesy of the USMA Library, taken from the Library Digital Collection, 1909 *Howitzer*
264	Thomas Selfridge Monument	Author
264	Thomas Selfridge *Howitzer* photo	Photo courtesy of the USMA Library, taken from the Library Digital Collection, 1903 *Howitzer*
264	B&W photo, Thomas Selfridge at controls of Wright Flyer	Photo courtesy of US Army Heritage and Education Center photo archives, Carlisle, PA
265	Rene DeRussy	Author
265	B&W photo of a painting of Rene DeRussy	Photo courtesy of the USMA Library, taken from the Library Digital Collections
266	Sylvanus Thayer Monument under tree cover	Author
267	Photo of cadet full dress coat	Photo courtesy of USMA Library, taken from Library Digital Collections
268	Color photo of Mom and Dad at Fort Benning	Author
270	Gaylyn Jones *Howitzer* photo	Photo courtesy of the USMA Library, taken from the Library Digital Collection, 1973 *Howitzer*
270	Gaylyn Jones headstone	Author
270	George Perkins *Howitzer* photo	Photo courtesy of the USMA Library, taken from the Library Digital Collection, 1973 *Howitzer*
270	George Perkins headstone	Author
270	Robert Morris *Howitzer* photo	Photo courtesy of the USMA Library, taken from the Library Digital Collection, 1973 *Howitzer*
270	Robert Morris headstone	Author
271	Pat Putignano *Howitzer* photo	Photo courtesy of the USMA Library, taken from the Library Digital Collection, 1973 *Howitzer*
271	Pat Putignano headstone	Author
271	Dan Edelstein *Howitzer* photo	Photo courtesy of the USMA Library, taken from the Library Digital Collection, 1973 *Howitzer*
271	Dan Edelstein headstone	Author
271	Robert Mair *Howitzer* photo	Photo courtesy of the USMA Library, taken from the Library Digital Collection, 1973 *Howitzer*
271	Robert Mair headstone	Author
272	Robert Kurrus *Howitzer* photo	Photo courtesy of the USMA Library, taken from the Library Digital Collection, 1973 *Howitzer*
272	Robert Kurrus headstone	Author
272	Richard Johnson *Howitzer* photo	Photo courtesy of the USMA Library, taken from the Library Digital Collection, 1973 *Howitzer*
272	Richard Johnson headstone	Author
272	Dave Blackerby *Howitzer* photo	Photo courtesy of the USMA Library, taken from the Library Digital Collection, 1973 *Howitzer*
272	Dave Blackerby headstone	Author
273	Herbert Mills *Howitzer* photo	Photo courtesy of the USMA Library, taken from the Library Digital Collection, 1973 *Howitzer*
273	Herbert Mills headstone	Author

Photo Credits **315**

Page	Description	Attribution
273	George Everett *Howitzer* photo	Photo courtesy of the USMA Library, taken from the Library Digital Collection, 1973 *Howitzer*
273	George Everett headstone	Author
273	Harry Campbell *Howitzer* photo	Photo courtesy of the USMA Library, taken from the Library Digital Collection, 1973 *Howitzer*
273	Harry Campbell columbarium marker	Author
274	Rich Dakin *Howitzer* photo	Photo courtesy of the USMA Library, taken from the Library Digital Collection, 1973 *Howitzer*
274	Rich Dakin columbarium marker	Author
274	Dave Kimball *Howitzer* photo	Photo courtesy of the USMA Library, taken from the Library Digital Collection, 1973 *Howitzer*
274	Dave Kimball headstone	Author
274	Class of '73 detail from Baker's headstone	Author

Index

Anderson, Brigadier General George S.
Anderson, Major General Robert
Barger, Colonel David H.
Barry, Major General Thomas H.
Bartlett, Professor William H. C.
Beebe, Major William S.
Benedict family
Bennett, General Donald V.
Benton, Colonel James G.
Bentz, Sergeant Louis
Benyaurd, Lieutenant Colonel William H. H.
Besson, General Frank S., Jr.
Biddle, Major General John
Black, Major General William M.
Blaik, Earl H. "Red"
Bryan, Lieutenant General Blackshear M.
Buford, Major General John
Bunker family
Butterfield, Major General Daniel
Buyers, Patricia
Cadet Monument, the
Church, Professor Albert E.
Clay, General Lucius D.
Comstock, Brigadier General Cyrus
Cota, Major General Norman "Dutch"
Coursen, First Lieutenant Samuel S.
Cushing, Lieutenant Alonzo
Custer, Lieutenant Colonel George A.
Cutler, Brigadier General Elliott C., Jr.
Davidson, Lieutenant General Garrison H. "Gar"
Davis, Glenn W.
Davis, Second Lieutenant Courtenay C.
Davison, General Michael S.
DeArmond, Brigadier General Edward H.
Derby, Captain George
DeRussy, Brigadier René E.
Devin, Brigadier General Thomas

Dixon, Margaret Mary "Maggie"
Donovan, Lieutenant Colonel Robert E.
Downing, General Wayne A.
Echols, Colonel Charles P.
Edwards, Major General Norman B.
Eisenhower, Brigadier General John S.
Esposito, Brigadier General Vincent J.
Eyster, Lieutenant Colonel George
Farman, Colonel Elbert E., Jr.
Feir, Major General Philip R.
Ferrara, Captain Matthew
Ford, Chaplain James D.
Gavin, Lieutenant General James
Gillespie, Brigadier General George L., Jr.
Gilman, Congressman Benjamin A.
Godfrey, Mary
Goethals, Major General George W.
Grady, Colonel Ronan C., Jr.
Grant, Major General Frederick Dent
Graves, Lieutenant General Howard D.
Green, James O., family
Harkins, General Paul D.
Hayes family
Heard, Brigadier General John W.
Heiberg family
Heintges, Lieutenant General John A.
Hitchcock, Major General, US Volunteers,
    Ethan Allen
Holden, Edward S.
Hottell, Major John A., III
Howze, General Hamilton H.
Howze, Major General Robert L.
Hudgins, Colonel Seth F., Jr.
Hudnutt, Colonel Dean
Hunt, Brigadier General Ora E.
Hunt, Major Edward B.
Infants, the

Irwin, Brigadier General Bernard J. D.
Jannarone, Brigadier General John R.
Jones, Major General Lawrence M., Jr.
Jones, Colonel Lawrence M. "Biff," Sr.
Kendall, Lieutenant General Paul W.
Kilpatrick, Major General Judson H.
King, Lieutenant Colonel William R.
King, Major General Edward L.
Kinnard, Brigadier General Douglas
Kobes, Brigadier General Frank, Jr.
Koehler, Lieutenant Colonel Herman J.
Koster, Major General Samuel W.
Krebs, Major Timothy E.
Kunzig, Brigadier General William B.
Lambka, First Lieutenant Todd
Leonard, Lieutenant Colonel Jaimie E.
Lewis, Francis W.
Lewis, Technical Sergeant William S.
Lillie, Major John
Losey, Captain Robert
Lucas, Lieutenant Colonel Andre C.
MacDonald, Colonel Stuart C.
Mahan, Master Sergeant James B.
Mahan, Professor Dennis Hart
Maher, Master Sergeant Marty
Marcus, Colonel David "Mickey"
Martin, Major Chancellor
Mathewson, Lieutenant General Lemuel
McCarthy, Brigadier General Joseph E.
McKenzie, Major General Henry
Merrill, Major General Frank D.
Metcalf, Captain Henry
Meyers, Brigadier General Charles R. "Monk"
Michie, Brevet Brigadier General Peter
Michie, First Lieutenant Dennis
Mills, Major General Albert
Moore, Major General Bryant E.

Index **317**

Mucci, Colonel Henry A.
Nappi, Master Sergeant Pasquale "Pat"
Newman, Major General Aubrey S. "Red"
Norton, Lieutenant General John
Nye, Colonel Roger H.
O'Connor, Lieutenant Colonel Mortimer L.
Palone, Coach Joseph M.
Pappas, Colonel George "Ike"
Parker, General Theodore W.
Patch, General Alexander M.
Penny, Professor William J.
Perez, Second Lieutenant Emily
Pinkerton, Charles C.
Pinkerton, George R.
Raymond, Brigadier General Charles W.
Reeder, Colonel Russel P. "Red"
Ridley, Major General Clarence
Rogers, General Bernard W.
Schempf, Colonel William H.
Schilling, Brigadier General Charles H.
Schulze, Lieutenant Walter H.
Schuyler, General Cortlandt V. R.
Schwarzkopf, General H. Norman, Jr.
Schwarzkopf, Major General H. Norman, Sr.
Scott, Lieutenant General Willard W., Jr.
Scott, Lieutenant General Winfield
Selfridge, First Lieutenant Thomas E.
Silver, Reverend H. Percy
Sladen, Major General Fred W.
Staser, Major General Bruce I.
Stilwell, General Joseph W.
Sutherland, Command Sergeant Major Mary E.
Tallman, Brigadier General Richard J.
Terry, Frederick G., Jr.
Terry, Frederick G., Sr.
Thayer, Brevet Brigadier General Sylvanus
Thompson, Brigadier General John T.
Tidball, Brigadier General John C.
Tow, Second Lieutenant George W.
Townsley, Major General Clarence P.
Trant, Ensign Dominick
Unknowns, the
Vauthier, Professor Louis
Viele, Brigadier General, US Volunteers, Egbert L.
Walker, First Lieutenant Laura M.
Walker, General Sam S.
Wang, Major General Chih
Warner, Anna

Warner, Susan
Weaver, First Lieutenant John L.
Webb, Brevet Major General Alexander S.
Weir, Professor Robert W.
Wen, Lieutenant General Ying-Hsing
Westmoreland, General William C.
White, Colonel Edward H., II
White, Colonel Lawrence K. "Red"
White, Major General Edward H., Sr.
Wilbur, Brigadier General William H.
Wood, Brevet Lieutenant Colonel Eleazer D.

During the publication process of the book, an additional classmate of the author from the Class of 1973 passed away and was buried in the cemetery. His addendum is below.

Ronald E. McConnell came to West Point from New Mexico and was commissioned in the Infantry upon graduation. His initial assignment was in the 82nd Airborne Division at Fort Bragg in the 2nd Battalion, 504th Parachute Infantry Regiment. Upon completion of the Advanced Course, Ron went to Germany where he commanded a company in the 1st Battalion 36th Infantry. He went back to graduate school at the University of New Mexico for a master's degree in mathematics, and subsequently was assigned to West Point to teach in the Math Department. While at West Point, he also completed the requirements for a master's in business administration. Ron then attended the Command and General Staff College at Fort Leavenworth. Upon completion of that course, he returned to troop duty and was assigned to the 1st Infantry Division in Germany. In 1989, Ron became the S-3 of the 1st Battalion, 16th Infantry. During Operation Desert Storm, he served on the VII Corps staff. After the war, he returned to Fort Leavenworth to teach until his retirement in 1994. Ron then returned to West Point and taught in the Math Department. Ron's wife, Elaine, works in the USMA Library and has a special connection to this book as she was instrumental in assisting the author in the research.

Robert Holcomb (Lt. Col., Ret.) was born on the grounds at West Point. He graduated from the US Military Academy in 1973. His parents are buried in the West Point Cemetery. Holcomb has a PhD in information technology and lives in Virginia.